Union Command Failure in
the Shenandoah

Other Books by Dave Powell

The Maps of Chickamauga.
An Atlas of the Chickamauga Campaign, Including the Tullahoma Operations,
June 22- September 23, 1863
(Savas Beatie, 2009)

Failure in the Saddle: Nathan Bedford Forrest,
Joseph Wheeler, and the Confederate Cavalry in the Chickamauga Campaign
(Savas Beatie, 2010)

The Chickamauga Campaign.
A Mad Irregular Battle: From the Crossing of the Tennessee River Through the
Second Day, August 22-September 19, 1863
(Savas Beatie, 2014)

The Chickamauga Campaign.
Glory or the Grave: The Breakthrough, the Union Collapse, and the
Defense of Horseshoe Ridge, September 20, 1863
(Savas Beatie, 2015)

The Chickamauga Campaign.
Barren Victory: The Retreat into Chattanooga, The Confederate Pursuit, and the
Aftermath of the Battle, September 21 to October 20, 1863
(Savas Beatie, 2016)

Battle Above the Clouds: Lifting the Siege of Chattanooga and the
Battle of Lookout Mountain, October 16-November 24, 1863
(Savas Beatie, 2017)

Decisions at Chickamauga: The Twenty-Four Critical Decisions that Defined the Battle
(University of Tennessee Press, 2018)

Union Command Failure in the Shenandoah Valley: Major General Franz Sigel and the
War in the Valley of Virginia, May 1864
(Savas Beatie, 2019)

All Hell Can't Stop Them: The Battles for Chattanooga –
Missionary Ridge and Ringgold, November 24-27, 1863
(Savas Beatie, 2019)

Union Command Failure in the Shenandoah

Major General Franz Sigel and the War in the Valley of Virginia, May 1864

David A. Powell

Savas Beatie
California

Library of Congress Cataloging-in-Publication Data

Names: Powell, David A. (David Alan), 1961- author.
Title: Union Command Failure in the Shenandoah: Major General Franz Sigel and the War in the Valley of Virginia, May 1864 / by David A. Powell.
Description: First edition. | El Dorado Hills, California: Savas Beatie LLC, [2019] | Includes bibliographical references and index.
Identifiers: LCCN 2018041968| ISBN 9781611214345 (hardcover: alk. paper) | ISBN 9781611214352 (ebk)
Subjects: LCSH: New Market, Battle of, New Market, Va., 1864. | Shenandoah Valley Campaign, 1864 (May-August)
Classification: LCC E476.64 .P69 2018 | DDC 973.7/36—dc23
LC record available at https://lccn.loc.gov/2018041968

First Edition, First Printing

SB

Published by
Savas Beatie LLC
989 Governor Drive, Suite 102
El Dorado Hills, CA 95762

Phone: 916-941-6896
(web) www.savasbeatie.com
(E-mail) sales@savasbeatie.com

Our titles are available at special discounts for bulk purchases. For more details, contact us at sales@savasbeatie.com.

Proudly printed in the United States of America.

To the Virginia Military Institute, which taught me much about life,

and

To my father, William D. Powell, who made that journey possible.

Table of Contents

List of Maps
viii

List of Illustrations
ix

Introduction
x

Chapter 1: Politicking for a Command
1

Chapter 2: Defending the Valley
25

Chapter 3: The Department of West Virginia
42

Chapter 4: Crook's Advance and the Battle of Cloyd's Mountain
65

Chapter 5: Sigel's Advance
87

Chapter 6: Skirmishing, May 12–14, 1864
109

Chapter 7: Commencement—Morning, May 15, 1864
133

Chapter 8: Climax—Afternoon, May 15, 1864
157

Chapter 9: Conclusion—Late Afternoon, May 15, 1864
183

Chapter 10: Aftermath
199

Appendix: Order of Battle
213

Bibliography
215

Index
225

Acknowledgments
231

List of Maps

1. Western Virginia   7

2. Grant's plan   44

3. Crook's advance and retreat   72

4. Battle of Cloyd's Mountain   82

5. The Lower Valley from Winchester to New Market   89

6. Sigel's advance   116

7. Battle of New Market: Morning Phase   153

8. Battle of New Market: Afternoon Phase   167

List of Illustrations

Lieutenant General Ulysses S. Grant   5

Brigadier General Benjamin F. Kelley   10

Major General Robert H. Milroy   14

Major General Franz Sigel   18

Brigadier General John D. Imboden   27

Major General Samuel Jones   32

Major General John C. Breckinridge   33

Major General George Crook in 1865   43

Major General Edward O. C. Ord   48

Colonel Rutherford B. Hayes and his staff at Cumberland
Maryland in 1864   67

Brigadier General Albert G. Jenkins   75

Brigadier General William W. Averell   85

Colonel John S. Mosby and members of the 43rd Virginia Cavalry   91

Captain John Hanson "Hanse" McNeill   92

Colonel Jacob Higgins   98

Mosby sutler train   112

Colonel David M. Strother, of Sigel's Staff   127

Brigadier General John D. Imboden   135

Colonel Augustus Moor   137

Brigadier General John Echols   139

Major General Julius Stahel   148

Colonel Joseph Thoburn   159

Colonel William B. Tibbits   176

Bushong House   179

Colonel George D. Wells   180

Brigadier General Gabriel C. Wharton   185

Lieutenant Colonel Scott Shipp   187

Brigadier General Jeremiah C. Sullivan   196

The 54th Pennsylvania Infantry Regiment's Monument at New Market   200

Introduction

As Civil War Battles go, the engagement fought at New Market Virginia on May 15, 1864, was a relatively minor affair. Two armies, each about 5,000 men strong, clashed amid rain and thunder and the defeated Federals fell back. It was a small but notable triumph for Southern arms, but not one that achieved any lasting success. Less than a month later that same Union army, reinforced and under new management, returned and marched the length of the Shenandoah Valley virtually unimpeded.

I first became aware of New Market when I matriculated at the Virginia Military Institute in the summer of 1979. Before I arrived, the school sent me a copy of William C. Davis's *The Battle of New Market* to better appreciate VMI's traditions. Already a Civil War buff, I read it quickly. In the four years that followed I spent numerous weekends at the New Market Battlefield as both a re-enactor and a living historian. I charged many times across the "field of lost shoes" and up the hill toward the waiting Union guns at the crest.

Despite its modest size and import, New Market contains drama enough to have sparked three separate campaign studies in the past century. The first, Edmund Raymond Turner's *The New Market Campaign*, published in 1912, Davis's aforementioned volume, which appeared in 1975, and most recently Charles R. Knight's *Valley Thunder*, an excellent examination of the battle published in 2010. All three are solid pieces of scholarship and writing.

I believe there is room for yet one more look at the campaign. All three of the previous works are told largely from the Confederate point of view. Turner's and Davis's books center on the VMI cadets by highlighting their exploits. Knight's work incorporates material from a broader scope, bringing the rest of the Confederate army to the field, and embraces additional Federal accounts.

The dramatic part played by the Virginia Military Institute Cadets on that stormy May afternoon couldn't help but come to dominate the story. Two of those young VMI men, Benjamin A. Colonna and John A. Wise, would go on to amass a great deal of eyewitness testimony from participants on both sides in their efforts to fully document the battle, but each focused primarily on the role of the cadets. This combined collection, now in the VMI Archives, has become the foundation stone upon which all subsequent writing of the battle rests. Certainly, Turner's and Davis's works both deploy the cadets at center stage.

Author Charles Knight acknowledges as much in his 2010 work, which is why his own monograph shifts the focus to the rest of the troops on the field. Knight broadens his lens, adding in rich source material from the ranks of both armies, but still focuses mainly on the Confederate perspective, their voices adding to our fuller understanding of the battle.

But what of the Federals, and especially of their commander, Franz Sigel? Sigel has been painted as more of a caricature than a commander. Almost every postwar account portrays Sigel as an obvious incompetent, and each of Sigel's decisions has been traditionally introduced as further proof of his battlefield negligence. The German general is blamed for being too slow in advancing up the valley, for dispersing his troops across too broad a front, and, most of all, for fighting the battle in a disjointed, piecemeal fashion that could only produce ruin. The rest of the Federal force (and especially their commanders) are reduced to little more than innocent victims of Sigel's blundering.

Blaming everything on Franz Sigel strikes me as far too simple an explanation for what happened on the Federal side of the line during that rainy, thunderous afternoon. It is by no means my intention seek to rehabilitate Sigel as the undiscovered military genius of the American Civil War. I do, however, think there is a great deal to be learned about why Sigel made the choices he did, and a close reading of history offers up valid reasons for many of those decisions. Sigel made significant mistakes, and those mistakes cost him the battle, but up to that point Sigel had also achieved much of what the Union higher command expected of him—a fact that goes largely unrecognized in the extant literature.

In my years of studying and writing about the battle of Chickamauga, I have come to appreciate the usefulness of the military staff ride and the tools it provides soldiers and interested civilians for better understanding the "why" of an event. In doing so, I have also come to appreciate that studying the mistakes and failures of one side or the other can be more illuminating to the student than examining success. We often learn more from failure, even if that failure is long in the past. While this book is not a staff ride per se, I try to apply those same concepts to Sigel's decisions. As readers will come to find, he was not merely a blundering fool, and not all of his decisions wrong-headed. In fact, many or even most of decisions were based on sound strategic thinking. Sigel was in fact executing his part in a strategy laid down by the Union overall commander, Major General Ulysses S. Grant. Moreover, Sigel alone of all the generals involved in Grant's planning came the closest to executing Grant's orders and meeting his overall intent. The lapses of others involved in that campaign had as much to do with the Federal defeat at New Market as did Sigel's own errors. Ultimately, of course, Sigel's mistakes outweighed his better decisions, but that should not preclude us gaining a clearer understanding of the Union side of the hill which has long remained mostly out of view.

I have striven to avoid neglecting the Confederates, especially the cadets of my Alma Mater who charged through that rain to glory 150 years ago, but I *have* tried to avoid burdensome repetition. I cover Rebel actions and decisions in at least enough detail to illuminate the corresponding decisions of their Federal counterparts, but not to the same level as the Federals. Instead I rely heavily on the views found in Turner, Davis, and especially Knight's modern study, which have so artfully cast a great deal of illumination on all the Confederates who fought there. To all three authors I must extend my thanks for having written their own works on the battle, and inspired me to go just a bit further with the story.

CHAPTER 1

Politicking for a Command

By the spring of 1864, the American Civil War was entering its fourth year of long and bloody struggle. Despite repeated seasons of sanguinary stalemate in the east, however, west of the Appalachians the Federal government had at long last good reason for confidence. Success at Vicksburg and Port Hudson the previous summer opened the entire length of the Mississippi River to Union vessels, a clear sign of progress. At the end of November, a smashing victory over the Confederates besieging Chattanooga ended the year on a high note. As a result, President Abraham Lincoln brought Maj. Gen. Ulysses S. Grant, the man largely responsible for both of those triumphs, to Washington and gave him overall command of the Union war effort. Grant also received an unprecedented promotion to the newly created three-star rank of lieutenant general. He superseded Maj. Gen. Henry Halleck, who became the general-in-chief in 1862 on the strength of his western achievements, but who had since proven to be a disappointment. Lincoln and Secretary of War Edwin M. Stanton wanted a commander, not a clerk: Halleck saw his role very differently, demonstrating time and again that he would not override the authority of the men in the field. Now Halleck would continue running the routine military machinery of the War Department, but Grant would direct the war.

Grant's rise typified the president's search for men who would fight and win. As a by-product of this process, the military rolls were littered with discarded officers who had been found wanting and relegated to distant posts, or sent home to "await orders" that never came. A good many of these men were determined to get back into the fight, hoping to save damaged reputations or win new fame. Among them were former army commanders like George B. McClellan, Don Carlos Buell, and William S. Rosecrans; all generals who felt aggrieved by their treatment at the hands of the administration. Dozens of other, lesser-ranked officers had been similarly shelved. With Grant's promotion, however, significant command shake-ups in both the east and west seemed likely. 1864 seemed to offer hope of redemption for many. Grant himself came east hoping to restore "officers who had been relieved from important commands to duty," but that sometimes proved easier said than done. Jealousy and pride proved difficult roadblocks.

When Grant offered Buell a second chance at redemption, that general refused to serve under officers whom he had previously outranked, which in turn rankled Grant: "The worst excuse a soldier can make for declining service," Grant later penned, "is that he once ranked the commander he is to report to." Not everyone felt like Buell. Others, less stiff-necked, would jockey for positions in the coming months. One of those open commands was the Department of West Virginia, which also encompassed the Shenandoah Valley.[1]

Though it had long been a burying ground for Federal military reputations, the Union could not simply ignore the Valley in 1864. Northern forces had to control at least the lower (northernmost) part of the valley, for self-protection if nothing else. Occupying the lower valley as far south as the towns of Martinsburg and Winchester achieved two objectives. First was protection of the vital Baltimore & Ohio Railroad, which served the Federal government as a critical direct link to the all-important large and resource-rich western states; and secondly, to shut down an invasion corridor that had repeatedly granted Rebel armies easy access to Maryland and Pennsylvania, or even posing a direct threat to Washington itself. Confederate General Thomas J. "Stonewall" Jackson drove the Federals from the valley and nearly invaded Maryland in the spring of 1862, creating an uproar in the Federal Capital. Robert E. Lee's Army of Northern Virginia did transit into Maryland in 1863, on the way into Pennsylvania. Lee also used the Valley twice in retreat—in 1862 after

---

1   Ulysses S. Grant, and John F. Marszalek, ed. *The Personal Memoirs of U. S. Grant. The Complete Annotated Edition* (Cambridge, MA: 2017), 473.

the standoff along the banks of Antietam Creek, and again on the way back from Gettysburg. By maintaining control of Winchester and sealing off this avenue of operations, the Union fulfilled important defensive goals.

But General Grant was not a man content to merely embrace the defense. He came east intending to prosecute an offensive war in Virginia, and the Shenandoah, he perceived, could play a role.

As long as the South could bring supplies out of the middle and upper Valley using the rails at Staunton and Roanoke, its rich fields remained a critical part of the Confederacy's supply chain. Armies needed vast quantities of food and forage, and by 1864, Virginia, ravaged by two years of conflict, was not producing much of either. Lee's army tapped resources as far away as Georgia to feed itself, which in turned denied those supplies to other Confederate armies in the west. The Shenandoah, however, was still a useful—if much abused—breadbasket. Farther south, Virginia salt and saltpeter were even more critical; for without them the South could neither preserve the meats nor produce the gunpowder its soldiers needed. Both sides had reason to pay attention to the valley or suffer the consequences.

By the spring of 1864, the Union effort had evolved beyond just restoring the Union at any cost. The Emancipation Proclamation, issued 18 months earlier and taking effect on January 1, 1863, made the elimination of slavery a Union war aim. Discarded as well was the idea that recalcitrant secessionists could be wooed back into the Union via a gentle hand and respect for their property. This policy of "soft war," promoted by men like Buell and McClellan, was ridiculed by many even at the time. Russian emigre and Union Brig. Gen. John Basil Turchin summed up his contempt for the policy when he derisively mocked the idea of "guarding potato patches" belonging to secessionists while their sons took up arms in rebellion. By 1864, Grant and many other Union commanders now espoused "hard war"—confiscation, retaliation, and emancipation. Partisan attacks were met with hangings and burnings. Soldiers were expected to forage off the local populace, and runaway slaves could join the Federal armies instead of being returned to their masters. Union Maj. Gen. William T. Sherman would become the most famous practitioner of "hard war" in his campaign through Georgia later that year, but similar policies had also come to Virginia.

With the arrival of Grant, not just a new man but a new spirit arrived. On March 9, 1864, Grant stepped off the train in Washington D.C., to accept his new rank and assignment. After meeting President Lincoln and his cabinet, Grant formally assumed command of all the armies of the United States. His task was to coordinate the movements of all Union armies for the upcoming campaign season. Originally Grant intended to remain out west, but once in Washington he perceived that his presence would be critical to success in Virginia. Leaving Sherman to command the forces opposing the Confederate Army of Tennessee defending Atlanta, Grant elected to personally supervise the massive Union Army of the Potomac in its seemingly endless—and so far fruitless—struggle with Robert E. Lee. "On to Richmond," the war cry of 1861, 1862, and 1863, was now a hollow slogan, tinged with irony and sarcasm; each previous effort having met only ignominious defeat. Grant intended to change that fact.[2]

While Grant superseded Halleck, assumed the latter's responsibilities, he had no intention of merely inheriting Halleck's desk in the War Department Annex building across 17th Street from the White House. Nor did he intend to replace the Union's principal field commander in Virginia, Maj. Gen. George Gordon Meade, currently commanding the Army of the Potomac. Instead, Grant set up a field headquarters, accompanying Meade, from which he could direct both field operations in Virginia and still coordinate the larger war effort. Halleck would be retained to handle the day-to-day paperwork and administrative duties of controlling the vast Federal forces, while Meade would continue to manage the affairs of the Union's largest field army. Freed from the mundane aspects of both burdens, Grant would focus instead on the strategy of winning the war, and of personally ensuring that the effort in Virginia was properly directed. Under a different general this arrangement might have resulted in a divided command and more of the same problems that plagued the Union war effort for the past three years, but Grant proved to have the right touch to make it all work.

Grant's and Halleck's relationship might have been a further complication, given that Halleck was once both Grant's superior and had sometimes worked to undermine Grant's standing in Washington. Halleck had a pre-war reputation for brilliance, and been given overall command of the Western Theater early in the war. Meeting with success in the summer of 1862, Halleck was ordered east and made general-in-chief—even though his victories were won largely by others, most notably Grant. Halleck, however, was an office maven, easily immersed in detail, who only rarely took the field. Previously he exercised command from an office in St. Louis, and only directly commanded his forces in the field for a month or so after

2   Ibid.

Lieutenant General Ulysses S. Grant. *Library of Congress*

the battle of Shiloh. During this brief foray in the field he assembled a huge force outside Corinth Mississippi, but did little with it, until he was called east. Once entrenched in his Washington office, Halleck never left, instead attempting to direct the war effort by telegraph. He effectively abdicated much of his authority, rarely making firm decisions, preferring instead to defer to the men in the field. The overall Union war effort floundered under his tenure. On March 10, Grant officially assumed his new duties. At last the war would have a unified strategy.

That strategy would be one of unrelenting pressure. Sherman would drive towards Atlanta, pressing the Rebels under Joseph E. Johnston. Grant and Meade would take the fight to Lee's Army of Northern Virginia and Richmond. Other Union armies would operate in support of these two main efforts. Grant envisioned an attack on Mobile from New Orleans, and Union troops in the Carolinas would be brought north to threaten Richmond from the southeast, in Lee's rear. In order to overwhelm the Confederate ability to shift troops from threat to threat—by which the Rebels offset Union numerical advantages in the past—Grant explained that "I arranged for a simultaneous movement all along the line."[3]

The Shenandoah Valley would not be overlooked. Here Grant envisioned another pincer movement. One force would move from West Virginia into the upper valley to threaten the Virginia and Tennessee Railroad, while a second column advanced south from Winchester in the lower valley, "covering the North from an invasion through that channel," while "every mile . . . advanced also gave us possession of stores on which Lee relied." Both columns would unite at Staunton, destroy all Confederate property there, and if possible continue eastward towards Gordonsville or Lynchburg—both of which served as bases for Lee's logistics. This operation, though secondary to Meade's movement, could potentially hamstring Lee's ability to oppose the main Union drive.[4]

Over the winter, Grant had already formulated much of his strategy for the Western Theater, since he assumed he would be conducting that effort personally. With the call to Washington, however, his plans changed. Several questions had to be resolved if all was to be made ready in time for the spring campaigning season. Finding the right officers to

3   Ibid., 473-474.

4   Ibid., 474.

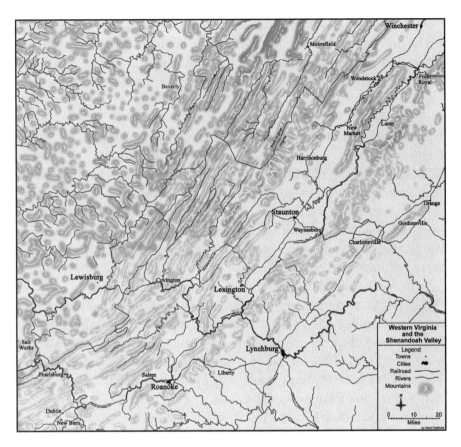

command the various offensives was critical. As noted, Grant hoped to draw on the talents of some of those idled officers. However, the new commander was not going to have an entirely free hand in choosing his subordinates. Clauswitz's famous dictum that "War is politics by other means" flowed both ways: 1864 was an election year in the North, and some officers would be selected more for their importance to the cause of political unity rather than for their military skill. Major Generals Nathanial P. Banks and Benjamin F. Butler, for example, could not be ignored. Both men were influential pre-war New England politicians, able to influence large blocks of votes in November, and so each would retain important positions.

Banks commanded the Department of the Gulf, headquartered in New Orleans. His offensive up the Red River used troops Grant originally intended to reinforce Sherman, and despite Banks's assurances that the

Red River affair would be finished before Sherman needed those men for his own march towards Atlanta, it was not to be. Banks's effort also meant that Grant's subsidiary drive towards Mobile, aimed at outflanking the Rebels in North Georgia, would also not come to pass.

Butler commanded along the Atlantic Coast, meaning that the attack on Richmond from the southeast originated within his department. He would command the newly formed Army of the James, 30,000 strong. Neither Grant nor Halleck was pleased with either of these choices. Banks and Butler had so far not displayed any great martial talents, but they were also civilians-in-uniform, not West Pointers; and but Grant's prejudice towards them was also influenced by the regular officers' disdain for amateur volunteer soldiers of any stripe. Given Lincoln's need for national political unity, Grant would simply have to accept them and make the best of the situation.[5]

Grant also hoped that any potential blunders committed by Banks or Butler might be mitigated by assigning trusted professional officers to accompany both men. Major General William B. Franklin was chosen as Banks's second-in-command. Franklin was a classmate of Grant's who had fallen afoul of the infamous Joint Committee on the Conduct of the War (JCCW) due to failings at the battle of Fredericksburg, and he left the Army of the Potomac under something of a cloud in the spring of 1863. Now in a position to help his old friend, Grant put Franklin forward for various Virginia commands. None of those assignments came to pass, but a transfer to the Department of the Gulf was approved. Franklin was given command of the XIX Corps, and soon won Banks's confidence.[6]

Similarly, Maj. Gen. William F. "Baldy" Smith, who also fell out of favor after Fredericksburg, was given a like position under Butler. Smith had previously impressed Grant with his work during the Chattanooga campaign in the fall of 1863, where Smith had been sent to take over the duties of chief engineer of the Army of the Cumberland. Smith was instrumental in re-opening a critical supply line to that besieged city prior to Grant's crushing victory over Confederate Gen. Braxton Bragg

---

5   The Red River expedition was pushed by Halleck at the behest of President Lincoln, and so went forward despite Grant's misgivings.

6   Mark A. Snell, *From First to Last: The Life of Major General William B. Franklin* (New York: 2002), 252-262.

at the end of November. Now Smith received his reward; command of the XVIII Corps under Butler.

Selecting a new man to head up the Department of West Virginia, and by extension, the Shenandoah Valley operation, became a bone of considerable contention. At least four men aspired to the appointment. Three of them had some connection with the region, but through misfortune or mismanagement had lost their commands. Those men were Franz Sigel, Edward O. C. Ord, Benjamin F. Kelley and Robert H. Milroy. Sigel and Ord were both major generals, while Kelly and Milroy each bore only one star. In Grant's opinion, Ord was the man for the job. He was another officer who had earned Grant's favorable opinion by dint of his service in the west. Ord hoped for a more prominent command now that his mentor was running things and was not above trying to obtain his patron's help. Grant further favored Ord because he was a West-Pointer, class of 1839. The other three were all volunteer officers, and Sigel was a foreigner to boot.

The Department of West Virginia was created on June 24, 1863. It was largely carved out of the pre-existing Middle Department, which was originally responsible for Baltimore, eastern Maryland, and the safety of the Baltimore & Ohio Railroad all the way to Ohio. That large region proved to be too geographically challenging for one commander to handle. Proof enough came in the spring of 1863, when, between April 20 and May 25 two Rebel cavalry brigades under Brig. Gens. William E. "Grumble" Jones and John D. Imboden rode through much of the newly created state of West Virginia with impunity, striking repeatedly at bridges, depots, and military warehouses. The raid created turmoil among West Virginia's politicians, sewing panic in the halls of the new state legislature. A feeble Union response, ineptly orchestrated by Maj. Gen. Robert Schenk from his departmental headquarters in far-away Baltimore, spurred the creation of the new command. Schenk was much more concerned with Confederate threats to Philadelphia, Baltimore or Washington than with events in West Virginia, and in any case would soon be caught up in the turmoil of Lee's invasion of Pennsylvania; he had little attention to spare elsewhere.

Benjamin F. Kelley, who was already responsible for the B & O Railroad's security, took command of the new department. Kelley was familiar with his enlarged responsibilities. He had overseen the "railroad

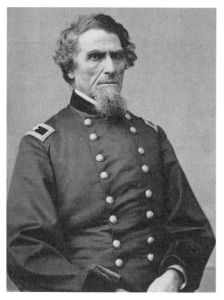

Brigadier General Benjamin F. Kelley.
Library of Congress

division" when it was still part of the Middle Department, assigned to guard the Baltimore and Ohio from Harper's Ferry to Marietta Ohio, and often acted independently of the remote Schenk. His duties would not change. At first glance Kelley probably seemed like the ideal man for the job. Born in New Hampshire in 1807, he moved to Wheeling Virginia as a young man. In 1851, he went to work for the railroad, and 10 years later, when war came, he raised a regiment of loyal Virginians for the Union cause. He was wounded at the battle of Philippi, a fight that also won him his star. He had so far spent his entire war in West Virginia, guarding the tracks of his old employer. He was brave, combat tested, and above all, knew the needs and vulnerabilities of a Civil War era rail company.[7]

Unfortunately, he lacked manpower. Virginia was a divided state. The creation of West Virginia in 1863 did not stop pro-Southern guerillas from raiding, nor prevent periodic incursions of Confederate cavalry. While 25,000 West Virginians served in Union blue, another 16,000 donned the gray. There were plenty of disgruntled secessionists willing to raid, bushwhack or abet others on that business even in the most loyal regions of the new state. As Union authorities had already discovered, guarding even a short stretch of rail through hostile territory required large numbers of garrison troops.[8]

Kelley, of course, had nothing like the forces needed to do that job. In July 1863, the Department contained 14,382 officers and men for duty.

7   U. S. War Department. *The War of the Rebellion: A Compilation of the Official Records of the Union and Confederate Armies,* 128 vols. (Washington D.C.: U. S. Government Printing Office, 1880–1901), Series I, volume 30, pt. 3, 299. Hereafter cited as *OR;* Ezra J. Warner, *Generals in Blue* (Baton Rouge: 1991), 260.

8   Darrell L. Collins, *The Jones-Imboden Raid* (Jefferson, NC: 2007), 19.

On paper, this was a substantial number, and if the only threat were small guerilla bands, they might have sufficed. However, the Confederates were equally alert to the importance of the B&O to the Federal war effort, and periodically sent larger forces raiding against the line.

Raids on the scale of the Jones-Imboden operation were rare, but lower level activity proved a more constant aggravation. Much of this action was directed by Confederate Guerrilla Capt. John Hanson McNeill. McNeill was born in 1815, in what is today Hardy County Virginia; but at the start of the war was a prosperous farmer and slave-holder living in Missouri. His initial war experience was all out west, fighting first at Wilson's Creek and in the nasty partisan bushwhacking that soon characterized Missouri warfare. Captured and imprisoned, McNeill escaped Union confinement and returned to Western Virginia sometime in 1862, where he formed his own company of partisan rangers. His roster strength never exceeded 210 men, and he usually operated in smaller bands. Like his more famous counterpart John Singleton Mosby, who waged a similar fight over in Fauquier and Loudoun Counties, McNeill's strong relationships with the pro-Southern civilians living in his home region provided him with safe havens, supplies, and intelligence sufficient to wage classic a guerrilla struggle. He made Unionist civilian life unlivable in the county seat of Romney, forcing the county government to relocate; and he struck repeatedly at the B&O around Cumberland Maryland. McNeill's Rangers had three primary objectives: "(1) to create general havoc among the Federal troops in the area; (2) disrupt traffic and communications on the Baltimore and Ohio Railroad; and (3) be a main source of supply in the foraging of beef cattle for the Confederate armies in the Shenandoah Valley." They proved remarkably successful in all three roles.[9]

As the Federal armies discovered in other areas where guerrilla activity was incessant, fending off these bands took a vastly disproportionate number of troops, especially when trying to protect something as large and as vulnerable as a railroad. Tracks could be torn up, bridges burned, trains derailed and captured. In response, the defenders had to disperse,

---

9   For more detail, see Simeon Miller Bright, "The McNeill Rangers: A Study in Confederate Guerrilla Warfare," *West Virginia History,* vol. 12, no. 4 (July 1951), 338-387. See also http://www.wvculture.org/hiStory/journal_wvh/ wvh12-1.html, accessed April 9, 2011.

building blockhouses every few miles and at vulnerable chokepoints like tunnels and bridges. Those garrisons had to be large enough to defend themselves against bands of up to a couple of hundred men. In addition, quick reaction forces—usually cavalry—had to be ready to ride at a moment's notice to relieve beleaguered outposts or chase marauders when they appeared. Such duty was onerous, exhausting, and manpower-intensive. Worst of all, troops dispersed in fixed defenses had no chance or time to drill as larger formations, and so their conventional combat skills deteriorated. Faced with these problems, Kelley managed the best he could, but he never had sufficient resources for the task.

In February 1864, one such Confederate raiding party captured Union Brig. Gen. Eliakim P. Scammon while he was asleep on a riverboat moored on the Kanawa River. Scammon himself was no great loss, but the repercussions of such an inglorious seizure reverberated through West Virginia. Kelley was already nervous about the threats to his department, perhaps overly so; he informed one of his staff officers, Col. David H. Strother, that he expected to "have a rough time in the spring and that the Rebels will make extraordinary efforts to retake Western Virginia." Strother, who better understood the realities of the Confederacy's resources, was dubious that the new state faced an actual invasion, but Kelley's opinion was shared by many nervous West Virginia citizens. For the West Virginia Senate, ensconced in Wheeling, the Scammon incident was the absolute last straw. On February 7, the body passed a resolution calling for Kelley's replacement. Initially, it requested either Robert H. Milroy or Franz Sigel by name. When that version proved difficult to pass, a revised draft simply requested any available major general. "The Senate could not have made a more ridiculous exhibition of itself . . . " fumed Strother.[10]

Kelley might have over-estimated the military capabilities of the Southern Confederacy by 1864, but clearly understood the political realities of his own situation. On February 18, Kelley informed Strother that the real problem lay not so much with a nervous state legislature, but instead in the fact "that there are fourteen major generals out of

---

10 *OR* 33, 109; Cecil D. Eby, Jr. Ed., *A Virginia Yankee in the Civil War: The Diaries of David Hunter Strother* (Chapel Hill, NC: 1961), 212. Scammon had been dismissed from the army in 1856. After he was exchanged, the War Department sent him to Florida for the duration of the war.

service drawing pay from the government. These will be dropped unless employed, and it is important to find a place for them. The Department of West Virginia is commanded by a brigadier. The place fits a major general; hence political influences are brought to bear on the president, who easily yields. . . ."[11]

One of those officers was Robert H. Milroy, who was a man seeking vindication. In the summer of 1863 Milroy commanded the 2nd Division of the VIII Corps; 6,900 men strong. Milroy's division was stationed at Winchester and tasked with suppressing Confederate guerrillas in the lower Shenandoah Valley. As far as Milroy was concerned, that spring the real war seemed far away, with the massive Union Army of the Potomac facing the enemy along the Rappahannock River opposite Fredericksburg. Then came the Union defeat at Chancellorsville. Following that success, Robert E. Lee decided the time had come to take the war north of the Potomac River and launched the campaign that would culminate at the battle of Gettysburg. At Winchester, Milroy's small force lay directly in Lee's path.

Between June 14 and 17, 1863, Confederate Lt. Gen. Richard S. Ewell's II Corps, Army of Northern Virginia (19,000 strong, including the attached cavalry) surrounded and crushed Milroy's command. Outnumbered nearly 3-to-1, Milroy's Federals should have been withdrawn, but no one would take the responsibility for doing so. Milroy believed that he could hold Winchester, a belief rooted in the idea that the main Rebel army could not move quickly enough to elude the Army of the Potomac, and all he would have to do was hold out for a day or so until reinforcements arrived. Halleck, who better understood the threat and should have overridden the decisions of both Milroy and departmental commander Schenk, characteristically refused to do more than advise Schenk to pull Milroy out of danger. Schenk, in Baltimore, demonstrated his own ineptitude when he neglected to do so. It took the direct intervention of President Lincoln to finally order the needed retreat. That decision came too late, and the result was predictable. Milroy lost 4,400 men, most as prisoners, while inflicting negligible Confederate casualties. Accused of both cowardice and incompetence, Milroy was relieved. In his own defense, he demanded a court of inquiry.[12]

11 Ibid., 213.

12 Bradley M. Gottfried, *The Maps of Gettysburg* (New York: 2007), 44; Stephen W. Sears, *Gettysburg* (New York: 2003), 77-78.

Major General Robert H. Milroy. *Library of Congress*

Eventually that court cleared him of wrongdoing, blaming instead both the War Department and the Army of the Potomac for losing track of Lee's army and allowing the disaster to unfold. The damage was done, however. Stanton and Halleck had no intention of returning Milroy to command. Instead, the general spent the rest of 1863 awaiting new orders, alternating his time between his Indiana residence and haunting the halls of Congress in Washington, agitating for restoration. In a letter to his wife Mary on December 31, Milroy recorded that the previous six months had been "the most intensely miserable half year of my life. I have been compelled to stand an idle useless spectator of the great events that were passing. . . ." Milroy blamed "the malice of Old Halleck" for his misfortunes, well aware of Halleck's obvious favoritism towards West Point men over volunteers. With a new year and the reconvening of Congress, however, Milroy vowed that "I will get my friends to work again" to seek re-instatement.[13]

Milroy was also the popular choice among the troops. Many of those captured men had now been exchanged and returned to duty. Far from blaming him for the disaster, the men who fought under him at Winchester regarded their general and themselves as unrecognized heroes, delaying Lee's advance into Pennsylvania for three critical days and allowing the lax Army of the Potomac time to catch up. Rightly or wrongly, it was a deeply held conviction. Years later, one such veteran opined that the delay gave "Gen. Meade time to perfect his disposition of troops, and select his position . . . an advantage which was worth more to the nation then the sacrifice it cost." In early February 1864, Milroy made an informal tour of the department, greeted everywhere with great enthusiasm. "Hundreds of Union Citizens came to see me whilst at Cumberland," he wrote on February 5, "& all expressed the strongest wishes for my return to command." At Martinsburg, there was more of the same. "My reception was sufficient to satisfy the vanity of a King. There are 7 of my old Regts there who were with me at different times since the beginning of the war. . . .The town of Martinsburg and the Camps of the soldiers . . . crowded to the hotel to see me. . . ." When touring those camps, noted Milroy, cries of "'we want you back' was heard on all sides from officers & soldiers & citizens." Lieutenant Colonel

---

13 "My Dear Mary," Washington D.C., December 31, 1863, Robert H. Milroy Papers, Jasper County Public Library, Rensselaer, Indiana.

Thomas F. Wildes of the 116th Ohio was one such sympathizer. Wildes noted that "no one . . . would have given more general satisfaction to the troops, but General Milroy was under the ban of the ogre General Halleck. . . ."[14]

Milroy certainly had his share of difficulties with "ogre" Halleck, but ethnicity also worked against him. The fact that he was not a German immigrant was more of a stumbling block. His nearest rival for the post, Franz Sigel, was both a German, and wildly popular within that émigré community.

Many Germans were recent arrivals to the United States, with large waves of them arriving in the 1840s and 1850s, fleeing old-world prosecution in the wake of the failed 1848 revolution. Motivated by the spirit of those revolts, the German-American communities tended to be socialist, abolitionist and militantly pro-Union. They viewed the Southern aristocracy as being a new-world extension of the old order they had tried to overthrow back home. As a result, German-Americans supported the Northern war effort in large numbers, and whole regiments were recruited out of cities like St. Louis, Cincinnati, Milwaukee, and Louisville. Germans were instrumental in helping keep both Missouri and Kentucky in the Union in 1861.

Not everyone was happy with the German presence, however. Germans faced significant discrimination from nativist American political elements before the war. Volunteering in ethnically German regiments for the Union was viewed as a duty, not just to prove their patriotism, but also because many Germans, having come of age in a militaristic society, felt that they were better soldiers than native-born Americans. Enlisting and proving themselves in combat was a way, once and for all, to silence nativist prejudice. The German vote, which under other circumstances would have been a natural constituency for the new Republican party due to their mutual hatred of slavery, was instead discouraged from voting for Lincoln in 1860 due to this same nativist prejudice. In 1864, with Lincoln running on an amalgam ticket—the Constitutional Union party—and facing dissatisfaction from elements within the Republicans, the incumbent now needed German votes more than ever.

---

14 Undated clipping from *The National Tribune*, John N. Waddell Papers, West Virginia State Archives, Charleston WV; "My Dear Mary," February 5, 1864, Milroy Papers; Thomas F. Wildes, *Record of the One Hundred and Sixteenth Regiment Ohio Infantry Volunteers in the War of the Rebellion* (Sandusky, OH: 1884), 79.

That sentiment carried up the chain of command and cut both ways. German regiments wanted to serve under German generals, and the highly active German language press agitated constantly for German-born officers to be given important assignments. Conversely, nativist-leaning papers argued that the stigma of defeats such as Chancellorsville or the first day's fighting at Gettysburg's could be blamed on the fact that much of the Union XI Corps was comprised of those self-same Germans. In response, outrage at being made scapegoats merely ratcheted up the pressure among the German-American constituency for greater political and military recognition. This pressure might not have mattered as much had 1864 not been an election year, but that fact could not be ignored. If Lincoln was going to be able to continue to prosecute the war to the end, he reasoned, he had to win the election first.

Franz Sigel was a central figure in the German struggle for acceptance. Born in Baden in 1824, Sigel was an 1843 Graduate of the Military Academy at Karlsruhe. In general, the military education at these *Kreigsacadamies* was superior to that to be had at West Point, focusing not just on tactics but providing more courses dealing with the theory and strategy of war. Sigel excelled at all aspects. Emerging near the top of his class, he then spent four years as a lieutenant in an infantry regiment. He also read up on politics and social theory. He gravitated towards liberalism, and eventually left the army for a career in law, but with the coming of the European revolts in 1848 he took up arms on the side of the revolutionaries. With their defeat, he fled to America. Thus, by the outbreak of the Civil War, he had a strong theoretical grounding in the art of war, practical experience in a professional army, and yet more practical experience in leading raw but highly motivated recruits. Less obvious was the fact that during those tumultuous months of active experience in 1848–1849, Sigel did not always shine on a battlefield.[15]

His record in the current war was spotty. He raised a regiment of St. Louis Germans in 1861, and led troops in combat at Carthage, Wilson's Creek, and Pea Ridge. Carthage was a small affair, more skirmish than real battle, and typical of many early-war collisions, but Sigel handled himself competently there and was subsequently hailed as a first-rate soldier. Wilson's Creek displayed him at both his best and his worst. As

15 Stephen D. Engle, *Yankee Dutchman: The Life of Franz Sigel* (Baton Rouge: 1993), 2-23.

Major General Franz Sigel. *Library of Congress*

a subordinate commander, part of a Union force facing a much larger Rebel army in southwestern Missouri, Sigel conceived and flawlessly executed a complicated two-pronged envelopment that, while it divided the Federal army in the face of the enemy (an extremely risky maneuver, especially with raw troops) if it succeeded would catch the larger Rebel army unawares, with a surprise attack. Despite the risk, Sigel delivered, his men appearing exactly when and where they were supposed to. "Sigel's accomplishment was stunning," according to the most definitive account of that battle. However, the march was only the half of it. There was still a fight to be won. While his initial attack was a notable success, Sigel neglected basic reconnaissance, and eventually a Rebel counter-blow all but routed his own men. Then, as problems mounted, Sigel went into a bit of a funk. The Federals were defeated, Union commander Nathanial G. Lyon was killed, and the Yankees retreated in disorder. Even though he would later get a reputation for masterminding that retreat, he in fact all but fled the field and left the task to others. When faced with adversity, Franz Sigel lacked the ability to react rapidly to changing circumstances. However, early news reports again cast him as a hero, and he emerged from the affair with his reputation enhanced.[16]

In March 1862, Sigel commanded half of the Union force at the battle of Pea Ridge, under overall command of Maj. Gen. Samuel R. Curtis. After Wilson's Creek Sigel took a sick leave, expecting to replace Lyon upon his return. Curtis's appointment came as an unpleasant surprise. Right from the start, the two men had an uneasy relationship, and the Union victory won at Pea Ridge did little to improve it. Quite the opposite, in fact.

Sigel again performed erratically. He initially over-extended his forces and had to conduct a fighting retreat to Curtis's main body on March 7, but he executed that retreat capably. On the 8th his two divisions attacked, after some prodding by Curtis, and routed the Rebels. During the fight Sigel displayed a great deal of personal bravery. His success masked certain flaws of deployment and judgment, but on the whole he turned in a very credible performance at Pea Ridge.

The real problems set in after the battle. Again, news reports, heavily influenced by German-born reporters (from both within the army and without) played up Sigel's role at the expense of Curtis. One correspondent went so far as to suggest that Curtis initially wanted to surrender and

16   William Garrett Piston and Richard W. Hatcher III, *Wilson's Creek: The Second Battle of the Civil War and the Men Who Fought It* (Chapel Hill, NC: 2000), 174-178, 191.

was swayed out of such a dire decision only by Sigel's determination to fight. Another insisted that the battle was won only because Curtis was persuaded to turn over command to Sigel. Naturally enough Curtis was outraged. After some days of mutual acrimony and suspicion between the two men, Sigel again took sick leave. He never returned and was eventually transferred eastward, rendering the problems between the two men moot.[17]

Sigel's main flaw in the eyes of his fellow officers was with his temperament. No one was more impressed with Franz Sigel's military talents than Sigel himself, and he was not loath to share his opinions on all things martial, often in abrasive terms. He was also quick to take insult, even where none was intended, and was constantly badgering his superiors to ensure that the respect he felt he was due was properly given.

As the overall commander in the west, Henry Halleck came to regard Sigel with a special disdain. Halleck considered himself the epitome of a professional; West Point educated, studious and well informed on military affairs, a man who had translated French military manuals for the United States Army's use and written his own treatises on strategy and fortification. Halleck considered himself without peer in understanding the art of war. His army nickname was "Old Brains." That pre-war reputation propelled him rapidly into the ranks of Union high command early in the war. He assumed command of the Department of Missouri in November 1861. From there he rose to command of all the Union armies in 1862, until superseded by Grant. In the early days of the war, he had much contact with Sigel.

Perhaps more than any other regular army officer, Halleck despised political generals, but despite Halleck's objections, Sigel was too popular to be sidelined. In the summer of 1862, Franz Sigel came east to assume command of what would eventually become the Union XI Corps. Sigel's eastern service began, however, under fellow western transplant Maj. Gen. John Pope, in the short-lived Army of Virginia. Pope's army was an assemblage of various independent commands, assembled at Halleck's direction. The army's only campaign culminated in the battle of Second Bull Run, fought in August 1862, in which Sigel played a significant role.

---

17 William L. Shea and Earl J. Hess, *Pea Ridge: Civil War Campaign in the West* (Chapel Hill, NC: 1992), 279-280.

Second Bull Run proved to be one of the more controversial battles of the war, a remarkable victory for Robert E. Lee; generating much recrimination and a famous court-martial on the Union side. For a change, Sigel was not at the center of any of it. In fact, he performed well under trying circumstances. Again there was tension with his commanding officer, for Pope also disliked the German, but Sigel proved to be a reliable subordinate. Sigel's corps fought almost alone on August 29, pressing home attacks ordered by Pope without much support for most of the day. On the 30th his men turned in an excellent performance on Chinn Ridge that probably saved the Union army from a sizeable disaster. One of his subordinates in that action was Robert Milroy.[18]

The fight under Pope was Sigel's last major battle at the head of his corps. The corps remained behind in the Washington defenses during the Antietam campaign, and missed Fredericksburg that December. Sigel did have time to cultivate political relationships; Union Brig. Gen., former Congressman and future President James A. Garfield visited, along with Kate Chase, daughter of Treasury Secretary Salmon P. Chase. Garfield came away with a very positive view of Sigel, who gave him a tour of the Second Bull Run battlefield, as well as a virtuoso performance on the piano.[19]

Sigel's pride proved his undoing. He further poisoned his reputation with regular army types by accusing fellow corps commander Irvin McDowell (West Point, 1838) of cowardice and even treason at Second Bull Run, and by spreading rumors to that effect in the press. During a subsequent court-martial McDowell was exonerated, largely because Sigel could offer no real evidence of any such scurrilous behavior. At the end of 1862, new army commander Ambrose Burnside made Sigel commander of the "Reserve Grand Division"; comprised of his own XI and the XII corps, a promotion which placed Sigel in command of nearly 25,000 men, more than he had ever led before. His command saw no combat, however, and then, in the wake of Burnside's defeat at Fredericksburg, Maj. Gen. Joseph E. Hooker (who replaced Burnside)

18 Pope accused Union Major General Fitz-John Porter of deliberately ignoring his orders in order to sabotage any success Pope might achieve, in hopes of restoring George B. McClellan to command.

19 Theodore Clarke Smith, *The Life and Writings of James Abram Garfield,* 2 vols. (New Haven, CT: 1925), vol. 2, 240-242.

dismantled the grand divisions. Sigel saw this as a demotion and a slur on his ethnicity. To compound matters, Sigel disliked Hooker and wasn't excited about serving under the new man.

The "demotion" returned him to command of the XI Corps, which turned out to be the smallest in the army. Larger corps were being commanded by men junior to him. His pride stung, Sigel began agitating for more troops. No troops were forthcoming. In February Sigel threatened to resign. Halleck promptly seized that opportunity to rid himself of the troublesome German and accepted his resignation. Unprepared to have his bluff called, Sigel found himself benched. Now, a year later, hungry for a command, he agitated unmercifully for reassignment, applying all the political pressure he could muster.

And that pressure was considerable. Sigel's popularity with the German-American community was strong enough to outweigh any personal shortcomings Sigel manifested as a general. Many Germans were becoming disillusioned with both Lincoln and the war effort. Several prominent ethnically German regiments, for example, had not re-upped as veterans in the spring of 1864, when their original enlistments expired. Given the intensity of their political leanings, this wave of Germanic disillusionment was a bad sign for the Lincoln administration.[20]

Grant, who cared little for the politics of the appointment, wanted neither Milroy nor Sigel. As noted, his choice was Maj. Gen. Edward Otho Cresap Ord for the job. Ord was a fellow West Pointer who had risen to command early, leading a brigade and then a division in Virginia from the fall of 1861 until the spring of 1862. He did not see combat, however. Ord, like Sigel, had trouble with McDowell. Serving in McDowell's corps, Ord despised his superior as incompetent, and feared he had been left in a backwater while the main army won glory elsewhere. He hoped to join Gen. George B. McClellan and the rest of the Army of the Potomac as it embarked on the Peninsula campaign against Richmond. Instead, he was ordered into the Shenandoah to help put down Confederate Gen. Thomas J. "Stonewall" Jackson. In a telling incident, Ord, when ordered to march one day, made a hash of it, his division moving only five miles. When McDowell demanded the reason

---

20 The 9th Ohio, 32nd Indiana, and 6th Kentucky—all German regiments—where among those who did not re-enlist.

for the delay, Ord apparently faked an illness and turned his command over to a subordinate.[21]

This was a damning performance, and it might have ended another man's career. But Ord was regular army and had friends in high places. Numbered among them was Henry Halleck, who had just risen to overall command. Eager to be out from under McDowell, Ord secured a transfer to the west. There another old friend, William T. Sherman, greeted him warmly. Ulysses S. Grant followed Sherman's lead in embracing Ord. In September 1862, at Iuka, Ord again fumbled badly, delivering yet another terrible march performance and missing his chance to attack a retreating Confederate column. Grant covered for Ord and blamed William Starke Rosecrans, whose troops bore the brunt of the fight, for the failure to trap the Rebels. In a later action, Ord was wounded and would not recover until May 1863. But his reputation, at least in Grant's eyes, remained untarnished. Ord rose to command the XIII Corps, replacing another troublesome politician, John A. McClernand. In the summer of 1863 Ord served at Vicksburg and Jackson, Mississippi, performing competently if without notable distinction. That fall he was sent to join Nathaniel Banks in Louisiana.[22]

Unsurprisingly Ord despised Banks and hated serving under him. Ord wanted to stick close to Grant, whose star was clearly rising, and where real fame might be won. Worse yet, McClernand managed to successfully argue his case and was returned to command of the XIII Corps, which would have meant a demotion for Ord. Again, he claimed illness and took leave. And again, his duplicity would be rewarded by Grant. The winter of 1863–1864 found Ord without a command, awaiting orders in Louisville Kentucky. With Grant's own promotion, Ord now sent a series of telegrams to his mentor, soliciting a job. On March 22, 1864 he wired, "Am without orders. Would rather have no corps with you than one away." In response, Grant summoned him to Washington.[23]

---

21 William B. Feis, "Grant's Relief Man: Edward O. C. Ord," in Steven E. Woodworth, ed., *Grant's Lieutenants from Chattanooga to Appomattox* (Lawrence, KS: 2008), 177-178.

22 Ibid., 180.

23 John Y. Simon, ed., *The Papers of Ulysses S. Grant*, 31 vols. (Carbondale, IL: 1982), vol. 10, 234. http://digital.library.msstate.edu/collections/document.php?CISOROOT=/USG_volume&CISOPTR=10823&REC=10, accessed April 16, 2011.

The summons came too late for Ord's hopes of an independent command. On March 10, 1864, Franz Sigel was appointed to the Department of West Virginia, which the bantam German viewed as both a personal triumph and a sign of professional vindication, though in reality he almost certainly got the nod because of his ethnicity, not due to his military skills. This didn't mean that Grant had no place for Ord, however. Just as he had done with Banks and Butler, Grant desired to place a trusted professional within the department who could act as a mitigating factor in case of any blunders Sigel might commit. Ord could be just the man. In fact, Grant seems to have assumed that Ord would be the field commander, with Sigel supposedly confining himself to mostly administrative duties at departmental headquarters. If so, Grant had completely misread Franz Sigel's character and intentions.

CHAPTER 2

Defending the Valley

By 1864, the Shenandoah Valley had become a burying ground for both Union soldiers and their commanders' reputations. In 1862, Nathaniel P. Banks came to grief at the hands of Thomas J. "Stonewall" Jackson, having been all but driven out of the valley by Jackson in May of that year. Thirteen months later, Gen. Robert Milroy's small force was nearly annihilated at Winchester as the Rebels marched towards Gettysburg. In between these larger campaigns, Confederate partisans waged a wearying guerrilla war against Federals occupying the northern half of the valley; a struggle that consumed resources, diverted manpower, and exasperated the Federal high command. This historic valley, carved by the Shenandoah River long ago, simply could not be ignored while the larger war in Virginia played out.

The Great Valley of Virginia stretches for nearly 200 miles, bounded on the north by the Potomac River and on the south by the headwaters of the James. It is narrow, usually no more than about 20 miles wide, with mountain walls to the east and west. When examined on a map, the Valley appears tilted, running northeast to southwest. Because the valley's namesake river flows from south to north, the standard geographical terminology has been flipped; a traveler goes "up" the valley when heading south, and "down" the valley if moving north.

By the time of the war, the valley was a rich agricultural center and well settled. In the north the towns of note were Harpers Ferry (where the Shenandoah River joined the Potomac) Winchester and Martinsburg.

Roanoke and Salem lay at the southern end. Harrisonburg, Staunton, and Lexington lay in between, with numerous smaller hamlets and settlements along the way. During the 1860s, no railroad ran the valley's length; instead, the main cultural and commercial artery was the Valley Turnpike, a macadamized roadway from Winchester to Staunton. Four railroads did connect parts of the valley with the outside world. The Winchester & Potomac ran between its namesake town and Harpers Ferry, linking to the Baltimore and Ohio. The Manassas Gap Railway connected the towns of Mount Jackson and Strasburg to Manassas Junction, intersecting with the Fredericksburg & Potomac. The Virginia Central hauled traffic from Staunton to Hanover Junction, just outside of Richmond. Finally, the Virginia and Tennessee Railway, which provided the Confederacy with its most direct link between Virginia and the war's Western Theater, ran through the upper valley at Roanoke before heading southwest to Salem, Kingsport, and Knoxville.

If the Federals could not ignore the Shenandoah Valley in 1864, neither could it be neglected by the South. In addition to the material resources the valley provided, it was also a fertile source of morale-building Confederate mythology. Stonewall Jackson rode to glory there, defeating enemy forces often exaggerated at many times his own strength. Even the most sober accounting of his record revealed an impressive string of successes, so much so that the Valley and Union defeat seemed synonymous.

This legacy also meant that any Confederate who followed in Jackson's footsteps would face inevitable comparisons to his legacy. In the South, both the public and the politicians would look to the valley's commander for victory, against even the steepest odds. Worse yet, given the Confederacy's dwindling manpower pool, by the conflict's third year few troops could be spared from more vital theaters to defend the place. As Robert E. Lee prepared to face Grant east of the Blue Ridge, he needed every man he could muster to offset the Union's strongest field army, now massing to oppose him. Only a handful of troops could be spared for western Virginia.

In the summer of 1863, the Valley's defender was Brig. Gen. John D. Imboden. A native of the region, Imboden was a logical choice; born and raised near Staunton; in adult life he practiced law in his home town. He knew the valley as well as anyone. Ironically, much like Franz

A postwar image of Brigadier General John D. Imboden. *Library of Congress*

Sigel, whom he would soon face in battle (and unlike many of his Scots-Irish neighbors) Imboden was also of German extraction; a third-generation descendent of immigrants from Wurttemberg and German-speaking Switzerland. Had his parents not emigrated, he could have been Sigel's Badener neighbor.[1]

Imboden prospered as a lawyer, active in both politics and the pre-war militia. His military involvement heightened in 1859, after John Brown raised the fearful specter of slave revolt at Harpers Ferry, an act which spurred Imboden to raise an artillery battery. He favored secession, an opinion that ran counter to that of many of his neighbors; Both Staunton and the rest of Augusta County leaned Unionist in 1861. However, as war neared the idea of secession became more palatable. As a prominent local political, civic, and military leader, John Imboden was at the forefront of this drift towards rebellion. In April 1861, converting words into action, Imboden and his militia battery helped capture the U.S. Arsenal at Harpers Ferry.

Imboden thrived in war as well. He and his gunners fought at First Manassas and were subsequently assigned to Joseph E. Johnston's Army of Virginia. In the spring of 1862, as guerrilla war raged in the mountains of western Virginia and there seemed to be little prospect of fighting between the main armies, Imboden's thoughts returned to his home county. He applied for and received authority to recruit a regiment of partisan rangers for Virginia service. The partisan rangers were a new concept, recently authorized by the Confederate Congress, units of local men raised in areas then occupied by the Federals in order to harass

---

1   Harold R. Woodward, Jr., *Defender of the Valley: Brigadier General John Daniel Imboden C.S.A.* (Berryville, VA: 1996), 1-4.

the enemy behind his lines. It was a concept that many Confederates—especially former officers of the pre-war regular army—would come to regret, for at times the line between partisan activity and mere banditry could be very thin indeed. Even worse, the new formations lured men away from regular service, for partisan rangers not only stayed close to home, but they also received prize money for captured war material. Eventually, many partisan units became havens for deserters, siphoning precious manpower away from the Confederacy's best combat commands. Those regrets came later, however; initially the idea was greeted with great enthusiasm. Imboden recruited the 1st Regiment, Virginia Partisan Rangers. It was a family affair. Brothers Francis and George Imboden both headed up companies in the new unit.

The regiment had a complicated organization, including both mounted and dismounted companies, and took half a year to flesh out. It was not sworn into Confederate service until September 9, 1862. In the meantime, Imboden took to the field with individual companies and battalion-sized fragments, fighting under Jackson at Cross Keys, Port Republic and mounting various raids against the Baltimore & Ohio. Here he first paired off against Union General Kelley, who was tasked with defending the tracks, and General Milroy, busily guarding the upper valley around Martinsburg.

By the spring of 1863 Imboden had expanded his command into a budding brigade. The mounted companies were re-designated as the 18th Virginia Cavalry, while the remainder of the regiment became the 62nd Infantry. The two units both functioned indistinguishably, as the 62nd were soon given horses and rechristened as Mounted Infantry. Other companies of partisans such as McNeill's rangers also sometimes rode under Imboden's command, and together the whole force was designated the Northwestern Brigade. In April 1863, under the overall command of Brig. Gen. William E. "Grumble" Jones, Imboden took part in a highly successful raid deep into West Virginia. His reputation soared further during the Gettysburg campaign when Imboden's men were charged with escorting Lee's wounded and 4,000 Union prisoners back to Virginia in the wake of that battle. Imboden successfully fended off Union attacks to bring that train of misery back safely to Virginia, and then at Williamsport helped keep the Federal army at bay until Lee crossed his whole army over the Potomac River. Having demonstrated success as both a raider and a more conventional cavalryman, Imboden seemed to be the perfect candidate to take over Stonewall Jackson's old job.

Imboden was assigned to command the Valley District on July 21, 1863, a week after the action at Williamsport. His command was part of the larger Department of Northern Virginia, which in turn was commanded by Gen. Robert E. Lee. That summer and fall, however, Lee's attention was focused on threats posed by the Union Army of the Potomac, leaving Imboden to act largely on his own hook. Lee's involvement in Imboden's command consisted primarily of prodding the junior man to launch various raids into Union territory, all intended to divert the Federals from attacking Lee directly.[2]

The Valley District embraced only about two thirds of the actual Shenandoah Valley. The territory south of Lexington was incorporated into a different department, that of western Virginia, commanded by Maj. Gen. Samuel Jones. Jones's primary responsibility was to defend the all-important salt and niter works located in southwest Virginia, so vital to Confederate war efforts, as well as protecting the Virginia & Tennessee Railway. In the fall of 1863, Jones's job was greatly complicated by the fact that the adjoining Confederate Department of East Tennessee was abandoned to Federal forces advancing on Knoxville and Chattanooga, as the Rebels desperately strove to combine forces to meet the threat against Chattanooga with something like equal odds. Suddenly, Jones's department had to worry not just about Union raids coming over the mountains from West Virginia or Kentucky, but also about a direct invasion looming from Knoxville.

During the winter, the Rebels made an unsuccessful effort to retake Knoxville with a force commanded by Lt. Gen. James Longstreet. When that effort failed Longstreet retreated towards Bristol Tennessee, on the Virginia state line, and almost within Jones's Department. The presence of Longstreet's 20,000 troops greatly eased Jones's fears of invasion, at least temporarily, but everyone expected that 1864 would bring a spring campaign in the area, and Jones's attention remained focused to his south. Thus, defense of the upper valley was split between various departments, each with larger problems focusing their attention elsewhere. Few troops or thoughts could be spared for Imboden's needs.

2   Ibid., 88.

Fortunately for Imboden, between October 1863 and March 1864 the war in the Valley was characterized mostly by partisan action, with both sides trading the occasional larger raid. Throughout, Robert E. Lee continued to urge Imboden to harass the Federals with yet more raids into the newly created state of West Virginia or against the Baltimore and Ohio. Lee's objective was simple: to tie up as many Federals as possible on guard duties, thus draining combat troops from his primary opponent, the Union Army of the Potomac.[3]

Imboden responded as best he could. While he lacked the resources to conduct a major raid matching the effort he and "Grumble" Jones jointly launched the previous spring, Imboden led or directed several smaller operations. The most notable of these came in October, when he made a sudden descent on Charlestown, capturing 434 Federals with minimal loss and throwing a scare into General Kelley.[4]

The Federals responded with raids of their own, mostly directed into Jones's Department of southwest Virginia, which forced Imboden to repeatedly call out local reserves. When Lee urged for yet more strikes at the B&O, Imboden prevailed upon him for additional cavalry, but no troops could be spared. As a result, Imboden turned increasingly to smaller bands of irregulars like McNeill's rangers or the six companies of partisan rangers commanded by Maj. Harry Gilmor, a Baltimore native who had cast his lot with the South and recruited his own band of adventurers.

By the winter of 1863–1864, most of Imboden's force was broken into smaller parties, distributed around the district, which were both easier to supply and able to conduct small raids more readily. However, dispersal also sometimes meant lapses in discipline, which would be an increasingly sore point in many regions of the South, and the Valley was no exception. Over time, Lee grew more critical of both the Western Department and the Valley District, both with the commanders and the men assigned to the units serving there. Things came to a head over one particularly troubling incident. In February 1864, Major Gilmor's battalion ambushed a train on the Baltimore & Ohio. In addition to whatever government property was seized, some of his men also robbed

---

3   West Virginia joined the Federal Union as a new state on June 20, 1863.

4   Woodward, *Defender of the Valley,* 92-94; *OR* 29, pt. 2, 352.

the passengers at gunpoint, relieving them of their private valuables. The *New York Times* claimed that Gilmor's men made off with up to $30,000 in cash and property, including "watches, diamonds, rings, and breastpins." A second outrage came just a few days later, when other members of Gilmor's band robbed a wagon caravan near Woodstock, taking "six thousand [dollars] in gold. . . ." When Lee got wind of the accusations, he ordered Imboden to investigate. Gilmor hotly denied the charges, blaming the outrages on deserters, but Imboden's inquiries suggested that not only had Gilmor's men been the culprits, but that Gilmor himself had a hand in the thievery. Gilmor was arrested and held over at Staunton for a military court martial, a trail that was still pending as the spring campaign opened.[5]

Imboden's other most reliable partisan chieftain, Hanse McNeill, also ran afoul of the courts. McNeill's crime was the misappropriation of public property, and for "knowingly receiving and entertaining a deserter from other than his own company and refusing to deliver him up." McNeill was exonerated, though just barely, but his command continued to be a refuge for deserters. One historian of the unit admitted that "the rangers accepted all who would join their troop, overlooking the fact that some were regular Confederate army men."[6]

By late 1863, most Confederate military officers were growing increasingly disillusioned with the concept of partisan irregulars. There was mounting pressure to disband these units and incorporate their manpower into regular formations badly in need of recruits and replacements. Imboden and his men were not exempt. In January 1864, Lee singled out Imboden's command, charging that it was filled with men who enlisted in the partisans purely to avoid conscription, and who often intended to desert at the first opportunity. These men, Lee insisted, "will be to a great extent lost to the general service. . . .I refer particularly to the commands of General Imboden, Col. William L. Jackson, and Maj. Gen. Sam Jones."[7]

5   Timothy R. Ackinclose, *Sabres and Pistols: The Civil War Career of Colonel Henry Gilmor, C.S.A.* (Gettysburg: 1997), 84-85.

6   Simeon Miller Bright, "The McNeill Rangers: A Study in Confederate Guerrilla Warfare," *West Virginia History*, vol. 12, no. 4 (July 1951), online edition, http://www.wvculture.org/history/journal_wvh/wvh12-1.html, accessed November 18, 2012.

7   *OR* 33, 1086.

Major General Samuel Jones. *Library of Congress*

In April, Lee went farther, condemning the idea of partisan rangers altogether: "Experience has convinced me that it is almost impossible, under the best officers even, to prevent them from becoming an injury instead of a benefit to the service, and even where this is accomplished the system gives license to many deserters and marauders . . . who commit depredations on friend and foe alike."[8]

Lee's low opinion of Imboden's command was furthered by reports from Maj. Gen. Jubal Early, who was dispatched to the valley in December 1863, after a particularly damaging Union raid there. Early remained until early February 1864. During his tenure Early found much fault with both Imboden and Imboden's troops. Early observed that the Northwestern Brigade was "inefficient, disorganized and undisciplined." Matters came to head when, while Early was at Staunton, "one of Imboden's lieutenants killed a sergeant on the streets" of the town. A steady stream of critical dispatches marked Early's time in the Valley. Lee took heed. "General Early states that his operations were impeded, and in a measure arrested by his inability to get service from General Imboden's men. . . .He could get no information about the enemy," Lee complained to President Davis, "because he could make no reconnaissance with these troops."[9]

The problems in Imboden's district, felt Lee, were mirrored in Samuel Jones's Department down in southwest Virginia. There, General Lee noted, "I have been disappointed in my expectations" of Jones's troops. Lee concluded that "I think a reorganization of [all] these troops necessary, and a change of commanders desirable." Lee wanted the Confederate War Department to both replace Jones and expand Jones's department

8   Ibid., 1252.

9   Jubal Anderson Early, *Autobiographical Sketch and Narrative of the War Between the States* (Philadelphia: 1912), 326; Woodward, *Defender of the Valley*, 100.

Major General John C. Breckinridge. *Library of Congress*

to include Imboden's command, hopefully selecting a new officer who could restore proper discipline to the troops in both sectors. Richmond agreed, because not only the South's leading military men were unhappy with Jones. As Confederate Secretary of War James A. Seddon explained, Jones had "ceased to command the general confidence of the people" in his department, "and discontent and apprehensions of hurtful nature were prevailing" among the citizens.[10]

Thus, it didn't come as a great surprise when a new man soon arrived to take charge. He was Maj. Gen. John C. Breckinridge, who had been officially relieved from duty with the Army of Tennessee that winter and ordered to report to Richmond for further assignment. The troops could sense change in the offing. In a letter home on February 8, 1864, Pvt. Thomas Fisher of the 51st Virginia informed his parents that "General Sam Jones has been relieved . . . and General Breckinridge is to take command of that department." Further, noted Fisher, "my opinion is that right here in this country will be the next fighting in the spring." Fisher's information was premature, but correct. Breckinridge was formally ordered to replace Major General Jones on February 25, though he would not arrive to assume his new command until March 5. With Early and his men returning to Lee's main army east of the Blue Ridge, Imboden would be subordinated to Breckinridge as well.[11]

Breckinridge was the most famous Kentuckian then serving the Confederacy. A pre-war lawyer and politician, he served as vice president of the United States under President James Buchanan from

---

10   *OR* 33, 1086; *OR* 51, 820.

11   "Dear parents," February 8, 1864, Thomas Winton Fisher Papers, http://ted.gardner. org/twfhome.htm, accessed November 18, 2012; *OR* 33, 1198, 1211.

1857 to 1861. Though a staunch defender of slavery, Breckinridge was initially an opponent of secession and worked hard to prevent it. Even though Kentucky ultimately remained loyal to the Union, however, Breckinridge soon despaired of reconciliation and decided that he must join the Confederacy to oppose the "moral or fanatical element" in the North that was pushing for Negro equality and what he regarded as the destruction of Southern society. Though he had no prewar military experience or training, he rose to high rank relatively early due to his political stature. He soon proved a capable soldier. He commanded the Reserve Corps at Shiloh (really a divisional-sized organization of three brigades) and served as a divisional commander in the western armies thereafter, fighting well at Murfreesboro and Chickamauga.[12]

However, Breckinridge did not win the favor of his army commander, Braxton Bragg. This is not surprising. Bragg had trouble with most of the senior officers in the Army of Tennessee. Wholesale controversy erupted after the failed Kentucky campaign of 1862, and for the next year would increasingly poison relations between Bragg and his top commanders. Breckinridge became involved in these internal struggles. Bragg appeared to bear a special enmity for Kentuckians, believing he had been deceived as to the actual loyalty of the state and the welcome he was likely to receive there when he marched north in the fall of 1862. Though Breckinridge was not with the army during that campaign (he was hurrying from Mississippi to join Bragg but failed to arrive before Bragg retreated out of Kentucky) Breckinridge was a loyal Kentuckian, and aligned with his fellow residents of the Bluegrass against Bragg's accusations and fault-finding.

Relations only worsened between the two men when on January 2, 1863, Bragg ordered Breckinridge to lead his division into what proved to be a bloody failure of an attack. Unsupported and outnumbered, Breckinridge's troops suffered heavily. The famed "Orphan Brigade" of Kentucky exiles in Confederate service took an especially hard pounding. Appalled at the pointless slaughter, Breckinridge blamed Bragg for issuing a badly conceived order; while Bragg blamed Breckinridge for incompetence in execution. This simmering animosity did not prevent Breckinridge from delivering an outstanding performance on the battlefield

---

12   William C. Davis, *Breckinridge: Statesman, Soldier, Symbol* (Baton Rouge: 1992), 212.

of Chickamauga on September 20, 1863, but again, his division was unsupported and driven back.

These difficulties came to a head two months later. Bragg's army triumphed at Chickamauga, but only managed to besiege the Union Army of the Cumberland in Chattanooga instead of destroying it. At the end of November, reinvigorated and reinforced, the Union forces decisively broke that siege, crushing the Rebels at Missionary Ridge. This defeat cost Bragg his command. Breckinridge, who by then had risen to corps command and defended a critical sector, was accused of being "dead drunk." Whether or not he was drunk (Breckinridge denied it, No one corroborated it, and Bragg never court-martialed him) Breckinridge had recklessly asserted that the army should defend in place instead of a more prudent retreat, advice that proved disastrous. To be fair, Bragg concurred, and then further complicated matters by stripping Breckinridge's line to a dangerous thinness before the Federals struck.[13]

Bragg was relieved of command, though not demoted. In fact, in February 1864 Confederate President Jefferson Davis brought Bragg to Richmond, appointing him "Military Advisor to the President." Despite Bragg's apparent vindication, Davis did not share Bragg's grudge against Breckinridge. Indeed, as Secretary of War James Seddon informed the unhappy General Jones, Davis regarded Breckinridge as "an officer of distinction in the western army, who has political as well as military influences to aid his administration" of the department. The orders announcing Bragg's appointment were published on February 24; Breckinridge's, the next day. The Kentuckian's transfer to Virginia represented a step up in authority and a chance to clear a besmirched name. It was also an enormous challenge.[14]

Upon taking command, Breckinridge discovered that his new department contained only 5,700 officers and men. They amounted to two brigades of infantry, under Brig. Gen. John Echols and Col. John McCausland; and two brigades of cavalry, one led by Col. William L. Jackson and a second nominally commanded by Brig. Gen. Albert G. Jenkins. Most of these troops were concentrated at the south end of the

---

13 Davis, *Breckinridge*, 395; Thomas L. Connelly, *Autumn of Glory* (Baton Rouge: 1971), 273.

14 Judith Lee Hallock, *Braxton Bragg and Confederate Defeat, Vol. II* (Tuscaloosa: 1991), 163; Davis, *Breckinridge*, 395-399; *OR* 51, 820.

department, near the Tennessee line, where they could protect the salt works and also bolster the Confederate defense of what remained of East Tennessee against Union incursion from Knoxville. Up until March 1864, the adjacent Confederate Department of East Tennessee contained nearly 20,000 men, including another of Breckinridge's infantry brigades led by Brig. Gen. Gabriel C. Wharton, loaned out during an earlier crisis and not yet returned. That would soon change.[15]

The Department of East Tennessee remained a separate command even after the fall of Knoxville, though doing so greatly complicated the defense of the region. In theory, it would have been better practice to combine southwest Virginia and East Tennessee into one command. Moreover, East Tennessee was almost a transient command. Currently it was led by Lt. Gen. James Longstreet, who ranked the normally assigned departmental commander, Maj. Gen. Simon Bolivar Buckner. Longstreet was there because prior to the battle of Chattanooga, Bragg sent him to retake Knoxville, more to get rid of yet another troublesome subordinate than in any real hope of returning East Tennessee to Confederate control. The bulk of the troops in the department belonged to Longstreet's Corps from the Army of Northern Virginia, a force which Lee only reluctantly agreed to send west to help Bragg just prior to the battle of Chickamauga. Now, with Grant's spring campaign looming in Virginia, Lee wanted those men back, and would soon get them. When it became apparent that the bulk of the Union troops in East Tennessee were being withdrawn to join either Sherman's or Grant's forces, so too did Longstreet return to Lee. By April Longstreet and 12,000 troops were at Gordonsville, Virginia.[16]

Many of the remaining 8,000 men in East Tennessee would also soon be transferred to other theaters, leaving a mere skeleton force under Buckner. Gabriel Wharton's brigade of Virginia Infantry was ordered to re-join Breckinridge, stripping eastern Tennessee of another 1,100 men. This left East Tennessee with a scattering of infantry, semi-organized organized into two brigades, numbering no more than 2,000 troops: these

---

15 *OR* 33, 1203, 1234. Jenkins was unfit for duty, recovering from a wound received at Gettysburg, and his regiments were widely dispersed.

16 J. Gary Laine and Morris M. Penny, *Law's Alabama Brigade in the War Between the Union and The Confederacy* (Shippensburg, PA: 1996), 230.

and three more small brigades of cavalry or mounted infantry comprised Buckner's entire garrison.[17]

Next to leave was Buckner himself. Buckner officially replaced Longstreet on March 8, but was ordered to the Trans-Mississippi on April 26, leaving Brig. Gen. William E. Jones in charge. By the beginning of April, the District of East Tennessee, far from being a strongly held buffer blocking Union threats coming into Breckinridge's sphere of command from the southwest, was instead a weak, poorly defended flank that opened up a new avenue of threat for Breckinridge to worry about.

In fact, Breckinridge faced threats from three directions. Federals held Knoxville, occupied Winchester, and were deployed all through West Virginia, the long western flank of Breckinridge's new command. While major incursions directly over the mountains were unlikely, once the weather cleared small columns of Federals could range across those ridges to strike almost anywhere in the Valley. Breckinridge's most important mission was to protect the long rail connection between Bristol, on the Virginia-Tennessee line, and Lynchburg, where the Virginia & Tennessee Railroad joined the Virginia Central. Loss of the salt works in southwest Virginia, or the loss of a rail connection to move that product would cripple the South's ability to supply troops in the field with meat. Almost as important was the Virginia Central spur line that ran to Staunton, where Imboden made his headquarters. Staunton was a town of 4,000 residents in 1860, though war swelled that population as refugees fled embattled areas. By early 1863, the village had become a hub of warehouses and factories. Food and other war materiel were stored here, not only for the use of those troops defending the valley, but also to support the much larger Army of Northern Virginia as Lee fought his campaigns east of the Blue Ridge. Defending everything with the forces on hand would be difficult.

Faced with myriad and complex problems, Breckinridge's first order of business was to personally survey his entire command. This trip involved a grueling "four hundred mile ride of his entire line . . . [which] took over three weeks, used up two horses, and thoroughly wore him out." However tiring, the journey did provide Breckinridge with a full understanding of his available resources, the chance to meet his subordinates, and reassure the citizenry that a competent man was now

17 *OR* 33, 1322.

on the job. His survey accomplished, Breckinridge could now formulate a strategy.[18]

Robert E. Lee already had some idea of just how Breckinridge might accomplish that mission. Lee thought that the Confederacy should protect only a bare minimum of territory, a strategy primarily intended to free up as many troops as possible with which to meet Grant. Accordingly, Lee suggested a defensive line first sketched out by Early over the winter, which unilaterally surrendered much of the existing department and instead relied on constructing earthworks to defend the most vital points. To aid in that labor, Lee offered up the services of the 700 men of the 1st Confederate Engineers, then stationed in Richmond. Breckinridge was loath to yield so much of his new command without a fight: doing so would hardly restore waning popular confidence. Instead, he chose a more ambitious line, which "generally . . . ran fifty miles in advance of Early's."[19]

Holding this new perimeter meant that Breckinridge would need to somehow significantly increase his available numbers, put those men already in the ranks into a more disciplined and combat-ready condition, and concentrate his forces in key areas so that they could be shifted to threatened points rapidly during moments of crisis. He couldn't defend everywhere, but by expanding the available defensive perimeter, in the event of an incursion Breckinridge reasoned that he could trade space for time in hopes of being able to concentrate against any emerging threats one at a time, defeat them, and move on to the next. The idea was sound strategic thinking, a smaller version of the strategy underpinning Davis's defense of the whole Confederacy. Pulling it off would also require a great deal of timely intelligence, some luck, and perhaps a dollop or two of Union incompetence.

The first order of business was to address the manpower issue. Stragglers, skulkers, shirkers and detailed men were at immediately ordered back to duty. Men now loose in the region were rounded up and returned to their units. Those existing regiments that had dispersed to their homes over the winter were expected to augment their ranks with new recruits. These efforts paid off. On the last day of February, the

18 Davis, *Breckinridge,* 409.

19 Ibid., 411-412.

department contained only 5,700 men. The March 30 return saw that number grow to 6,900 troops, andby the end of April the Department of Western Virginia could boast 9,555 men under arms, though this last increase was in large part due to the return of Wharton's 1,100 troops and the transfer of Maj. J. D. Kirkpatrick's 800-man battalion (comprised of the survivors of Brig. Gen. John Hunt Morgan's cavalry division, which had been captured during a raid into Ohio the previous year.) Simultaneously, Imboden's Northwestern Brigade increased to a respectable 1,568 effectives. Over the course of a bare two months, Breckinridge's efforts added 2,500 men to the ranks over and above the 1,900 reinforcements sent to him. All in all, it was an impressive effort.[20]

Nor was this all. In addition to the roughly 11,000 troops now available among the regular forces, every effort was exerted to improve the numbers and equipment of the local reserve and home guard units. While these men were either too young, too old, too crippled or desperately needed in critical war endeavors to take the field for more than short periods of time, they could turn out in critical emergencies to man local defenses until the regular troops arrived. In the Valley district alone, these elements amounted to a little over 850 rifles, including the 261 cadets of the Virginia Military Institute. Similar local defense forces were mustered in southwest Virginia. Thus, by April Breckinridge might expect to be able to call on 12,000 or 13,000 total defenders, of which about 10,000 were his effective field force.[21]

The core of Breckinridge's little army were his three infantry brigades under Echols, McCausland, and Wharton. Together they amounted to roughly 5,000 infantry, all Virginians, most of whom had seen long service but little action for many months. The force consisted of five full regiments, the 22nd, 36th, 45th, 51st, and 60th; and four more separate battalions, the 23rd, 26th, 30th Sharpshooters, and 45th. With two exceptions, none of these troops had been in a battle since 1862, and some of them not since 1861. Most recently, the 22nd Regiment and 23rd Battalion had both seen combat at Droop Mountain in November 1863. However, the Confederacy did not prevail in that action, and neither formation met with much success there. The fight resulted when Brigadier General

---

20 *OR* 33, 1250; Steven H. Newton, *Lost for the Cause: The Confederate Army in 1864* (Mason City, IA: 2000), 185, 189-191.

21 Newton, *Lost for the Cause,* 185.

Echols attempted to head off a Union raid with his 1,700 men, only to meet a much superior Federal force of 7,000. Echols was soundly defeated, suffering 275 casualties. His troops were effectively routed. "We fought four to one & where whipped very badly," sadly concluded James Hardin of the 23rd.[22]

Of the rest, the 45th Virginia Regiment last saw action at Carnifax Ferry in September 1861. The 36th and 51st regiments had previously only faced General Grant in the disastrous affair of Fort Donelson, February 1862, barely escaping capture there. The 60th Virginia saw heavy fighting during the Seven Days outside Richmond in June of 1862, but then had been transferred out of A. P. Hill's famous Light Division to help defend western Virginia and seen no action since. The 26th Battalion was formed out of several companies of the 59th Regiment who managed to escape capture at Roanoke Island, also in February 1862. The 30th Battalion Sharpshooters and the 45th Battalion had yet to see any serious combat, though they did contain some veterans from other units within their ranks, including, in the case of the sharpshooters, at least two companies of Virginians who had been captured at Donelson, then paroled and eventually returned to service. It could be said that while Breckinridge's infantry was reasonably seasoned, much of that seasoning came in the form of battlefield defeat; a potentially demoralizing state of affairs. 1864 promised a much livelier campaigning season ahead.

Desertion remained a concern. Many of these troops were locally raised, and after years in the army the lure of a visit home was strong. The 30th Virginia Sharpshooters provides a case in point. In April 1863, the battalion was ordered to depart their camp at Narrows, Virginia, and move to Saltville. While the distance was less than one hundred miles, in just three days, between April 18 and 20, 35 men left the ranks. Only eight of those men would voluntarily return, and absenteeism continued to be a problem. While Breckinridge hoped to get some of these men back with local recruiting and appeals to patriotism, his arrival also heralded a tightening of discipline and increased use of the stick as well as carrot. One such example came on April 15, 1864, when James Peters and his comrades of the 30th sharpshooters witnessed the execution of Pvt. John H. Jones of Company E for the military crime of desertion. Similarly,

---

22 "My Dear sister," November 11, 1863, James Hardin Papers, Preston Library, Virginia Military Institute, Lexington, VA; Hereafter VMI.

Imboden was forced to make an example of Pvt. John Mick of the 62nd Virginia Mounted Infantry. Mick, who left the ranks to join a band of Union sympathizers, was executed by firing squad on March 18, 1864, while the assembled Northwestern Brigade looked on.[23]

The lack of suitable cannon was probably the Department of Western Virginia's greatest weakness. Breckinridge's artillery totaled approximately 26–30 guns in 7 batteries. At least two batteries did not report the condition or number of their guns, leaving their complement open to speculation, but both of those companies also reported very few men present; they could not have crewed many guns in any case. The remaining 5 batteries reported 23 cannon available, mostly of unspecified caliber. Of those that did report type, only 8 pieces could be considered modern; either 12-pound smoothbore Napoleons or three-inch rifles. The rest were older models, Mexican War era pieces like 6-pound smoothbores or Model 1841 12-pound howitzers; gun types now largely replaced in the main Confederate armies. In addition, Imboden's district included one battery of six pieces, four of which were modern three-inch rifles. Additionally, the VMI Corps of cadets included a two-gun section of the antiquated six pounders. If it came to an artillery duel, Breckinridge's forces would be powerfully outgunned.[24]

All in all, Breckinridge's and Imboden's forces faced daunting challenges. Manpower shortages, morale problems, and equipment deficiencies remained significant concerns. Despite all those troubles, however, Breckinridge remained optimistic. He intended to make a stubborn fight of it, wherever the blow landed, and he intended to win.

23   Jack L. Dickenson, *Diary of a Confederate Sharpshooter: The Life of James Conrad Peters* (Charleston, WV,:1997), 87-88; Woodward, *Defender of the Valley*, 102.

24   Newton, *Lost for the Cause*, 185, 189-191.

CHAPTER 3

The Department of West Virginia

G rant's promotion would bring change and activity to every Union
department, and West Virginia was no exception. On January
31, 1864, the Department included 24,959 officers and men present for
duty. This force was organized into four divisions of varying sizes, each
a mixed command of artillery, infantry and cavalry. That mix included
roughly 16,000 foot, 8,000 horse, and 122 cannon. On March 29, after
having had a chance to personally assess his new command, Sigel
reported that the department now contained 23,397 men. Infantry and
artillery numbers remained essentially unchanged, but mounted strength
had declined to 5,441 (likely due to unserviceable horses rather than a
loss of men.) Additionally, he was about to lose another 1,000 troops
because one of his brigades had just been ordered to re-join the Army
of the Potomac.[1]

While on paper Sigel's forces appeared substantial and well organized;
the men were widely scattered, distributed largely with an eye towards
railroad defense, not field operations. Each of the existing divisions
would require significant reorganization into separate infantry and
cavalry commands to undertake active campaigning. To do so, many
men would have to be stripped away from the rail garrisons. The troops
themselves needed extensive drilling, having been too long in stationary
positions or dispersed into small garrisons; their battlefield skills had

---

1   *OR* 33, 479, 762.

Major General George Crook in 1865. *Library of Congress*

grown stale. Regiments would have to be uprooted from existing camps and barracks and brought together in larger camps of instruction, so that they could re-learn their trade. This in turn would expose much of the state to greater harassment from guerrillas and raiders, a prospect that alarmed both the West Virginia governor and the state legislature, who after all had petitioned for a change of commanders to have more protection, not less. Indeed, immediate offensive operations seemed out of reach. All in all, Sigel concluded, it was about all he could do "to make the troops efficient, to defend and strengthen my position, and to protect the people."[2]

Grant, of course, had other ideas. Sigel's mission was attack, not defense. "Whilst the long line of railroad you have to guard may require all the force you have," admitted the General-in-chief, "for a movement towards the enemy it looks to me that almost everything except a small force judiciously distributed . . . might be spared." Grant reasoned that by taking the war to the enemy, the Confederates would have little opportunity to embark on an offensive of their own. While this might be true enough for Breckinridge's limited conventional forces, Grant was seriously underestimating the havoc smaller raiding parties might wreak.[3]

Late in March, Grant summoned Maj. Gen. George Crook to his new headquarters. Crook was a proven soldier, with much experience leading both infantry and cavalry. In 1862, he had seen service with the IX Corps in West Virginia and at Antietam. For much of 1863 he served in Tennessee, under William S. Rosecrans, seeing action at the battle Chickamauga, where he commanded a cavalry division. In January

2   Ibid., 765.

3   Ibid.

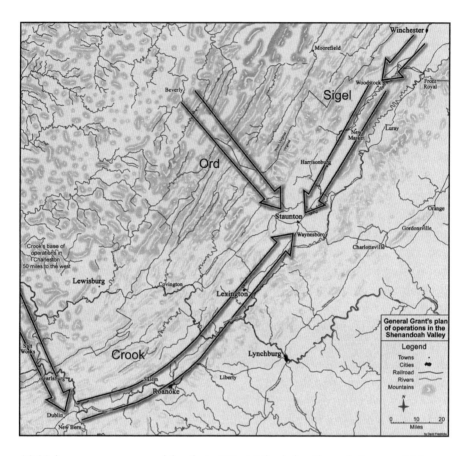

1864 he was summoned back to West Virginia, though he would have preferred to remain in Tennessee where he thought he might have a shot at commanding a full cavalry corps as part of Sherman's upcoming campaign.[4]

While at Grant's headquarters, Crook met Edward Ord. Grant explained to both men his plans for the coming spring. The new chief envisioned a pincer movement, converging on the Valley's heart at Staunton. Crook was to command an expedition against the rails in southwest Virginia. Crook remembered later that "it was agreed that I was to . . . destroy the bridge across the New River, and then move along that railroad, destroying it en route until I met General Sigel's force, which was to move via Staunton for the same railroad." If the New River Bridge

---

4   George Crook, *General George Crook: His Autobiography* (Norman, OK, 1946), 114.

could be destroyed, then southwest Virginia and hopefully, the bulk of Breckinridge's force would be isolated from the lower Valley. Once this was accomplished Crook could move north towards Staunton in relative safety. He need not worry about his line of retreat, for once united with Sigel, his supply line would stretch northward to Winchester, not back through the mountains into West Virginia.[5]

Now Grant added a twist. He informed the two men that he wanted another column to move eastward from the town of Beverly—with 8,000 infantry and 1,500 cavalry—threatening Staunton from the northwest and further dividing the limited Confederate resources available to defend the Valley. This was the force Crook was supposed to meet. It was intended to be Sigel's in name only: Ord was to be the actual field commander. Both columns were expected to live off the land as much as possible, though Grant expressly warned against "indiscriminate marauding." Sigel's role was reduced to that of an administrator. He was to provide the troops for Ord's expedition, stockpile 10 days' supplies at Beverly, and ensure that Ord had a pontoon train if possible. Sigel's only active role would be lead a re-supply convoy from Winchester to Staunton with provisions for both Ord's and Crook's columns. Clearly, the commanding general intended to limit Sigel's field duties as much as possible. As of yet, Sigel knew nothing of this new variation.[6]

Grant's interference would have a profound impact on the coming campaign, and not for the better. His decision to create a third column was based only on map study, augmented by information obtained second-hand. Having never served in Virginia, the new boss had no real appreciation for the terrain. Nor did he consider the effect of the weather, where Virginia was having a wet, cold spring. Neither Crook nor Ord could offer any recent knowledge, since Crook hadn't campaigned in the region for two years and Ord knew the country not at all. Shortly after this meeting, Crook and Ord traveled together back to West Virginia, staying overnight in the District of Columbia. They resumed their travels the next day. Ord de-trained at his home town of Cumberland Maryland, now the site of Sigel's headquarters, and Crook continued to Charleston.[7]

---

5   Ibid.

6   *OR* 33, 765.

7   Ibid., 874.

Whatever Grant intended to accomplish by inserting Ord into the mix, he in effect delivered a poison pill to Sigel's command. Arriving at departmental headquarters on March 29, Ord's appearance fell on Sigel like a bombshell. "General E. 0. C. Ord arrived . . . " the little German indignantly sputtered, "with a letter from General Grant, saying in Substance that I should immediately assemble 8,000 infantry, 1,500 cavalry ('picked men'), besides artillery, provided with ten days' rations, at Beverly, for the purpose of marching by Covington to Staunton; the troops to be under the command of General Ord, who supplemented the letter by saying, on the on the authority of General Grant, that the column should start within ten days."[8]

The timing was stunning. Sigel had only assumed command less than three weeks earlier. Previously, Grant had alerted him that Sigel would need to assemble 20,000 men and be ready to take the field by the middle of April—already a tall order. Ord's arrival moved that timetable up by at least a full week, to April 8 at the latest. The task, already difficult, just became virtually impossible.

To make matters worse, Ord's attitude was disputatious, verging on insubordinate. Ord understood the commanding general intended for him to have Sigel's job, an appointment that was stymied only by political machinations, and that it would only be a matter of time before he replaced Sigel and assumed departmental command in his own right. Armed with that foreknowledge, Ord proved unable to control his arrogance or temper. In a candid letter to his wife Molly, Ord admitted that he had been "excessively vexed" at the idea of serving under Sigel right from the outset, an attitude that he made no effort to hide. For his own part, Sigel—by nature suspicious and jealous—was incensed at being so obviously shelved. "All dispositions were made in such a manner," he recalled, "as if I did not exist at all."[9]

Sigel's objections to these new orders were not merely rooted in damaged vanity. Sigel immediately understood that the idea of a Beverly expedition was poorly conceived. As Stonewall Jackson discovered back

---

8   Franz Sigel, "Sigel in the Shenandoah Valley in 1864," *Battles and Leaders of the Civil War*, 4 vols. (New York, 1956), vol. 4, 487.

9   "Dear Molly," April 20, 1864, Ord Papers, University of California at Berkeley, hereafter UC Berkeley; Sigel Papers, Western Reserve Historical Society, Cleveland, OH, hereafter WRHS.

in the winter of 1861, even limited movements through the mountains of western Virginia could be nigh impossible during bad weather. And in the spring of 1864, bad weather ruled the day. Winter seemed reluctant to leave, with frequent cold rains, turning to snow at higher elevations. The roads were churned to muddy impassibility by the passage of even a few troops. On April 12, Sigel wired Grant, explaining the difficulties of moving through 147 miles of nearly trackless mountains, in foul weather, dependent only on wagons for resupply. Sigel grasped that Crook's column would have a much shorter approach to Staunton from the Kanawha River valley, via Lewisburg. By contrast, "a column advancing by Beverly and coming to a standstill [in the mountains] will be a lost power, as it can neither assist us in the Shenandoah nor cooperate well with General Crook."[10]

After unproductive consultations with Sigel, Ord departed Cumberland on April 6, to take command of the new force assembling at Beverly. Once there, he discovered that only two thirds—6,500—of the requisite 9,500 troops were present. Ord was sure Sigel was to blame, deliberately withholding men to derail Ord's role in the campaign. Both Grant and Ord seriously over-estimated the numbers of troops Sigel could free up from rail protection. Despite his personal feelings, Sigel had in fact had done everything in his power to muster the required force at Beverly, leaving the B&O dangerously exposed in the meantime.

To make matters worse, Ord was greatly dismayed at the quality of the troops he found waiting for him. Their lack of drill and efficiency was obvious, and he balked at the idea of leading them into combat. Grant's timetable was clearly unrealistic, but Ord didn't want to be the one blamed for delaying things.

Confronted with these realities, Ord privately quailed. He reverted to his old habit of ducking responsibility, this time without even the fig leaf of illness to cover his tracks. The troops at Beverly needed a firm military hand to instill discipline and confidence, and who better to provide that guidance then a proven professional officer with what seemed to be a solid combat record? Instead, Ord immediately sought to escape what he expected to be a disaster before blame could be laid

---

10   James I. Robertson, Jr., *Stonewall Jackson: The Man, The Soldier, The Legend* (New York, 1997), 305-318, highlights the difficulties Jackson's troops encountered during their winter campaign. *OR* 33, 844.

Major General Edward O. C. Ord. *Library of Congress*

at his feet. He immediately applied to Grant for a transfer, asking to be sent to Wheeling, far from the scene of any impending battle, or to be excused duty in the department altogether. "I . . . have not had a delightful time 'mit Sigel' and think I shall get out of this as soon as I can" he informed Molly on April 9, less than three days after laying eyes on his new command. On April 11 he protested to his wife that he was only trying to do his duty as he saw it, but four days later he revealed his true motives: "I would like to be relieved . . . of any of the responsibility of events to come." Ord soon got his wish, much to Sigel's evident relief. "General Ord, who was every day in my headquarters became so diffident in regard to the whole matter that he asked General Grant to be relieved. His request was granted on the 17th of April. . . ." Ord spared no time in departing, but the turmoil left in his wake would reverberate in the weeks to come.[11]

Even as his intended plans for West Virginia crumbled into ruin, Grant continued to harbor misapprehensions about the difficulties the campaign faced. Grant expected any Rebels Sigel's forces met to flee rather than fight. On April 13 he airily informed Sigel that "a movement up the Shenandoah Valley . . . will not require much more than an escort for the wagon train." This was a wholly unrealistic assertion, especially given how much partisan activity there was in the lower Shenandoah at this stage of the war.[12]

Perhaps Grant expected little result from Sigel's venture, especially given Ord's private request to be absolved of responsibility, but even

---

11 Charles R. Knight, *Valley Thunder: The Battle of New Market and the Opening of the Shenandoah Campaign, May 1864* (New York, 2010), 29-30; Letters of April 11th and 15th, Ord to Molly, Ord Papers; Sigel, "Sigel in the Shenandoah Valley," 487.

12 *OR* 33, 858.

so, there was still merit to the operation. Grant hated the idea of having any troops standing still, even if needed to control occupied territory. Besides, action on Sigel's part could still help Crook, who in Grant's view had by far the most important mission: that destroying the New River Bridge and cutting the V & T Railroad at a stroke. As Grant famously explained to Lincoln, "these troops could perform this service just as well by advancing [as standing still] . . . and . . . they would compel the enemy to keep detachments to hold them back or else lay his own territory open to invasion . . . " Lincoln grasped the idea at once: "if a man can't skin he must hold a leg while someone else does." With Ord gone, Sigel himself would have to do the leg-holding.[13]

Sigel faced three problems in executing Grant's scheme. First, there simply weren't enough troops for three expeditions, and those that were present were in dire need of both training and re-equipping. Second, bad weather persisted well into April. That month was wet enough to bring creeks and rivers out of their beds, rendering them un-crossable, and turned roads to quagmires of mud. Snow continued to fly as late as the beginning of May, greatly complicating travel in the mountains. Third, Confederate partisans had no intention of ignoring Sigel's logistical tail as his men marched up the Valley to Staunton.

In a dispatch to Grant on April 12 Sigel outlined his manpower problem, explaining that he had only 23 regiments of infantry in his whole department. Six of those were already tasked to go with Crook's column, and 10 more were now assigned to Ord (who had not yet secured his desired transfer.) Four more regiments would have to be retained to guard the Baltimore & Ohio. Crook was additionally to be reinforced by the 36th Ohio, then on veteran furlough at Marietta and about to return to the front, but this left only three regiments available to escort the re-supply train when it departed Winchester, hardly a sufficient force.[14]

The cavalry was also bedeviled with problems. Crook informed Sigel that he was still badly in need of remounts, and further, that "it is essential that both my raw men and horses be trained a little before commencing this difficult move." One brand new regiment, the recently-arrived 20th Pennsylvania Cavalry, was completely unready for field duty. The 20th's

13 Ulysses S. Grant, "Preparing for the Campaigns of '64," *Battles and Leaders of the Civil War,* vol. 4, 112.

14 *OR* 33, 845-846.

1,000 men shared "only 150 horses" between them "and [had] no arms except sabers." With grand offensives being readied in both Virginia and North Georgia, few troops or supplies could be spared for Sigel's needs.[15]

In response to Sigel's litany of woes and Ord's abrupt request for re-assignment, Grant hurriedly dispatched Col. Orville E. Babcock to Cumberland in hopes of clarifying matters. Babcock bore a dispatch aimed at placating the German, and approving Ord's demand to be excused. In this dispatch, Grant tacitly conceded that the Beverly expedition might have been unreasonable, writing "that it is not necessary that the exact line marked out by me should be followed." If other, better routes were available, he noted, "I have no objections. . . ." To Grant, only objectives mattered: Sigel must support Crook's expedition, put pressure on the lower Valley, and prevent the Rebels there from reinforcing Lee. Sigel could "confer freely with Colonel Babcock . . . to settle unalterably the line to be pursued by your forces." Once a new plan was worked out, Sigel could wire Grant for final approval.[16]

Babcock arrived on the 17th. Ord departed the same day, new orders in hand. He had been part of the campaign for a little more than two weeks, and in time wreaked an impressive amount of mayhem. With Ord gone, Sigel and Babcock soon settled upon a new strategy, outlining it to Grant via the telegraph the next day. Sigel's views were largely adopted. The Beverly expedition was abandoned, reducing the number of columns to a more realistic two. Sigel's own expedition would assemble at Martinsburg. From there they would occupy Winchester and advance as least as far as Cedar Creek, some 15 miles farther up the valley. Crook was to use part of his force to seize Lewisburg, and from there move against the New River Bridge. Crook was also tasked with destroying the works at Saltville, if possible.

Since Sigel felt that the Rebels were already aware of the growing troop concentration at Beverly, a small force should be retained there in order to fool any Rebel observers into thinking that an expedition from that place was still likely. Sigel also thought that Crook's column should be strengthened and offered up Brig. Gen. William W. Averell and 1,000 more cavalry as reinforcements. Averell's force, originally part of the

---

15 Ibid., 844.

16 Ibid., 874.

Beverly concentration, was already halfway to Crook's command and could join him once the roads dried. Babcock concurred with all these changes, and the new plan was approved. Crook would begin moving on May 2, once all his forces were in place, while Sigel thought his own troops "should start a few days earlier to divert the enemy's attention." The revised plan had much merit, and a reasonable chance of success.[17]

In the meantime, the core of what would have been Ord's column had only come into being a week or so earlier, on April 9, when Sigel created the 1st Infantry Division. Brigadier General Jeremiah C. Sullivan was assigned to command. Sullivan was an 1848 graduate of Annapolis and former naval officer who left the sea in 1854 to practice law in his home state of Indiana. The turn to a legal career was a natural move given that his father was a famous jurist and member of the Indiana Supreme Court. In 1861, Sullivan went to war with the 6th Indiana, serving in West Virginia under William Rosecrans. His first experience in the Shenandoah was in early 1862, when he commanded a brigade at the battle of Kernstown. He was transferred west and again served under Rosecrans in the fall of 1862, leading a brigade into action at the battles of Iuka and Corinth. He returned to West Virginia in the fall of 1863. He was the son-in-law of General Kelley, then commanding the department, which might have had something to do with his return to the theater. Sullivan was demonstrably a brave man, serving at Iuka and rallying troops by personal example in the thick of the fight at Corinth, where he suffered a minor wound. However, in neither affair had he had much chance to exercise tactical dexterity or demonstrate a grasp of more complex martial skills.[18]

Sullivan's division consisted of eight regiments, formed into two brigades. Colonel Augustus Moor commanded the 1st, which contained the 18th Connecticut along with the 28th, 116th, and 123rd Ohio. Colonel Joseph Thoburn's 2nd brigade included the 1st and 12th West Virginia, the 34th Massachusetts, and the 54th Pennsylvania. All eight regiments were large by the standards of 1864, each having between 500 and 600 men in the ranks. The largest, the 116th Ohio, weighed in at 766 rank

---

17 *OR* 33, 901; Franz Sigel, "Sigel in the Shenandoah Valley," 487.

18 Warner, *Generals in Blue,* 487-488.

and file. The 1st West Virginia was the smallest, mustering 387. Sullivan total force amounted to about 4,500 bayonets.[19]

Moor was a capable officer, another exiled German who fled the revolution for Cincinnati, where he opened a beer garden. Instrumental in raising the ethnically German 28th Ohio, Moor served as their first colonel. Initially deployed to western Virginia, in 1862 the 28th saw action at South Mountain and Antietam. Though not heavily engaged in either action, the men performed well. Theodore F. Lang, a Federal West Virginian who had served on Milroy's staff and was now doing the same service for Sigel, noted that Moor was "intelligent . . . [an] efficient officer and gallant soldier, [who] was well liked by [both] officers and men." Seniority elevated him to brigade command, but this was not his first time acting in that capacity. Moor had led a de-facto infantry brigade under General Averell in the fight at Droop Mountain the previous November, leading a spirited attack on the Confederate left that turned the enemy out of a strong defensive position. Moor's role proved instrumental in securing that victory. Despite their shared German roots, Moor was not automatically a fervent supporter of Sigel. The beefy colonel preferred to reserve judgment.[20]

Colonel Joseph Thoburn was Irish-born, but he grew up in Ohio. His family immigrated to America when he was just an infant. Having studied medicine prior to the war, Thoburn began his military career as an army surgeon, leaving behind an established practice in Wheeling.

---

19 Brigade Return, May 10, Augustus Moor Papers, Illinois Historical Survey, University of Illinois, Urbana IL; Charles J. Rawling, *History of the First Regiment Virginia Infantry. Being a Narrative of the Military Movements in the Mountains of Virginia, in the Shenandoah Valley and East of the Blue Ridge during the War of the Rebellion, of the First Regiment Virginia Infantry Volunteers—Three Months' and Three Years' Service* (Philadelphia, 1887), 168; William C. Davis, *The Battle of New Market* (New York, 1975), 188-189, gives substantially different numbers for some units, especially among the West Virginians: Davis shows the 1st numbering 700 and the 12th numbering 989. No sources are provided for these strengths. However, the return in *OR* 37, pt. 1, 571, shows a divisional total of 4,400 for the end of May. The division lost 716 casualties in battle at New Market, but also had those losses effectively replaced with the addition of two new units, a Maryland regiment and a battalion of New York heavy artillery. The 12th West Virginia had been in service since 1862, and more likely numbered around 500 officers and men.

20 Theodore F. Lang, *Loyal West Virginia from 1861 to 1865, With an Introductory Chapter on the Status of Virginia for Thirty Years Prior to the War* (Baltimore, 1895), 106; *OR* 29, pt. 1, 506.

When his regiment, the 1st Virginia (later to be known as the 1st West Virginia after statehood) reorganized from a three-month unit to a three-year enlistment Thoburn forsook the green sash of a medico for a colonel's eagles and assumed command. Thoburn saw active service against Stonewall Jackson, both in the 1862 Valley campaign and again at Cedar Mountain that August. He and his regiment then spent the next year and a half in West Virginia, doing more marching than fighting. He was competent in his current position, but, like General Sullivan, had so far been given few chances to demonstrate notable tactical acumen.

As for the men in the ranks, the regiments comprising the division might be up to snuff numerically but varied greatly in quality. Of the eight regiments in the division, four of them had fought at Second Winchester under Milroy: the 18th Connecticut, 12th West Virginia, 116th and 123rd Ohio. While "Milroy's weary boys" felt their stand played a vital role in delaying Lee on the way to Gettysburg, most of the rest of the army looked at them askance for having been captured. More significantly, all four regiments were crippled in terms of leadership. While the enlisted men had been paroled and exchanged, most of the officers remained in enemy hands to await freedom under an ever more increasingly problematic exchange cartel.

The 123rd Ohio's problems were typical. The regiment was raised in October 1862; Winchester was their first action. A full-strength regiment included 34 line officers, not counting positions such as surgeon or chaplain. One captain and two lieutenants staffed each of the 10 companies, while a major, a lieutenant-colonel, and the colonel rounded out the field grade roster. The regimental adjutant, while not technically a line officer, also played a significant role in unit training and discipline; for many young officers the adjutant's slot was a stepping stone to regimental command. Of these 34 positions, however, the 123rd had only eight officers present in April 1864. Twenty-one more men were still in enemy hands or under parole, and a couple of positions were completely vacant. Fortunately, Maj. Horace Kellogg and Adjutant William V. McCracken were still present, but only 6 line officers out of the 30 company-grade officers allotted were ready for duty. As if to exacerbate the shortage, 128 new recruits came in over the winter to swell the 123rd's ranks to just over 600 effectives, but those new men would need constant drilling to integrate them into the regiment and teach them the complex maneuvers expected of them on a battlefield. In January and February, "when the weather permitted, drilling by company and squad occurred daily," noted regimental historian C. M. Keyes, but on March 1 that training regimen came to an end when the 123rd's "companies were distributed as guards" along the line of the B & O Railroad "between Harper's Ferry and Monocacy Junction." Short of officers, with 20 percent of their numbers made up of green men, and with little chance to drill above the company level, the 123rd was wholly unprepared for the rigors of active combat.[21]

Despite these shortcomings, the 123rd was assigned railroad duty to replace their fellow Buckeyes of the 116th, who were even less prepared. The 116th had spent the last seven months detailed as rail guards, serving continuously from August 1863. During this time, noted Lt. Col. Thomas F. Wildes, "the field and staff officers soon found themselves 'more ornamental than useful.'" Having not practiced regimental maneuvers for half a year, the regiment was extremely rusty. Once relieved by the 123rd, the 116th embarked on a crash course of drilling, though the lingering winter weather greatly hampered those efforts.[22]

Both the 12th West Virginia and 18th Connecticut found themselves in similar straits. The West Virginians lost 233 officers and men at Winchester (191 of them captured) out of about 675 engaged, though the regimental history noted that the 12th was the only infantry regiment that "retain[ed] their organization." Recruiting and exchanges probably built the 12th back up to between 600 and 700 rank and file. Fortunately, with all 10 companies assembled at Cumberland, the 12th also found a little more time to drill. Lieutenant William Hewitt, later the regimental historian, noted that "in the forepart of February, Col. Curtis received orders to take the regiment and go into camp on a hill west of the city. . . .[T]he Colonel found time to thoroughly drill the regiment in battalion drill, the manual of arms, and dress parade." Less fortunate was the 18th, which also numbered about 600 men, but had only Maj. Henry Peale, Adjutant Benjamin Culver, three captains and two lieutenants still with the colors.[23]

21 C. M. Keyes, *The Military History of the 123rd Regiment Ohio Volunteer Infantry* (Sandusky, OH, 1874), 52-53, 59-60.

22 Wildes, *Record of the One Hundred and Sixteenth Regiment*, 107.

23 *OR* 27, pt. 2, 53; *OR* 27 pt. 3, 296; William Hewitt, *History of the Twelfth West Virginia Volunteer Infantry, the Part It Took in the War of the Rebellion 1861–1865*

The skills of the remaining four infantry regiments in Sigel's main body were of a similarly mixed bag. The 34th Massachusetts was a splendid-looking command, well dressed, well equipped, superbly drilled; as well as noted for its excellent band. So far, however, the regiment had spent almost its entire career in the defenses of Washington, they had yet to see combat. Colonel George D. Wells tasted gunpowder, having served previously with the 1st Massachusetts until July 1862. In that time, however, he had been in only one really sharp fight: the limited action of Oak Grove, fought outside Richmond on June 25, an engagement that was soon overshadowed by the much bloodier Seven Days' fighting between Lee and McClellan; by which time Wells had already returned home to raise the 34th. When Wells and his men arrived in Washington, they were incorporated into the capitol defenses, and would remain there for the next year. The 34th gained some field experience in the fall of 1863, sent to Harper's Ferry after Gettysburg, but saw only very limited skirmishing with guerrillas. Their mastery of drill was all well and good, but they were not battle-tested.[24]

When the 34th found out they were to serve with the likes of the 116th and 123rd Ohio, there was considerable consternation among the New Englanders. "Heaven help us!" exclaimed Lt. Col. William Lincoln; "except for the 34th, this infantry is neither drilled nor disciplined!" Lincoln also spoke disparagingly of the 12th West Virginia's propensity to travel with lots of baggage, another sign of poor discipline. The 34th had some unauthorized hangers-on of their own. Because of the static nature most of the regiment's service, the 34th had more than the usual number of dogs. Regimental dogs were not uncommon in the war, many soldiers made pets of strays or even brought some from home. However, the 34th seems to have been over-supplied in that regard. "Our dogs," said Lincoln, "of which we have an army . . . howl at every bugle call, [and] all bark in chorus when the drum corps makes its presence known. . . . Many are regular in their attendance at all drills, and one

---

(Charleston, 1892), 47, 98; William C. Walker, *History of the Eighteenth Regiment Conn. Volunteers in the War for the Union* (Norwich, 1885), 174.

24 The 1st was present at First Bull Run, but not engaged in the main fight. They suffered only one man killed and one wounded. At Williamsburg they were close to the fight but again not engaged. As part of the Union III Corps, the Bay-Staters were also only peripherally engaged at one of the Seven Days' actions, at Glendale on June 30th. Of the 154 casualties suffered during the Peninsula campaign, 126 of them fell at Oak Grove.

of these sings second whenever our colonel's voice is heard delivering
. . . command[s]."[25]

The remaining three regiments were at least veteran units. The 28th
Ohio had seen much combat and done well. They were probably the best
of all the regiments in Sigel's budding army, reliable and effective. The
1st West Virginia, also veteran, was not without blemish. On September
11, 1863 all or part of five companies—nearly half the command—were
captured by McNeill's Partisan Rangers, with hardly a shot fired. Major
Edward W. Stephens led an ad-hoc battalion to Moorfield West Virginia,
ordered to occupy the region and suppress McNeill. Instead the 23-year-
old Stephens ended up suppressed. On the night in question, Stephens
sent out a patrol of 100 men to run down a report of partisan activity,
which is when McNeill chose to strike. The Rebels approached Stephens's
bivouac from an unexpected direction, slipping past a line of sleeping
pickets to descend on the main camp in a pre-dawn rush. Tabulations
of the exact number of men captured vary. The 1st's regimental history
reported that McNeill took 230 captives, while Rebel General Imboden
recorded a haul of 146 prisoners. Either way, the loss all but gutted
the regiment, reducing it to a small battalion. Stephens was cleared of
wrongdoing in a subsequent board of inquiry, but morale in the 1st was
clearly shaken by the disaster. When their time expired in February 1864,
only about half of the men re-enlisted to serve out the rest of the war.[26]

The 54th Pennsylvania could also boast of long service, virtually all
of it in West Virginia. Recruited in the fall of 1861, after a brief stint
in the forts of Washington, D.C., in March of 1862 the 54th was sent to
join the garrison Harper's Ferry. They narrowly escaped capture when
Stonewall Jackson invested that place just prior to the battle of Antietam,
and thereafter were assigned to General Kelley as guards for the B & O.
So far, their entire service involved guarding the tracks and skirmishing
with guerrillas. They had yet to see a stand-up fight. Moreover, like
several other regiments assigned to railroad duty, wide dispersal meant
that there was little opportunity for drilling to polish the maneuvering
skills they would need on a battlefield.

---

25 William S. Lincoln, *Life with the Thirty-Fourth Mass. Infantry in the War of the
Rebellion* (Worcester, 1879), 247, 249.

26 Rawling, *History of the First Regiment Virginia Infantry*, 168; Roger U. Delauter,
Jr., *McNeill's Rangers* (Lynchburg, 1986), 53.

In addition to whipping the infantry into shape, Sigel also needed someone to bring order to his mounted arm. That officer might have been William W. Averell, since by 1864 Averell had considerable experience leading cavalry raids in the region, but Averell was already part of Crook's expedition. For Sigel, Averell's absence cleared the way to bring in his own favored man: Maj. Gen. Julius Stahel. Stahel was a fellow European revolutionary, a Hungarian of Germanic descent who settled in New York after the 1848 revolts were crushed. Stahel had already led a regiment, a brigade, and a division in combat, serving in the Valley and with the 11th Corps under Sigel in 1862; he'd even temporarily commanded that corps, though not in active service. In 1863 Stahel headed up a cavalry division in the Middle Department, until, around the time of Gettysburg, his division was incorporated into the Army of the Potomac and he was replaced by Judson Kilpatrick.

In the eyes of Maj. Gen. Alfred Pleasonton, who headed up the Army of the Potomac's Cavalry Corps at the time, Stahel suffered from two defects that rendered him unfit: the Hungarian was foreign-born, and his commission ranked Pleasonton's own by three months.

On June 27, just days before Gettysburg, Maj. Gen. Joseph E. Hooker acceded to Pleasonton's request and relieved Stahel, writing that Stahel's "presence here as senior major general will much embarrass me and retard my movements." If Stahel harbored any resentment at being relieved on the eve of what seemed to be the crisis of the war, he kept them to himself, but he must have been simmering with frustration over the slight. Sigel had a high opinion of the Hungarian and was delighted to have him, expecting much. Others were not so sure.[27]

David Strother found Stahel to be "a very young man of mild and polite manners . . . " who "received his commission when the fury for foreigners was at its height and when the German influence was high in Washington. Stahel is a very good fancy cavalry officer who has never done anything in the field and never will do anything. He is entirely too mild and amiable for any such position." At least, concluded Strother, "he is a sensible man, and honorable, and in no way mixed up in politics or speculations." Stahel must have looked to be younger than his age, for he was 38 years old when he arrived in the department; hardly a young man in civil war cavalry circles. He was also personally brave,

---

27 *OR* 27, pt. 1, 59-60.

as he would demonstrate beyond question at the battle of Piedmont later that year, where he was awarded the Congressional Medal of Honor.[28]

At least one of Stahel's subordinates avoided the common nativist prejudice against the Hungarian and held him in high opinion. Just the previous month Col. John E. Wyncoop, then commanding his 20th Pennsylvania Regiment at a cavalry camp of instruction in New Cumberland, had lamented Stahel's departure for a field command; "my personal esteem for you as a man," wrote Wyncoop, "renders my regret at not having an interview with you ere you left, the more poignant." Moreover, felt Wyncoop, Stahel had taken a personal interest "in the perfection of my command," impressing both officers and men. Hopefully the Keystoners would get the chance to serve under Stahel in the field, with Wyncoop urging that the general not forget them and "endeavor to have the 20th Penna. Cavalry in your new sphere of operations." Wyncoop was a veteran officer, having seen much service in Tennessee, rendering his opinion of Stahel especially interesting. The 20th soon got their wish, leaving New Cumberland within days to report to Sigel's department, placed again under Stahel's command.[29]

Stahel's task was daunting. In little more than a month, the Hungarian had to organize and train a new division of cavalry. Sigel's mounted force was, if anything, even rawer than his infantry. On paper they numbered roughly 3,000 men, again organized in two brigades. The first, commanded by Col. William B. Tibbets, included the 1st New York (Lincoln) and 1st New York (veteran), the 21st New York, the 1st Maryland Potomac Home Brigade, and the 14th Pennsylvania Cavalry. The 2nd Brigade went to Wyncoop. It consisted of detachments drawn from the 15th New York, 20th and 22nd Pennsylvania cavalries. None of these eight regiments was present in their entirety. The necessity of guarding outposts, escorting trains and chasing guerillas meant that various companies and battalions were scattered across West Virginia. More men lacked serviceable horses and were stationed at the huge cavalry remount depot in Geisboro Maryland, awaiting remounts. Just as

---

28 Strother, *Virginia Yankee,* 223.

29 Colonel John E. Wyncoop to Julius Stahel, March 26th, 1864, Julius Stahel Papers, Library of Congress.

with the infantry, scattered service for the cavalry meant that discipline, training and effectiveness all suffered.

Few of these mounted units had been together for very long in the first place. Only the 1st New York (Lincoln) cavalry had been formed in 1861. Four companies of the Marylanders and a battalion of the 22nd Pennsylvania cavalry were also recruited during the first year of the war, but each of those formations had then been fleshed out into full regiments only in February 1864. The majority of the troopers in their ranks were brand new to the soldier life. The next longest service was to be found in the 14th Pennsylvania, which was raised in the fall of 1862. The 1st New York (Veteran), the 15th and 21st New York, as well as the 20th Pennsylvania all had similar histories. They all began recruiting in the late summer or early fall of 1863, but filled their ranks very slowly. None of them were ready to take the field until that December, with the last of their companies coming into the camps as late as February 1864. The few real veterans like the Lincoln cavalry viewed many of these Johnny-come-latelies with disdain, because their ranks included many bounty men. The 15th New York, for example, offered enlistment bounties of up to $477 for signing up, and still had trouble filling their ranks. No one enlisting in 1861 got any such inducement, and those men all resented the idea of patriotism for sale, a resentment that was somewhat mollified when bounties were offered to re-enlisting veterans that winter.

The 20th Pennsylvania had a most unusual service trajectory. It was hastily raised in June 1863, an amalgam of seven companies of six-months' men and a further five companies of emergency militia. The 20th took the field on July 7 at Greencastle Pennsylvania, ordered to join the Army of the Potomac in following Lee's army as the Rebels retreated from Gettysburg. Within a few weeks, the emergency men went home, leaving only the six-months' men still in the field. Suddenly shrunken by half, the remaining companies were assigned to help defend the B & O Railroad. This meant that the regiment never served as a unit beyond the first couple weeks of its existence, but instead, just like the infantry, was deployed one or two companies at a time across western Maryland. The troopers saw only limited action. When their time expired in late December the half-regiment returned to Harrisburg and was mustered out in early January. Immediately Col. John Estill Wynkoop set about reorganizing the 20th as a three-year regiment. He met with some success, recruiting a good number of the newly mustered out troopers, but the re-organized command would not be ready to take the field again until February.

Wynkoop saw previous service in the 3rd and 7th Pennsylvania cavalries. He gained most of his combat experience with the 7th, serving in Tennessee under General Rosecrans in the Army of the Cumberland. After the battle of Stones River Wynkoop returned to his hometown of Philadelphia on recruiting duty, hoping to replenish the 7th's thinned ranks. Then Lee invaded Pennsylvania, and in the emergency, he was assigned to command the newly raised 20th, a position that became permanent with the three years' reorganization. Lieutenant Colonel Gabriel Middleton transferred in from the 2nd Pennsylvania cavalry, where he had previously been captain of Company E; however, he took up the reins of his new responsibilities only on February 23, 1864. He would almost immediately inherit command of the 20th when Wynkoop stepped up to brigade leadership.

Colonel William B. Tibbets of the 21st New York was also a veteran officer, albeit not with cavalry. Tibbets served as major of the 2nd New York Infantry until that unit mustered out in May 1863. Tibbets and the rest of the 2nd returned home to Troy, New York, but Tibbets intended to continue his service, preferably with a promotion and a change of branch. A friend of New York Congressman John A. Griswold, Tibbets used his connections to secure the promise of a colonelcy and command of the newly forming 21st, also to be known as the Griswold Light Cavalry. Just as with Wynkoop, seniority soon thrust Tibbets into brigade command, for the previous ranking officer, Col. Andrew T. McReynolds of the 1st Lincoln, was currently detached to command a cavalry camp of instruction near Harpers Ferry. McReynolds was also under a bit of a cloud, having been arrested the previous summer for suspected Rebel sympathies (he was accused of being too lenient towards Rebel prisoners, among other things) and even though he was cleared of those charges, he was not summoned to the front to take command of his regiment in the forthcoming campaign. McReynolds was a pre-war army officer with service in the Mexican War and plenty of experience in the current struggle; he probably would have been more effective at molding such a polyglot gaggle of troopers into a cavalry brigade, but for the moment, that job fell to Tibbets.[30]

Only in artillery could Sigel's expedition said to be well supplied. His field force amounted to 5 batteries mounting 28 guns, all under Capt. Alonzo Snow. These included Battery B of the 1st Maryland, Battery B of the 5th U. S. Regulars, Batteries D and G of the 1st West Virginia, and the 30th New York Independent Battery. All the guns were modern, including 22 rifled three-inch ordnance pieces and 6 Napoleons in the New York Battery. Captain Snow of the 1st Maryland might have been nominally listed as Sigel's chief of artillery, but according to Capt. Henry du Pont of the Regulars, Sigel made no tactical use of him in that capacity, instead parceling his batteries out to the various brigades. This, thought du Pont, was a serious mistake: "throwing away the advantages of proper selection of position, concentration of fire, and general 'ensemble' of operations which so greatly enhance artillery efficiency."[31]

The Marylanders, du Pont's Regulars and Battery D, 1st West Virginia were assigned to Moor's brigade. Captain Alfred von Kleiser's New Yorkers (a German unit) were assigned to Thoburn, leaving the four rifles of Battery G, 1st West Virginia to support Stahel's cavalry. At least all five batteries had already seen substantial service, including some combat. Since artillery was of less use in chasing guerrillas than were the other branches, the batteries also had the benefit of serving and training together in between campaigns. They were among the most dependable components of Sigel's budding expeditionary force.

Sigel's army gathered at Martinsburg during the last half of April. They might have been assembled much sooner had Ord not been involved, since during the first fortnight in April, Sigel was struggling to ship troops to Beverly, as per Grant's meddling. For many of the men involved, the trip to Beverly was an arduous one. Rain and unseasonable cold turned the roads to mud and made the men miserable. Surgeon Alexander Neil accompanied his regiment, the 12th West Virginia, during this march.

30 John C. Bonnell, Jr., *Sabres in the Shenandoah, the 21st New York Cavalry, 1863–1866* (Shippensburg, PA, 1996), xii-xiii.

31 Knight, *Valley Thunder*, 251-252; Henry A. Du Pont, *The Battle of Newmarket, Virginia, May 15, 1864* (Washington, D.C., 1923), 7.

In a letter home on April 5, Neil wrote that the 12th reached Philippi only after toiling over "the worst roads and deepest mortar [mud] I ever saw. . . . It is a terrible thing on the soldiers, as it rains and snows all the time, and many fall by the way." The first part of the movement had been via the railroad, Neil recorded, but even then, it wasn't an easy journey. At Grafton they passed "through the mountains where the snow was two feet deep."[32]

Three days later Neil and his comrades finally reached Beverly, but things had not improved much. "The roads are in such a condition that it seems almost impractical for the artillery and wagons to get along." Even more frustrating, however, were the orders issued on the night of the 8th: "For some reason unknown, we are ordered . . . to be in readiness to Webster [towards Philippi]." Little did Neil know, but this was the moment when General Ord decided he wanted no part of the coming campaign and asked for a transfer. As a result, Neil and his fellow West Virginians, along with all the other Federals making their arduous way to Beverly, now had to retrace their steps and return to Martinsburg. If anything, the march back to Philippi was worse: "I wrote you from Beverly," Neil penned, "since which we have had some terrible marching, indeed, my horse is about give out."[33]

Once back in Philippi, the men at last received a break, resting there for the better part of a week to recover their strength while the roads dried out. Neil recorded that the 12th didn't arrive back in Martinsburg until April 23, "after traveling hundreds of miles by rail and road." All told, they spent nearly a month in transit, wasting valuable time that should have been put to drilling, and needlessly wearing out equipment.[34]

Even the troops not tasked to join the Beverly column had a tough slog ahead of them. On April 17, Charles H. Moulton of the 34th described his regiment's toils with the mud. Moulton, whose writing and clerical skills had long since secured him a headquarters job at Harpers Ferry, took no delight in foot soldiering. "This plodding through mud with a 40-pound knapsack . . . and leading a 'pack mule's' life I don't fancy, exactly, no sirree!" he wrote. "Now our boys . . . when they had orders

32   Richard R. Duncan, ed., *Alexander Neil and the Last Shenandoah Valley Campaign: Letters of an Army Surgeon to his Family, 1864* (Shippensburg, PA, 1996), 16-17.

33   Ibid., 18.

34   Ibid., 20.

to leave Martinsburg, were obliged to march 30 miles with the mud some 10 or a dozen inches deep."[35]

Despite Ord's indictments, Sigel made every effort to comply with Grant's intentions. The force assembled at Beverly demonstrated the German's willingness to fully cooperate with his new commander even though Sigel himself had grave doubts about the wisdom of the venture; given the weather, terrain, and Ord's obstreperousness. Sigel also correctly surmised that the Rebels knew all about the intended concentration at Beverly, meaning that there was no hope of retaining the element of surprise. A much better use of that time would have been to assemble the column at Martinsburg in early to mid-April, where the time could have been used for training. The diversion to Beverly was a blunder, forced on Sigel against his will, and one compounded by Ord's unsoldierly decision to quit the campaign even before it had rightly begun. To Sullivan, Sigel lamented that "there must have been great confusion occasioned by the fact that the whole movement . . . had to be interrupted and stopped when it had already commenced."[36]

On April 27, Sigel ordered his assembled command paraded for the first time, as part of a garrison review. The result displayed some basic shortcomings. "Such a time as we had," noted the 116th Ohio's regimental history, "finding our places in the line. . . . The brigades had never been in line together before, and all questions of rank had to be settled . . . before anyone knew or would take [their] place in the line. After all preliminaries were settled, the review went off very well." Doctor Neill of the 12th witnessed the spectacle, escorting some of the ladies of Martinsburg to the review. To him the troops seemed in high spirits. "The scene . . . [was] magnificent beyond description. As Genls Sigel & Stahel with their respective staffs & orderlies rode up and down the lines the heavens were almost rent with cheers."[37]

35 Lee C. Drickamer and Karen D. Drickamer, eds., *Fort Lyon to Harper's Ferry: On the Border of North and South with "Rambling Jour": The Civil War Letters and Newspaper Dispatches of Charles H. Moulton (34th Mass. Vol. Inf.)* (Shippensburg, PA, 1987), 178.

36 *OR* 33, 875.

37 Wildes, *Record of the One Hundred and Sixteenth,* 37; Duncan, *Alexander Neill,* 21.

Remarkably, despite all these challenges, Sigel was ready to move on time, as promised. On April 30 Corp. Andrew Powell of the 123rd Ohio noted that "we left Martinsburg yesterday and came here [Bunker Hill, Virginia, a few miles north of Winchester] with a force of at least 10,000 men and the number still fastly increasing." Powell's confidence was buoyed by the sight of the whole force on the move. "We have a fine army, the best looking and largest we have ever been in. . . . We are in fine spirits as now 'we fights mit Sigel.'" The next day, May 1, the Federals marched into Winchester. Sigel's command now posed a threat to the Valley, that John D. Imboden and Robert E. Lee could not ignore.[38]

38   "Dear Bro." Camp of Bunker Hill, Va., April 30, 1864, Andrew Powell Letters, Rutherford B. Hayes Presidential Library and Archives, Fremont, Ohio.

CHAPTER 4

Crook's Advance and the Battle of Cloyd's Mountain

hile Sigel was assembling his army at Martinsburg, George Crook was doing the same at Charleston, readying for the intended descent on the upper Valley. Crook's army, about the same size as Sigel's, also contained a fair number of new and inexperienced men. His command included 6,155 infantry and approximately 2,500 cavalry, plus two batteries of artillery. In addition to holding overall authority Crook also retained direct command of the infantry division, while General Averell led the cavalry force. Both men were professionals. They soon developed a solid working relationship. Crook's trust in Averell extended to sending him and virtually all the cavalry off on what amounted to an independent expedition towards Saltville while Crook, with the infantry and only about 500 mounted men, made for their main objective, the New River Bridge.[1]

Aside from augmenting Crook's strength by the addition of Averell, Ord's abrupt departure from the campaign had less effect on Crook's plans then it had on Sigel's. Instead of meeting Ord's column angling in from Beverly, Crook simply had to rendezvous with Sigel's column coming from Martinsburg. The plan still called for a juncture around Staunton. Sigel's force was already moving during the last few days of April, while Crook's own expedition was to be underway by May 1.

---

1   *OR* 37, pt. 1, 10, 41.

Crook's understanding of his role in the forthcoming campaign diverged from Sigel's in one critical respect: Sigel expected that Crook would first advance on Lewisburg with all or part of his force, capturing that place either in conjunction with or before moving on to destroy the New River Bridge. By first taking Lewisburg, Crook would in turn help further divide the Confederates opposing both columns. Crook, however, rejected that idea. The New River Bridge lay almost due south of Crook's jumping-off point, while Lewisburg lay nearly due east. If he captured Lewisburg first, Crook was adding many miles and several extra days' marches to his route. If he divided his forces and tried for both objectives simultaneously, neither column would likely be strong enough to overcome the Rebels they encountered. Accordingly, while Crook would send a small force eastward as a diversion, he intended to march his main force directly south. He failed to inform Sigel of this change in his plans.

Crook's largest advantage in the forthcoming expedition was that the core of his infantry command was built around a dependable, veteran division; men who had served under him before. The 12th, 23rd and 36th Ohio were all proven veterans, having fought together in the IX Corps under Crook's leadership at South Mountain and Antietam. Indeed, the 36th Ohio was Crook's very first command, now nicknamed "Crook's Regulars." The 36th went west with Crook in 1863 and fought at Chickamauga, though by then Crook had been transferred to a cavalry command. Now, re-assembled in the Kanawha Valley, Crook turned to his veterans for leadership as well as fighting prowess. Two of his three brigade commanders were Cols. Rutherford B. Hayes of the 23rd and Carr B. White of the 12th, who both knew and trusted Crook from those earlier campaigns.

The men of all three regiments were delighted to be returned to Crook's purview. On April 26, they presented Crook "with a dress sword they had purchased for the princely sum of seven hundred dollars, raised by contributions from the ranks."[2]

Crook's third brigade commander was Col. Horatio G. Sickel of the 3rd Pennsylvania Reserves, who brought his own regiment and the similarly designated 4th Reserves to join the expedition. Despite their

2   Paul Magid, *George Crook: From the Redwoods to Appomattox* (Norman, 2011), 181.

Colonel Rutherford B. Hayes (center, seated) and his staff at Cumberland Maryland in 1864. *Rutherford B. Hayes Presidential Library*

odd nomenclature, the Pennsylvania Reserves had been in the war from the first, where they amassed a solid combat record with the Army of the Potomac. Initially raised in excess of their state's required militia levy in 1861, the reserves formed a separate combat division, fighting in all that army's major battles. From the reserves' ranks sprang both

Maj. Gens. John F. Reynolds (killed at Gettysburg) and the Army of the Potomac's current commander, George Gordon Meade. Sickel's Pennsylvania regiments were as solid as any veterans Crook could have asked for, as was Sickel himself.

Distributed among these five veteran outfits were several regiments of West Virginians and one more of Ohioans, men who had served most of their time in the Department of West Virginia but had seen little action. This melding of veteran and inexperienced units, all under veteran brigadiers, was a proven method of integrating new troops into combat formations. It was efficacious here as well. The 91st Ohio, 9th and 14th West Virginia regiments were assigned to White's 2nd Brigade, while Sickel's ranks were augmented by the 11th and 15th West Virginia infantry.

As was typical across the rest of the department, odd detachments abounded. For example, the 34th Ohio infantry was now a hybrid: Seven companies were mounted, while the remaining three companies remained afoot. As a result, the bulk of the regiment was assigned to Averell, while the dismounted men were temporarily merged into the 36th Ohio. The 5th and 7th West Virginia Cavalry were also recently converted from infantry—formerly known as the 2nd and 8th West Virginia regiments, respectively, until January of 1864—and still lacked horseflesh for many of their soldiers. There were sufficient mounts for only about 400 of them. The remainder of each regiment, despite the changed nomenclature, continued to march along as foot soldiers in Hayes's brigade.

The mounted companies of each regiment were merged into a single battalion, commanded by Col. J. H. Otey of the 7th. When he first clapped eyes on them, General Crook was dismayed. Otey's men, he noted, "were the odds and ends of several regiments, many with broken down horses, and were not in a condition for the service that was required of them." Realizing that in its current condition Otey's battalion had no chance of keeping up with Averell's fast-moving cavalry raiders, Crook decided that the mounted element of the 5th/7th would remain with his own infantry column. In fact, they were the only mounted troops Crook retained under his direct control. All his other cavalry would be with Averell.[3]

The relative lack of cavalry in Crook's column potentially blinded him, limiting his ability to send out scouts and screen his movements, if it were not for one other contingent. In the summer of 1863, to counter-

---

3   *OR* 37, pt. 1, 11.

act the omnipresent threat of Rebel partisans, Col. Carr White created an independent anti-partisan detachment of about 100 hand-picked men. The unit operated successfully for several months, but since they never had any official status, they were officially disbanded late that fall. When Crook returned to West Virginia, he reformed the command, equipping them with cutting edge firepower in the form of new repeating carbines. These scouts, now 80 men strong and led by Lt. Richard Blazer of the 91st Ohio, were eager to take the fight to enemy bushwackers. Blazer and his independent scouts excelled in the counter-guerrilla role. Blazer had his pick of all the best men, each clamoring to swap the drudgery of regular infantry service for relative independence and the excitement of anti-partisan work. By the spring of 1864, Blazer and his men were intimately familiar with the area of operations and proven in irregular warfare. Crook would make substantial use of them in the upcoming expedition.[4]

By late April, Crook had completed his preparations and finalized his plans. He intended to march his column first to Gauley Bridge, at the junction of the Kanawha and New Rivers. By establishing a base at Gauley, Crook could rely on river steamers to supply his army to that point. Beyond Gauley, things would be more difficult; he would be forced to rely on wagon transport through the mountains, augmented by whatever supplies his men could forage from the sparsely settled countryside. The move to Gauley fit in perfectly with Sigel's understanding of Crook's plans.

From Gauley Bridge, However, Crook's strategy diverged greatly from what Sigel expected. Instead of moving east to seize Lewisburg, Crook intended to only to feint in that direction. As noted, Crook planned to march his main body due south towards the town of Princeton. From Princeton, Crook's route would slide eastwards through the mountains to descend on the New River Bridge from the north. To create an additional diversion, Crook ordered Averell to parallel the infantry's march, heading southwest from Charleston via Logan and Wyoming Courthouses, ultimately moving towards Tazewell, Virginia. Once at Tazewell, Averell could attack the critical works at Saltville from the northwest while Crook appeared to apply pressure from the north. Ideally, this two-pronged

---

4   Darl L. Stephenson, *Headquarters in the Brush: Blazer's Independent Union Scouts* (Athens, OH, 2001), 60-61.

threat would hold the Rebel defenders in place while Crook's infantry sidestepped eastward to their real objective. Unfortunately for future operations, Crook did not discuss his intentions with Sigel beforehand. The German fully expected that Crook's troops would take Lewisburg in the opening days of the campaign and based his own campaign decisions on that assumption.[5]

Opposing Crook, Breckinridge's Confederates were dispersed along the newly drawn and still unrecognized (at least by the Confederacy) Virginia-West Virginia border. Breckinridge's headquarters was at Dublin depot on the Virginia & Tennessee line. John Echol's brigade, numbering 1,500 bayonets, was stationed near Lewisburg and charged with watching the approaches to Staunton. John C. McCausland's brigade, of similar strength, was stationed at Narrows Virginia, about 25 miles east of Princeton. Unbeknownst to Crook, at the beginning of May Confederate Brig. Gen. Gabriel Wharton's brigade (1,100 strong) arrived from East Tennessee, ordered to replace McCausland at Narrows so that McCausland could shift his force to Princeton, directly onto Crook's intended route.[6]

Additionally, two brigades of Rebel cavalry were still operating in the area, struggling to recruit men and procure re-mounts after the hard winter. Colonel William L. Jackson's brigade of Virginia cavalry was stationed up in Bath County, northeast of Lewisburg. The three regiments and two separate battalions of Albert G. Jenkins's cavalry brigade were dispersed in and around Saltville. Jenkins, who had been badly wounded at Gettysburg, only returned to duty in the fall of 1863, and he and his men operated for a time in East Tennessee. Now they were back in the Old Dominion, but their horses were worn out from hard service. His regiments were widely dispersed; the 14th Virginia Cavalry, locally recruited, even kept their livestock at their homes because the army couldn't provide forage. On May 1 Jenkins ordered the 14th to fetch those animals and prepare for active operations, but it would take a week or so for the 14th to be ready for action.

With less than 9,000 men of all arms, Crook did not feel he could send much of a diversionary force towards Staunton. The road east from Gauley Bridge ran through Lewisburg to Covington, and then

---

5   *OR* 37, pt. 1, 41.

6   Ibid., 708.

on to Lexington, home of the Virginia Military Institute. Staunton was another 30 miles north of Lexington. Originally, Ord's Beverly column was supposed to simultaneously threaten Staunton from the west, but with Ord out of the picture and most of his column reverting to Sigel's control, any diversion eastwards would have to come from Crook's own resources. This was a key reason that Sigel agreed send Crook Averell and the extra cavalry.

To make the effort towards Lewisburg, Crook selected Col. Abia A. Tomlinson's 5th West Virginia Infantry, augmented by Blazer's scouts. Together the two units numbered less than 600 men. The previous December, when an entire Union brigade advanced on Lewisburg, they found that not only was the town held by Rebels, but that the whole region between that point and Gauley Bridge was so thick with partisans that couriers required heavy escorts in order to travel securely. It was certain that any new Federal movement towards the town would be quickly reported (and hopefully exaggerated) to Breckinridge or his subordinates in the Valley, likely provoking an equally rapid reaction. Crook enhanced the illusion with an additional ruse, reinforcing Tomlinson with the field musicians and regimental bands from other commands, their instructions to "'make noise enough for an army of ten thousand men.' Each night each band bivouacked apart from the rest, built [a] great camp and made the mountains echo with their martial music."[7]

In the last few days of April Crook's forces deployed to Gauley Bridge, and from there moved on to Fayettesville, West Virginia, named as the new point of departure for his expedition. On April 30 Crook finally telegraphed Sigel of his changed plans, and that he would be marching south, not east. With that Crook left Charleston, heading upriver to Gauley and beyond the immediate reach of any reply. Sigel would not see this dispatch until May 2, by which time both expeditions were under way, leaving the diminutive German no choice but to press on and hope for the best.

As they began to move, Crook's men were plagued with still more foul weather. On April 29, the 23rd Ohio left Charleston to much fanfare, under "a cloudless spring sky." The troops marched along the Kanawha with the rest of Crook's 1st Brigade, while Mrs. Hayes and other regimental ladies kept up via a chartered steamboat. This idyllic

7   *OR* 37, pt. 1, 41; Stephenson, *Headquarters in the Brush*, 87-88.

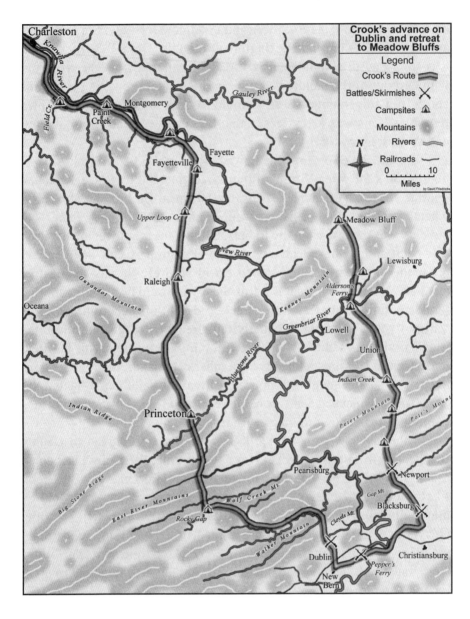

beginning soon came to an end. That night, "a cold winterish rain"
began, falling all through April 30 and into May 1. By the time they
reached Gauley Bridge the troops were drenched and shivering. The 2nd
began well enough, with some sun and a warming trend, but halfway to
Fayettesville the cold, stinging rain returned, morphing into sleet and

then snow; which lasted into the night as they made camp. It was, noted Col. Rutherford B. Hayes, "a rough opening of our campaign."[8]

With his field force finally assembled at Fayettesville, on the morning of May 3 Crook began the next stage of his advance. That morning, Robert B. Wilson of the 12th Ohio recalled, again "with colors flying and bands playing," the column departed Fayettesville. Alert to enemy scouting parties, Crook's men made 14 slushy miles that day. The advance guard repeatedly traded shots with Confederate bushwackers, capturing two of them. Similar marches brought Crook's men to Raleigh Courthouse by the evening of the 4th, and to the summit of Flat Top Mountain on the 5th. Once there, the weather finally warmed up, but so did the opposition; with Rebel partisans becoming even more numerous.[9]

All the while, Tomlinson's diversionary mission towards Lewisburg pushed east, Blazer's scouts leading the way. The small force soon ran into serious opposition. Tomlinson's route lay through the heart of the 14th Virginia Cavalry's home territory, whose troopers now converged on the encroaching Federals. Though still short of horses, the 14th still mustered an impressive 36 officers and 576 men on April 20, 1864, giving them numerical parity with Tomlinson's expedition. The Union scouts waged a cat and mouse fight with these familiar foes for several days, up and down both Big Sewell and Little Sewell Mountains. Each side suffered casualties. Tomlinson's aggressiveness served its purpose, however, drawing Rebel attention and the rest of Jenkins's brigade in to oppose him.[10]

Averell's was the last Federal column to move. Originally supposed to begin in conjunction with Crook's and Tomlinson's departures, Averell's parting was plagued with last minute delays. Wagons were his chief concern. According to his subsequent report, Averell intended to bring six days' rations and four days' forage with him on the expedition, but, "owing to the miserable condition of the teams and horses furnished,"

---

8   Howard Rollins McManus, *The Battle of Cloyd's Mountain: The Virginia and Tennessee Railroad Raid, April 29–May 19, 1864* (Lynchburg, VA, 1989), 9-11, 12. McManus's history of Crook's Campaign is an excellent study of this little-known operation.

9   Robert B. Wilson, "The Dublin Raid," *G. A. R. War Papers* (Cincinnati, OH, 1891), 100; McManus, *Cloyd's Mountain*, 12-14.

10   Stephenson, *Headquarters in the Brush*, 88.

he could haul only four days' rations and barely a day and a half's worth of forage. Futile attempts to remedy this situation consumed several days, delaying Averall's departure from Logan Courthouse until May 5. Finally, the cavalryman decided he could delay no longer, though his supply situation had not improved. Once under way, the cavalry pressed hard and made good time, reaching Wyoming Courthouse by the 6th and moving into Tazewell County on the 7th. There Averell had his first significant contact, skirmishing with and subsequently capturing a picket of the 8th Virginia Cavalry.[11]

Sigel's, Crook's, Averell's and Tomlinson's movements all produced excitement and alarm among the Confederates. Throughout the first few days of May, telegrams flew up and down the Valley and beyond, to both Robert E. Lee at Orange Courthouse, where he was expecting Grant's advance to begin at any moment, and to President Davis in Richmond.

Both Lewisburg and Princeton lay within Breckinridge's defensive scheme of fortified points. Once Wharton's troops arrived at Narrows, Breckinridge ordered McCausland's brigade onward to Princeton, ordered to complete a partially finished earthwork there and hold the town. McCausland's infantry reached Princeton on May 3, though work on the fort was hindered by the fact that the troops had very few entrenching tools.[12]

On the 4th, everything changed. That day, Davis wired Breckinridge the following terse message, which, while brief, completely re-oriented Breckinridge's plans. "Information received here," noted the Confederate president, "indicates the propriety of your making a junction with General Imboden to meet the enemy on his movements towards Staunton. Communicate with Gen. R. E. Lee and General Imboden." Sigel's force had reached Winchester, and both Lee and Davis regarded that as the greater danger. All the rest of that day, the wires hummed with traffic, as Breckinridge struggled to comply. Lee's view that Sigel's advance was the key threat was further enhanced when Grant's army began to cross the Rapidan.[13]

---

11 *OR* 37, pt. 1, 41.

12 McManus, *Cloyd's Mountain,* 15.

13 *OR* 37, pt. 1, 712.

Brigadier General Albert G. Jenkins. *Library of Congress*

Lee's messages revealed a concern not just for Staunton's safety, but with Sigel slipping down the valley and hitting his own army's western flank just as Grant and the Army of the Potomac moved against his front. In one dispatch, Lee worried that, according to Imboden, "Sigel will probably cross [the Bull Run Mountains] at Chester Gap and move on [The Army of Northern Virginia's] left." In response, Lee urged Breckinridge, "if you cannot by counter moves occupy him [Sigel] in [the] Valley, leave sufficient troops to guard against movement from Kanawha [Crook] and push forward your troops to Orange Court House. . . ." In a second dispatch, Lee was even more emphatic. Sigel appeared to be moving on Front Royal with 7,000 men, and, said Lee, "these are the forces I wish you to meet, or by some movement to draw back before they get on my left. . . . Try and check this Valley movement soon as possible."[14]

Breckinridge, who until now had been focused on defending his department against threats from the south and west, was now directed to completely re-orient his forces and rush as much combat power as he could spare 100 miles to the northeast. He reacted with alacrity. On the 5th Breckinridge ordered all three of his infantry brigades to move to Jackson River Depot on the Virginia & Tennessee. From there, 4,000 men and 12 cannon would take the trains north into the lower Valley. Crook would have to be stopped by Jenkins's and Jackson's cavalry, along with whatever additional support Brig. Gen. William E. "Grumble" Jones could provide from East Tennessee. Almost as an afterthought, since he was personally headed to Staunton with the infantry, Breckinridge informed Jenkins that the latter officer was now in command of the Department of

14 Ibid., 713.

Southwest Virginia and responsible for its defense. This must have come as quite a shock, especially since Breckinridge was taking virtually all the department's available troops with him.[15]

Princeton now had to be abandoned. McCausland's 1,500 infantry marched out less than 48 hours after they arrived, leaving only Capt. James S. A. Crawford's squadron of the 17th Virginia Cavalry to defend newly christened "Fort Breckinridge." They would not be nearly strong enough to stop Crook's army. When Crook's men approached Princeton on May 6 Captain Crawford, hopelessly outnumbered, could only fall back skirmishing. At 10:00 a.m. that morning, Crawford sent off a dispatch informing Jenkins of the town's loss and of Crook's strength. Crawford now split his own small force further, sending part of it eastwards along "the road to the Narrows," with the rest "fall[ing] back on the Wytheville Road" to the south. "[I] will keep you posted as to their movements. My courier will know where to find you," Crawford concluded. Unfortunately for the Confederates, Crawford's dispatch was in error. Either through a blunder or necessity, no one covered the Wytheville Road. Instead most of Crawford's patrol fell back southwest towards Tazewell, leaving Jenkins to note that "I am left with nothing but infantry pickets" to shadow Crook's advance.[16]

The Federals spent the night in Princeton, rummaging through hastily abandoned Rebel camps and re-naming the local fort. McCausland's men had, as a finishing touch, laid sod on the face of the earthwork to spell "Fort Breckinridge," but jubilant Yankees soon re-christened it "Fort Crook." Buckeye Andrew Stairwalt, a musician in Company F of the 23rd Ohio, noted that Crook's men helped themselves to what was useful and burned the rest. When the Yankees departed, noted young Stairwalt, Princeton was "in a state of dilapodation."[17]

Crook wasted little time on either celebration or rest. At 4:30 a.m. on the 7th, the Federals marched out again. Instead of following the McCausland's line of retreat towards Narrows or towards Tazewell, Crook ventured due south on the Wytheville Road over Wolf Creek Mountain to Rocky Gap. This path was not nearly as good as either

---

15   Ibid., 716.

16   Ibid., 719-721.

17   *OR* 37, pt. 1, 721; McManus, *Cloyd's Mountain,* 16.

of the other roads, but it was the most direct—and shortest—route to Crook's objective.

Fewer miles did not mean an easier march. The terrain was rugged, the road poor, and there were at least enough Confederates to skirmish with Crook's column all day. Now Col. Horatio Sickel's brigade led the way, their own skirmishers deployed ahead and on each flank. The topography was ideal for a small force trying to delay or harass a larger one, reducing progress to a crawl, especially once they neared Rocky Gap. Here Crook ordered Col. R. H. Woolworth to take his 4th Pennsylvania Reserves on a flanking movement to the left, which proved to be quite an ordeal for the Keystoners. Wolf Creek, fast running, knee-deep and icy cold, had to be forded several times. The capper for the Pennsylvanians proved to be scaling Wolf Creek Mountain; "1,400 feet high, the men and officers displaying great courage in crossing the latter, which was very rugged." Neither side sustained casualties in the day's fight, but the Federals didn't secure the gap and fall into camp until 6:00 p.m., after more than 13 hours of marching and skirmishing.[18]

Those troops toiling in the rear, guarding Crook's supply train, had nearly as bad a time, though they were at least not taking enemy fire. To Ohioan R. B. Wilson, a member of that rear guard, the day was exhausting. At one point "the descent was very steep, and the narrow road, in many places hanging over precipices of great height, required expert driving and cool nerve." Here Wilson noted the fall of a mule, who tumbled off the slope and then stood "imprisoned among great boulders, apparently unhurt" but also, apparently, beyond rescue. The column had no choice but to march on, abandoning the poor animal to its fate. It was well after nightfall when the rear-guard passed through the gap to go into camp with the rest of the army, the dark so profound that they could only negotiate the path "by painfully keeping touch of the cliff on one side, and holding on to the tail of the blouse of the man in front. . . ."[19]

Once through Rocky Gap, however, Crook's options improved. He could strike due south for Wytheville, turn west towards Saltville, or move east, thereby outflanking the small Rebel garrison force at

---

18 *OR* 37, pt. 1, 32.

19 Wilson, "the Dublin Raid," 102-103.

Pearisburg and strike for Dublin Depot, with the New River Bridge just a few miles farther on. He chose the eastern option. May 8 promised to be a day of results.

John C. Breckinridge had himself left Dublin late on May 5, headed for Staunton. "The situation of affairs in my Department was precarious," he later reported, "and nothing but the necessity of preserving Staunton and the left of Gen. Lee's line of communications justified its temporary abandonment to the . . . enemy." Abandonment seemed very likely. Aside from the cavalry, the only organized infantry left in the entire department were the 700 men of the 45th Virginia Infantry, guarding Saltville. Some companies of partisan rangers were also present, and Breckinridge hastily called out the local militia before he left, but these forces would amount to only a few hundred men at best. Albert Jenkins seemed destined to lose his new command within days of inheriting it.[20]

Breckinridge turned to William E. Jones in East Tennessee for additional help. Jones had "4,000 cavalry," said Breckinridge, which Jenkins mistook as the disposable force that Jones would be able to send north. In fact, that number represented nearly Jones's whole strength, only part of which could be spared elsewhere. Commendably, Jones did what he could. The Kentuckians of Brig. Gen. John Hunt Morgan's brigade were available, and already intended for transfer to Southwest Virginia. These men were the survivors of what used to be Morgan's cavalry division, which had never been fully reconstituted after that officer's disastrous expedition into Ohio the previous summer. Jones got the Kentuckians moving quickly.[21]

Nor was that all. Jones also dispatched two artillery batteries, though at least one of those units would continue northward to join Breckinridge, not move to help Jenkins. Finally, Brig. Gen. John C. Vaughn's brigade of Tennessee Mounted Infantry was also ordered to Staunton to help defend

---

20   John C. Breckinridge, "Report of Operations," New Market Collection, VMI; *OR* 37, pt. 1, 719.

21   *OR* 37, pt. 1, 719. Morgan had spent much of the last few months in Richmond, petitioning the Confederate Government for the return of his scattered units so that he could resume operations in Kentucky. The overall strength of this force is hard to determine. James A. Ramage, *Rebel Raider: The Life of General John Hunt Morgan* (Lexington, KY, 1986), 211, gives Morgan's strength as 2,000, of which 800 were unmounted, and 400 without weapons. Like many other Confederate partisan forces, Morgan's reconstituted force suffered from poor discipline.

the lower Valley against Sigel. This last reinforcement would have no immediate effect on either part of the campaign. Realistically, Vaughn's troops were in no condition for immediate action, being scattered to their homes. Originally raised in East Tennessee, the brigade was captured at Vicksburg. Paroled and allowed to go home until formally exchanged, it took Vaughn a great deal of effort to reassemble his men and restore military order. Several weeks, in fact, were required to gather them from their homes and camps in the mountains. Jones was probably happy to release them, since their indiscipline and looting were causing Jones immense headaches, but Vaughn's roughly 1,400 Tennesseans would not arrive in the Shenandoah for almost another month.[22]

With his own cavalry also widely dispersed, Jenkins could muster barely 200 men (mostly from the 17th Virginia) to defend Dublin Depot and the rail line. The militia might double that number, but against Crook's column, estimated by the Rebels at 5,000 strong, Jenkins had little hope of stopping the Yankees without a great deal of additional help. On the 6th, Jenkins commandeered Capt. Crispin Dickenson and his Ringgold Light Artillery—a Virginia battery then en route to join Robert E. Lee. Desperate, Jenkins sent Dickenson's guns five miles north to Cloyd's Mountain, with orders to defend that approach into Dublin. Next, Jenkins revoked McCausland's movement orders, since his infantry were still at Dublin waiting for their turn on the trains. Jenkins made a last-minute appeal to Breckinridge to keep them at Dublin. This request was granted early on May 7, first by Breckinridge, who only authorized Jenkins to "retain Colonel McCausland a day if absolutely necessary"; and subsequently by Richmond, where Gen. Braxton Bragg told Jenkins to keep McCausland "until the danger is over."[23]

This change caught Colonel McCausland in the very act of loading his men. At once the colonel reversed course and began ordering his artillery off the flatcars. The brigade camped just outside town that night, awaiting developments. On the morning of the 8th, once it was ascertained that Crook was approaching via Cloyd's Mountain, Jenkins ordered McCausland to reinforce Captain Dickenson. Home guard members

22 *OR* 37, pt. 1, 723; Larry Gordon, *The Last Confederate General: John C. Vaughn and his East Tennessee Cavalry* (Minneapolis, 2009), 84-85.

23 McManus, *Cloyd's Mountain,* 19; *OR* 37, pt. 1, 723.

were by now arriving in Dublin as well, all of which were formed into companies and sent to join the growing Rebel force.

Additional succor was also at hand: Grumble Jones, Morgan, and approximately 2,000 troops from East Tennessee raced up the tracks on May 7 to help defend both Saltville and Wytheville. These reinforcements freed up the 45th Virginia Regiment in turn, to rush to Dublin and rejoin McCausland's brigade. Jones's troops would protect Saltville from Averell's troopers while Jenkins attempted to meet and blunt Crook's advance. Once at Saltville, Jones determined that he had sufficient force to defend the place and ordered Morgan to send a further 750 men of the 5th Kentucky Cavalry onward to Jenkins's aid. By now the rails were becoming overloaded with traffic. The 5th Kentucky's Col., D. Howard Smith, reported that he received this order on the 8th, but it wasn't until midnight that enough cars could be found to move even 400 of Smith's men. A derailment entailed additional delay. Smith's Kentuckians did not reach Dublin until 1:00 p.m. on May 9. By then, battle had already been joined.[24]

On the 8th, meanwhile, Crook's column left Rocky Gap, marching east to Shannon's Bridge, where the Pearisburg-Dublin Road crossed Walker Creek, on the north side of Cloyd's Mountain. The Yankees camped here that evening, just 10 miles from Dublin. The day's march was again marked by constant skirmishing. Crook intended to cross the mountain and descend into Dublin on the morning of the 9th, which every Federal was sure would bring on a fight. Crook expected the Rebels to make their stand where the road crested the mountain, but instead McCausland chose to defend at the southern foot of the mountain, on a north facing ridge behind Back Creek. Only a detail from the 36th Virginia contested the crest, and the Federals did not get a good look at their opponents until they had driven those men down the south slope. Crook described the enemy's position as being "posted on a bluff, with an open bottom between us . . . [and] a stream with a muddy bottom running close under the bluff." Having sized up the foe, he decided to attack immediately.[25]

---

24 *OR* 37, pt. 1, 66.

25 Crook, *Autobiography,* 115.

Jenkins, who had been present with McCausland on the 8th, returned to Dublin that night, hoping to hurry on both reinforcements and the evacuation of those stores that could be moved quickly. With the morning, however, he returned. Jenkins's mood was fretful. He was doubtless deeply worried about the coming fight, but he was also feeling confident enough to offer battle. His latest intelligence estimated Crook's strength at only "five regiments of infantry, ten pieces of artillery, and two companies of cavalry." If true, this was good news, for it meant that Jenkins's assembled forces were nearly of a size with the Federal column. Upon his arrival, Jenkins found some fault with McCausland's dispositions, shifting units around on the bluff, bracing himself for the coming blow as best he could. The line was further enhanced by hastily constructed breastworks of dirt and rails. At 9:00 a.m. the 45th Virginia arrived, bringing Jenkins's overall numbers up to about 2,400 bayonets. The 45th's appearance allowed Jenkins to strengthen his center, and certainly buoyed Rebel spirits. A dispatch reflecting Jenkins's suddenly-found optimism was sent by Maj. Charles A. Stringfellow at Dublin, who wired Breckinridge the latest update: "Our men in splendid spirits, anxious for the fight, and perfectly confident."[26]

That confidence was misplaced. Crook led 11 of regiments of infantry, not five; and his force included the equivalent of a full regiment of cavalry. Only in artillery was the Rebel estimate accurate: 12 guns in 2 batteries. Crook's overall force exceeded 6,500 men, nearly three times Jenkins's number. Crook decided to use those numbers to advantage by sending one of his brigades eastwards to turn Jenkins's right flank, that move supported by an assault all along the line once the flanking effort opened the action. Brush and tree cover on the north side of Back Creek hid this movement from the Confederates. For a time it seemed to the waiting Rebels that Crook's whole army disappeared, and some Rebels began to think that no battle would occur that day.[27]

They were soon dissuaded of that notion. Crook's attack was made ragged by the difficult terrain, but still achieved complete success on the Rebel right, and after about three hours of at-times severe fighting, the Confederate line was broken and thrown into disordered retreat. Casualties

26 *OR* 37, part 1, 725, 727; McManus, *Cloyd's Mountain,* 21-23.

27 McManus, *Cloyd's Mountain,* 27.

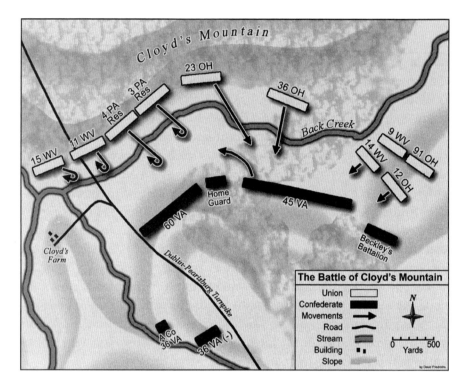

were heavy on both sides. Union losses totaled 688 killed, wounded, and missing; while Rebel losses amounted to 538. Though overall casualties were higher among the Federals, as a percentage, the Confederate loss was much more severe, nearly shattering some formations.[28]

Crook was sure the enemy's losses would have been much higher had he "but 1,000 effective cavalry," but all he had were Otey's "broken-down" troopers. Now he probably regretted—at least privately—sending his best horsemen with Averell. However, the lack of effective pursuit might also have had something to do with the fact that Crook himself fainted from exhaustion at the climax of the battle, just as the Confederate line broke for the last time. The Union general decided to personally lead the charge of his 1st Brigade, struggling across Back Creek at the head of the 23rd Ohio. "For a brief but critical period," noted biographer Paul Magid, Crook's army was effectively without a commander.[29]

28 Ibid., 81-82.

29 *OR* 37, pt. 1, 11; Magid, *Crook*, 186.

The Union army wasn't the only side rendered leaderless. Early in the action, General Jenkins suffered a severe wound, a bullet "shatter[ing] his left arm near the shoulder." This wound eventually killed him. McCausland assumed command, while the stricken Jenkins was moved to a large farmhouse nearer to Dublin.[30]

With Crook at least temporarily *hors-de-combat*, Colonel Hayes of the 23rd took charge of an advance guard—roughly 500 men—and pushed on to Dublin, encountering the late-arriving Confederate 5th Kentucky along the way. Colonel Smith and his Kentuckians met McCausland retreating from the field, who ordered Smith to act as rear guard. Smith noted that his initial fire checked Hayes's impromptu pursuit, holding the Federals at bay for more than an hour so that Dublin depot could be at least partially evacuated.[31]

The Rebels then retreated through Dublin and across the New River Bridge to halt on the north bank. Crook's column entered Dublin that night, seizing great quantities of stores, burning what they could not carry off. On the morning of the 10th Crook moved on to the all-important bridge. Along the way they uprooted and destroyed six miles of track, burning the ties and twisting the heated rails. At the bridge, McCausland offered resistance with his artillery. Crook ordered up his own guns and the two sides dueled for several hours. In the end, however, the Confederates retreated before the Federals could figure a way across the river to outflank the defenses, leaving Crook in sole possession of the structure. The bridge presented the Federals with something of a problem, for while the flooring and tracks could be easily destroyed, the stone piers proved invulnerable. They resisted all attempts to topple them, impervious even to cannon fire. With the piers intact, the bridge could be easily rebuilt rather once the Federals departed, which proved to be the case. In less than three weeks Rebel trains would be running across the New River again.[32]

---

30 McManus, *Cloyd's Mountain,* 37, 47-48. Jenkins's treatment was not the best. He was captured by Union soldiers, but not examined by a Union surgeon until May 13. By then the wound was gangrenous, and amputation was the only answer. The surgery was successful, but on May 24, while having his injury dressed, the wound hemorrhaged, and Jenkins quickly bled to death.

31 *OR* 37, pt. 1, 67.

32 McManus, *Cloyd's Mountain*, 50-54.; and Magid, *George Crook,* 187-188.

McCausland's command retreated northward up the railroad to Christiansburg, where they prepared to make another stand, though there was no hope of reinforcement. At Dublin, Crook faced a difficult choice. His original orders now called for him to follow McCausland, moving northward through the upper Valley and ultimately, unite with Sigel's column at Staunton. For the moment, enemy opposition was not a factor, since Jenkins's little army had been badly mauled, losing 23% of those engaged. The survivors seemed utterly demoralized, but how long could that demoralization last? Dublin depot had yielded more than provisions and other loot; the telegraph office also contained several messages which reported Lee winning a great victory over Grant on May 7 and 8, at the battle of the Wilderness. If Grant was suddenly retreating, how many Rebels might be freed up to rush south and deal Crook's army? Instead of continuing towards Staunton, Crook reported that this news "determined me to move to Lewisburg as rapidly as possible." In fact, Crook was heading for a place called Meadow Bluff, some 20 miles west of Lewisburg (likely at least a day-and-a-half's march from that town, given the rough terrain) and a very long ways from Staunton. By doing so, he would not be in position to unite with Sigel any time soon.[33]

This was a fateful decision. There would be no effort to move on Staunton or to affect a juncture with Sigel. Crook 's own force was now low on ammunition and food, despite the captures at Dublin, and burdened with wounded. Some of those Federals, too injured to move, would have to be left behind, eventually to become prisoners. Crook's livestock and wagons were also in poor shape, having suffered much during the march south.

However, a retreat to Meadow Bluff was not without difficulties. This route would take the army back through that same difficult country, mountainous and with few opportunities for forage. Pressing on to Staunton, while certainly a more daring choice, would have offered up both an easier route (through the valley instead of over the Blue Ridge Mountains) where Crook's men could forage in well-settled farmland. Additionally, Staunton was a major Confederate depot, like Dublin; capturing it would allow Crook to live off the enemy's supplies. Indeed, Staunton was a far juicier prize than was Dublin, and its loss would have done significant damage to Lee's logistics at a critical moment in his

33   *OR* 37, pt. 1, 12.

Brigadier General William W. Averell. *Library of Congress*

struggle against Grant. Moreover, Crook would still be marching toward a supply line, not away from one, for establishing contact with Sigel meant both an immediate resupply and a new line of communications down the Valley to Winchester.

The idea of marching on Staunton must have seemed too daunting, for pressing on meant taking some very significant chances, but doing so also offered up a real chance to damage Lee's supply line, far more than what had already been accomplished. It mirrored Grant's own decision to strike inland after landing at Port Gibson, south of Vicksburg, in 1863. Crook, however, was not Grant. He chose to retreat into West Virginia, towards his existing base along the Kanawha.

And what of Averell? While Crook was trouncing Jenkins and McCausland, Averell was finding hard going towards Saltville. The reinforcements sent by "Grumble" Jones proved sufficient to block Averell's advance. Early on May 11, amid a "saturating rain," Crook received word of Averell's situation. "A detachment of Averell's cavalry, escorting fifty Confederate prisoners," reached Dublin: their commander informed the general that the Averell elected not to attack Saltville, but was going to still try for Wytheville to further damage the railroad. Crook called off that effort, sending a courier to inform Averell that his infantry column was headed back northeast towards Blacksburg, and from there, to Meadow Bluff. Averell was to join him as soon as he could.[34]

Averell had already thought better of a major strike at Wytheville and was now headed for Dublin, intending to link up with Crook's main body. He made one last attempt at Wytheville on the afternoon of May

34 McManus, *Cloyd's Mountain*, 63.

10 but, short of the town, he ran into Jones and Morgan, with a force rumored "to have numbered 5,000." A sharp engagement ensued. The battle lasted four hours, cost Averell 114 casualties, and convinced him that further effort to press forward would only get his entire command captured. He broke off the action and rode to find Crook. Averell captured Christiansburg on the 12th, doing a bit more minor damage to the railroad, and then turned north, rejoining the main column on the May 15.[35]

Crook's command was now burdened with many of their own wounded, 300 Rebel prisoners, and a swarm of runaway slaves who greeted the Federals as liberators. Heavy rains through much of May 10, 11 and 12 made the march more difficult, though initially the region was ripe with forage. Once they left Blacksburg, however, the roads over the mountains proved highly unsatisfactory, and at one point Crook was forced to abandon some of his wagons and captured provisions. The last week of the retreat to Meadow Bluff was a grueling experience, made worse by the lack of rations. The Confederates made one more effort to interfere, producing a skirmish on May 12, but the worst obstacle by far proved to be the rain-swollen Greenbriar River. It took the army three days to cross this raging stream, using an old flatboat as a ferry. To further complicate matters, By May 16 Crook's rations were exhausted, and foraging parties were returning empty-handed.[36]

On May 19, Crook's ragged, hungry band marched to Meadow Bluff, there to await a new supply convoy from Gauley Bridge. Their part of the campaign was now ended. Though Crook had won a battle and achieved his initial objectives, His failure of nerve at Dublin would have larger ramifications on the rest of Grant's overall plans.

35   *OR* 37, pt. 1, 43-44.

36   Wilson, "Dublin Raid," 119.

CHAPTER 5

Sigel's Advance

n May 2, the day Crook's column set out towards Fayettesville, Sigel's Army of the Valley occupied Winchester. This once-thriving market town at the lower end of the Valley, less than 25 miles south of Martinsburg, would boast of being the municipality that changed hands the most times over the course of the war. The population was a mixed bag of ardent Secessionists and die-hard Unionists, but Sigel's troops treated it as hostile territory, a precedent set by General Milroy the previous year. Upon arrival, the Federals initiated house-to-house searches, turning up "a large collection of old guns, swords and accoutrements" which were confiscated and promptly destroyed. Sigel also issued a proclamation forbidding civilians from gathering on the streets or "the talking of Politics," sealing the town in hopes of preventing any intelligence of his movements or intentions from reaching the Confederates. Entry in or out was allowed only via passes issued by his headquarters. Twenty-one-year-old Kate Sperry, one of those ardent Secessionists, complained to her diary that "Old Sigel is worse than Milroy . . . not a soul has been permitted to leave the town or one person come in. Sigel has arrested every boy and man he can find out in the country and a good many of the townspeople."[1]

---

1   Keyes, *The Military History of the 12rd Regiment Ohio*, 54; Garland R. Quarles, *Occupied Winchester 1861–1865* (Winchester, VA, 1991), 93.

Sigel's occupation of the town was bloodless, for General Imboden chose not to contest the place. On May 2 he and his men were camped 70 miles to the south, at Mount Crawford. As the campaign opened, Imboden's force numbered only 1,492 officers and men; the Federals outnumbered him several times over. At Sigel's advance, Imboden sent word to both the local reserves and to Superintendent Francis H. Smith of the Virginia Military Institute, alerting them that they might be called upon for immediate operations. Then Imboden rode north, but only as far as Woodstock, 33 miles short of Winchester.[2]

With Winchester's civilians well cowed, Sigel ordered Stahel's cavalry to push another 20 miles south, securing the towns of Strasburg and Front Royal but venturing no farther. Here the Valley bifurcated, split into two narrower vales by the bulk of Massanutten Mountain. Nearly 3,000 feet high, Massanutten was a long ridge running southwestward for 50 miles, ending just north of Harrisonburg. A fork of the Shenandoah River ran through each valley. The Valley Turnpike ran down the western side, to Woodstock and then onward to the hamlets of Edinberg and New Market. Massanutten could only be easily crossed at New Market, two thirds of the way from Strasburg to Harrisonburg, where a winding mountain road connected that village with the eastern community of Luray.

Massanutten posed a considerable problem for any advancing force. An army moving up or down on one side of the mountain could suddenly find itself trapped if a foe were to move more quickly up or down the other side. If Sigel's army marched up the turnpike from Strasburg to Woodstock, a Rebel force could move down the eastern valley, emerge at the northern end of Massanutten at Front Royal, and then strike for either Winchester or Strasburg, cutting off the Federals from their base. The solution to this geographical dilemma was to either advance up both sub-valleys simultaneously or leave strong garrisons at Front Royal and New Market to secure the eastern valley's exits. Thus, moving south beyond Strasburg meant that Sigel would have to bleed off substantial strength from his army as he went, dividing his limited forces in the face of the enemy not once, but twice. This strategic conundrum had hamstrung Union operations in 1862, even with forces far larger than Sigel now commanded.

---

2   John D. Imboden, "The Battle of New Market, VA, May 15th, 1864" *Battles and Leaders,* vol. 3, 480.

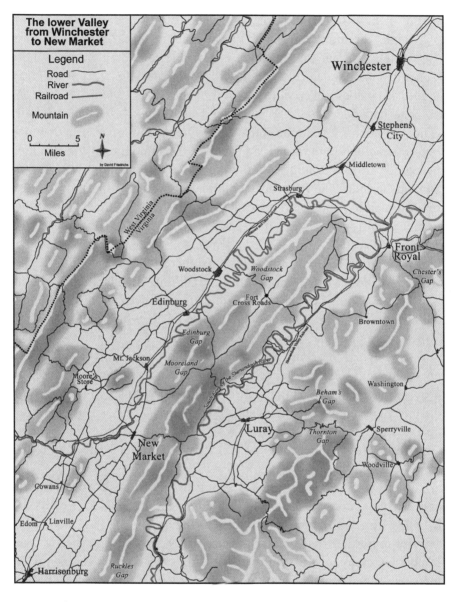

The lower Valley from Winchester to New Market

Legend
Road
River
Railroad
Mountain

0 — 5
Miles

by David Fredrichs

Winchester
Stephens City
Middletown
Strasburg
Front Royal
Chester's Gap
West Virginia / Virginia
Woodstock
Woodstock Gap
Fort Cross Roads
Browntown
Edinburg
Edinburg Gap
Mr. Jackson
Mooreland Gap
Moore's Store
the Shenandoah River
South fork of
Beham's Gap
Washington
Luray
Thornton Gap
Sperryville
New Market
Woodville
Cowans
Edom / Linville
Harrisonburg
Ruckles Gap

By 1864 the Valley held special terrors for Federals, given how many prior expeditions came to grief between those mountain walls. Even troops not caught up in earlier disasters were subject to the general mood. "It is the general impression that we are to await at Winchester," pessimistically noted Lieutenant Colonel Lincoln of the 34th Massachusetts for "instructions from Grant[.] . . . [T]he hope is strong, at least on the part of *many* of the officers, that we are not to advance *far* up the Valley. . . . Banks, Fremont and Shields have each, in turn, been driven from this Valley: and our present force is a smaller one than either of those Generals commanded. . . . Sigel, with his present force, will be lucky indeed if he does not have to 'get out of this.'"[3]

The Federal pause in Winchester lasted a week. Despite Colonel Lincoln's hopes, it is doubtful that Sigel intended to loiter even that long before heading south, but in addition to the impediment Massanutten posed for Union strategy, another series of problems now beset the bantam German. The first such complication was his receipt of Crook's revised plan to head south instead of first moving on Lewisburg. Sigel immediately forwarded this message to Grant with a lengthy addendum. Sigel might well "wish him [Crook] success," but with the likelihood of uniting the two columns now a diminishing prospect, the German also wanted to know what Grant now desired of him. "I understand that I am to occupy the line of Cedar Creek, [which flowed from west to east across the Valley just north of Strasburg] and to advance up the Shenandoah Valley if circumstances will allow me to do so." But, he pointed out, "to advance beyond Strasburg with my present force is hardly possible." To do so he would need to leave a "strong force opposite Front Royal to prevent the enemy marching into my rear. . . ." With 8,000 troops, Sigel did not have enough manpower to both continue his advance deeper up the Valley and secure an ever-lengthening line of communications. Grant concurred. "I do not want you to move farther south than Cedar Run [Creek]."[4]

For Sigel, the security of his supply line was to prove a constant concern. For more than a year, Confederate Col. John S. Mosby and his 43rd Virginia Battalion of partisan rangers operated against Union activity in northern Virginia. The heart of "Mosby's Confederacy" was Loudoun County, just east of the Blue Ridge, but it was a simple matter for Mosby and his men to slip into the lower Valley. Raids against Sigel's supply line began almost immediately. On May 1 Mosby struck a supply convoy at Bunker Hill, and penetrated the horse corrals in Martinsburg that same night, stealing stock from under the Federal garrison's very nose. During the first week in May, with Grant's army also stirring,

3   Lincoln, *Thirty-Fourth Mass. Infantry,* 260.

4   *OR* 37, pt. 1, 368-369.

Colonel John S. Mosby and members of the 43rd Virginia Cavalry. *Library of Congress*

Mosby was forced to divide his battalion, taking two companies back east to pester the Army of the Potomac, but he left his other two companies in place to plague Sigel.[5]

Further there was still the need to secure the Baltimore and Ohio. With the rail guards stripped from their posts to form Crook's and Sigel's expeditionary forces, manpower, as ever, was the issue. One welcome new arrival was the 12th Pennsylvania Cavalry, a supposedly veteran regiment—500 strong—which had just returned from their re-enlistment furlough in Philadelphia. They were slated to go to Martinsburg. Once there, Sigel immediately detailed them to move instead to join Gen. Max Weber at Harper's Ferry, from whence they would be assigned as rail guards. Unfortunately, when Weber clapped eyes on them, he was filled with dismay. As it turned out, the 12th had only 130 men mounted and fully equipped; roughly 10 men per company. The remaining 400 men were raw recruits, completely untrained and in Weber's opinion, "good for nothing—worse than useless." More and better troops would have to be found for this mission.[6]

5   Jeffry D. Wert, *Mosby's Rangers* (New York, 1990), 160.

6   Ibid., 70.

Captain John Hanson "Hanse" McNeill.
Library of Congress

In the meantime, Mosby's men were having a substantial impact. "A number of guerrillas and horse thieves are infesting the road between Winchester and Martinsburg," worried Sigel, who ordered Martinsburg commander Col. Robert S. Rodgers "not to send out trains without an escort." Martinsburg was held by only about 100 infantry of the provost guard and a battery of artillery, complained Rodgers, forcing him to make up escorts drawn from "convalescents, stragglers, %c." It was a stop-gap measure, one that would soon prove wholly inadequate.[7]

Rail security would become an even more pressing issue on May 5. Early that morning, Capt. Hanse McNeill and 60 partisan rangers descended on the town of Bloomington Maryland and the nearby rail depot at Piedmont West Virginia. This raid was a stunning Confederate success. Both locales were lightly defended, allowing the raiders free reign. Piedmont was full of repair facilities, a roundhouse, and huge amounts of stores. McNeill's men destroyed nearly a million dollars' worth of property, including seven different railroad shops, nine locomotives, 22 loaded freight cars, and some 2,000 feet of track. Henry Truehart, a Texan riding with McNeill, was awed by the scope of the damage, boasting of it in a letter to his brother, then serving with Lee: "[We] burned seven R. R. Locomotive & machine establishments said to be the most extensive and valuable on the Balt. & O RR together with 85 RR cars 9 engines large quantities of oil turpentine & paint . . . we sent six other engines down the road at full head of steam & going at a fearful rate of speed with no one to control them. . . ."[8]

7   *OR* 37, pt. 1, 71-72, 378.

8   Richard R. Duncan, "The Raid on Piedmont and the Crippling of Franz Sigel in the Shenandoah Valley," *West Virginia History*, vol. 55 (1996) Online edition:

The Piedmont raid sent alarms singing across the telegraph wires both east and west. In Ohio, Republican Governor John Brough was organizing 17 regiments of new short-term men, most of whom were slated to join the garrison in Washington DC. Two of those units were already tasked to go to Parkersburg, West Virginia. With this new disaster, Maj. Gen. Henry Halleck diverted no less than 10 more regiments to the state: "Four . . . to Charleston, three to New Creek and three to Harper's Ferry." Nearly 10,000 additional troops should provide a sufficient force to guard the railroad against further raids, but they were all green, and would take time to finish outfitting and reach their assigned locales. In the meantime, the tumult raised by McNeill's success had more immediate effects.[9]

On May 5, before word of the Piedmont attack even reached him, Sigel detached 600 mounted men from his main body, sending them back down the Valley to Martinsburg, an effort aimed at securing his rear against Mosby's depredations. From there half of that force would go to Harper's Ferry—to supplement the wholly inadequate 12th Pennsylvania—and the other half were to patrol the road between Martinsburg and Bunker Hill. This detachment amounted to 20 percent of his total cavalry force, but he saw no other choice: both the B&O and his own supply lines must remain open, especially if there was to be any chance of still linking with Crook.

The next day, responding to McNeill's success, Sigel ordered Col. Jacob Higgins to take elements of the 15th and 21st New York, along with part of his own 22nd Pennsylvania Cavalries, in all another 500 men, and march west towards Moorefield. Sigel reasoned that Higgins could cut off McNeill's retreat and perhaps end that menace once and for all. Higgins departed early on the 7th.[10]

Meanwhile, the pause at Winchester was also really the first time that Sigel had a chance to hone his disparate command into an effective unit. The shambles of a review at Martinsburg revealed considerable problems, both in regimental training and in the skill set of the brigade commanders, who had little chance to maneuver even a full regiment in

---

www.wvculture.org/history/journal_wvh/wvh55-2.html; Edward B. Williams, ed., *Rebel Brothers: The Civil War Letters of the Truehearts* (College Station, TX, 1995), 192-193.

9   *OR* 37, pt. 1, 383.

10   Ibid., 384.

the past year. The week's interlude now gave Sigel a chance to work on refining those skills. During this same time, the officers and men got to know Sigel and his staff. It was not a harmonious experience.

Not everyone was pleased with Sigel's choice of staff officers. Sigel tended to embrace the flourishes of a European headquarters, a trait which often rubbed native-born Americans the wrong way. Colonel Strother was one, becoming disillusioned with Sigel's choice of former Europeans as aides, especially as they seemed to have only a limited grasp of English. In addition, Strother was taken aback by the "set of low scouts, spies, detectives, and speculators" that swarmed Sigel's command tent. Strother himself was out of sorts for he had so far been unable to procure a suitable mount, messing arrangements, or a personal servant for his needs on campaign; all of which left him feeling gloomy and filled with premonitions of failure.[11]

Sigel used the time to drill his army incessantly, improving the rusty skills of the troops and officers. The troops drilled at least three hours per day, with regimental evolutions in the morning and brigade exercises in the afternoon. Weather permitting, these sessions were frequently extended. One panting West Virginia private noted that "they keep us . . . four to five hours a day. I do hate to drill these hot days." Inspections and reviews were also part of the program. Sigel was trying to compensate for months of inattention in a single week, but to many of the men the frantic activity seemed pointless. In combat, however, any unit that could not maneuver effectively on a battlefield was nearly useless.[12]

Sigel also added a twist that few Civil War commanders adopted; he tried to make the training more realistic by staging mock battles. This play-acting also drew ridicule, but it also highlighted important defects in the skills of the units involved. The first of these sessions, held on May 5, was a fiasco. "Few of the colonels knew anything about brigade drill, and some of them very little even about battalion drill. One of the first things that was done was to deploy and start out the 34th Massachusetts as skirmishers, and then General Sigel undertook to maneuver the infantry, cavalry and artillery as if on a field of battle.

11   Eby, *Virginia Yankee*, 221.

12   Swiger, *Joshua Winters*, 105.

. . . It was the funniest farce ever witnessed anywhere," concluded Lieutenant Colonel Wildes.[13]

The mock battle soon deteriorated into complete confusion. Wildes's own regiment, the 116th Ohio, launched a disordered "charge" and promptly dissolved into a yelling mob. They were howling so loud they were unable to hear "recall" on the bugle, forcing some of Sigel's "leather breeches Dutch staff officers" to chase after them. The 34th Massachusetts, deployed as skirmishers, was accidently left on the field at the end of the day, with no one remembering to order them back to camp. Wildes and his fellow Ohioans blamed Sigel, sneering at his incompetence, but in fact the day's action (and a similar drill held the following afternoon, with only slightly less chaotic results) suggested serious defects among the field grade officers. If the troops couldn't be controlled on a drill field, how would they fare on a battlefield? Even the well-trained 34th clearly had much to learn: it was the duty of a skirmish line to maintain contact with the main line, both to provide warning of an enemy and to react to their own battle line's movements. How could the 34th's commanders fail to note the conclusion of the day's action? Clearly, they were not in contact with the brigade as they should have been. The Bay-Staters marched back to camp hours after everyone else quit the field, well after dark, seething and disgruntled. They also blamed Sigel for the lapse, but their own officers were at fault. The 34th might have been drilled to parade perfection, but the regiment was not ready for combat. Each day provided one more chance to improve skills and sharpen badly needed combat-effectiveness.

A second effort on May 6 fared no better. Colonel Wells of the 34th Massachusetts feigned illness rather than participate again, disgustedly ordering Lieutenant Colonel Lincoln to "take your regiment and do with it what you please. I've lost all interest in it and the service." Lincoln did so, describing a difficult afternoon's work in which Sigel, imperious, issued incorrect orders and brooked "no suggestions from Battalion Commanders!" Problems were soon compounded when the other regiments in Lincoln's brigade managed their part of the exercise very poorly, failing to leave proper intervals between units and falling into general disorder. Colonel Wells, who was not too sick to observe the whole mess, sarcastically remarked to Lincoln on the lieutenant

13 Wildes, *Record of the One Hundred and Sixteenth,* 84.

colonel's return that he had "seen a movement or two by the 34th, as a battalion; and a good deal of running about, in a confused sort of way, by the other regiments."[14]

Wells's disdain was misplaced. His duty was with his men, not pouting on the sidelines. His recalcitrant attitude, rooted in prejudice, proved detrimental to his own regiment's improvement, and would all too soon get men depending on his marital skills needlessly killed.

The cavalry spent less time in drill, but they were hardly inactive. Between the guerrilla threat and the need to keep Rebel raiders at bay, Sigel kept his mounted arm in constant motion, much to the dismay of some. Lieutenant Colonel Charles Fitzsimmons of the 21st New York disgustedly described the cavalry's activity during this period as wearing indeed: "Although it was well known that there was no force of enemy in our front," sneered the New Yorker, "day and night [Sigel] kept his cavalry in motion, detailing them in parties from fifty to a hundred men, and sending them out in all directions, east, west, north, and south, with no definite instructions or apparent object." Like Wells, Fitzsimmons's contempt was misplaced. Writing in 1882, he was both mistaken about the size of the force Sigel led into Winchester—placing Sigel's strength at 13,000—and about the need for such patrolling. Partisan attacks were a constant, and Sigel simply had too few cavalry to execute his mission properly.[15]

Not all officers blamed Sigel for everything. Wells's indifference towards his duties and Fitzsimmons's deprecations did not go unnoticed, causing further tension within the command. In 1867 letter to Sigel, Col. Jacob Campbell of the 54th Pennsylvania (one of those regiments so disdained by Wells) attributed much of the German's difficulties during this period to being "surrounded by many who would sacrifice the country's cause for the purpose of bringing you into disrepute. . . . [T]hose who desired to be true . . . " lamented Campbell, "were under the ban of these men." Campbell's accusation named no names, but the implications were clear.[16]

---

14 Lincoln, *Thirty-Fourth Mass. Infantry*, 264, 266-270.

15 Charles Fitz-Simmons, "Sigel's Fight at New Market, VA." *Military Order of the Loyal Legion of the United States,* 70 vols. (Wilmington, NC, 1992), vol. 12, 62.

16 Jacob Campbell to Sigel, May 1, 1867, Sigel Papers, WRHS; Engle, *Yankee Dutchman,* 173.

The weather also continued to work against any advance. It was warmer now, but still precipitation came nearly every day. "The rains have been almost continuous since we came out of Martinsburg," noted Strother, leaving "the side roads . . . very muddy . . . and the streams swollen." The Valley Pike was macadamized, and thus useable even in wet weather, but foraging and flanking patrols that left the pike for the side roads would struggle in the excessive mud. An end to the rains would hopefully let the roads dry and improve the army's prospects for a speedy advance.[17]

All this delay was not without cost. Initially, outside of the intense partisan and guerrilla activities, Rebel opposition was scant. Union intelligence reported that Imboden had only about 3,000 troops defending the lower Valley, and that he couldn't afford to move against the Federal main body. With the Federal infantry ensconced in Winchester, however, and the Blue cavalry dispersed and so active, Imboden felt there was some chance at picking off one or more of the many Union detachments. One such opportunity beckoned when Colonel Higgins led his 500 troopers out to chase down Hanse McNeill.

Colonel Higgins's column was, as was typical with cavalry operating in this department, an amalgam of various units rather than a single regiment. This was usually because each individual regiment had too few mounts to field all their manpower, or there were too many different missions for the number of regiments involved. Instead, ad-hoc battalions were organized, with men chosen for expeditions based on whose mounts were ready for the ride, or because column commanders wanted to cherry-pick the better soldiers from among their commands. This outing would be no different. Higgins selected 200 men from the 15th New York, "a small detachment from the 21st" with the balance of his 500 sabers drawn from the newly expanded 22nd Pennsylvania. Affairs seemed to begin well. On May 8 Higgins nearly caught McNeill at Moorefield, nearly 60 miles west of Winchester. The Federals managed to ambush McNeill's men, but the Rebel partisans scattered, escaping with little loss. Confounded, Higgins rested his main body at Moorefield on the 9th while patrols scoured the area looking for the enemy, to no avail. While Higgins loitered, however, more Rebels were descending on his small force.[18]

17 Eby, *Virginia Yankee*, 224.

18 Bonnell, *Sabres in the Shenandoah*, 43.

Colonel Jacob Higgins. *Library of Congress*

Confederate signalers atop Massanutten Mountain had a clear view of Sigel's dispositions, and they informed Imboden about the Union column moving west on the Moorefield Road almost as soon as it departed. Immediately, Imboden sensed an opportunity. While the Confederate couldn't hope to engage Sigel's entire command on anything like equal terms, he could strike against elements of it that ventured beyond the security of the main force. Acting quickly, Imboden moved to do exactly that. With the 18th and 23rd Virginia Cavalry regiments, 800 men, Imboden set off in pursuit. McNeill's scattered men joined him on the march.[19]

Now it was the Confederates' turn to ambush Higgins. They did so shortly after dawn on the 10th, just after the Union column departed Moorefield, at a place called Lost River Gap. The Rebel attack was a complete success. The Yankees were completely routed, fleeing northward, abandoning equipment and supplies as they went. While Higgins suffered only 50 casualties, the Federal colonel also lost his entire supply train, in what amounted to a stinging defeat. Higgins's panicked troopers continued their demoralized retreat for the next 36 hours, tearing through Romney, and ultimately making their way all the way back to Cumberland, Maryland, finding sanctuary among the garrison there. When they arrived, they needed an extensive refit, requiring rest, food, weapons, horseshoes, and in many cases, new horses to replace animals worn out from continuous riding. To add to Union ignominy, for most of this shameful retreat they were pursued only by McNeill's handful of now-triumphant rangers, a fraction of their strength; shortly after the fight, Imboden turned back towards Woodstock in case Sigel took advantage of his absence.[20]

19 Roger U. Delauter, Jr., *18th Virginia Cavalry* (Lynchburg, VA, 1985), 17.

20 Bonnell, *Sabres in the Shenandoah*, 44; Williams, *Rebel Brothers,* 193.

Between Higgins's defeat and the need to send other cavalry back to Martinsburg, Sigel effectively lost more than 1,000 troopers before he had even properly begun his foray up the Valley. Moreover, the performance of Higgins's column seemed to confirm Sigel's worst fears about the troopers in blue; they were too prone to panic and not tactically proficient in the face of an aggressive opponent. Cumberland was roughly 70 cross-country miles from Winchester—more than 100 if by rail via Martinsburg. For the time being, Higgins's 500 sabers were out of the campaign.

Despite these alarming distractions, Sigel remained commendably focused on his assigned mission. On the morning of May 7 he received heartening news from Crook, which suggested that a junction would be possible after all. In this dispatch, dated 2:00 p.m., May 4, Crook informed Sigel that while he could not predict exactly when he would reach Lewisburg—"Depends entirely on what obstacles I encounter"— if all went well "I will either be there or in communication within ten days." If Crook kept to that timetable he would be at or near Lewisburg by May 14, looking for Sigel's men. The next day, Sigel wired Grant: "If I received no orders to the contrary, I will move up the Shenandoah Valley and try . . . and form a junction with General Crook. . . ." Grant, who had just finished fighting one titanic battle in the Wilderness, and commenced a second engagement at Spotsylvania Courthouse, of course had no objections. Sigel must move south.[21]

As noted, Sigel's movement provoked a flurry of communications across Confederate-held Virginia; a telegraphic round-robin of communication between Lee, President Davis, Breckinridge, and Imboden. By May 4, Breckinridge was hastening north, all but abandoning southwest Virginia to Crook to meet what Lee considered the much greater threat of Sigel's advance. Sigel's pause at Winchester seemingly played directly into Rebel hands, giving the Valley's defenders time to achieve the concentration Lee intended. This is why, while reinforcements sped their way to him, Imboden felt confident enough to go chase after Colonel Higgins. That effort nearly proved costly, for while Imboden was smashing Higgins' column; Sigel, heartened by Crook's news, was also on the march.

On the 9th Sigel ordered his army to close up on Strasburg. One of the tasks accomplished during the past week was to lighten the army's

---

21 *OR* 37, pt. 1, 401.

marching load. The movement from Martinsburg to Winchester proved that each regiment carried far too much baggage, taking up valuable wagon space and slowing the pace to a crawl. Now orders reduced the baggage even further.

The day also proved to be hot, a rarity so far in this cold, rainy campaign. That heat struck down a fair number of men. The day was "suffocating," complained Cpl. Andrew Powell of the 123rd Ohio, in Moor's brigade, writing home the next day. "The sun [was] hot and the roads very dusty. Over a half dozen [men] were prostrated yesterday by sunstroke . . . 34 ambulances convoying near 175 men were filled by the 34th Mass. 18th Conn. and a few of 116th Ohio Regts while but one man of the 123rd rode." Powell took this as a sign that the "down easterns" made poorer soldiers than "Buckeyes Hoosiers and the like."[22]

The army made 12 miles that day, camping along the banks of Cedar Creek. Sigel established his headquarters at Belle Grove, a famous (and historic) mansion dating from the 1700s. Strother described the limestone house as "of baronial size," and noted a casual bit of looting, in the name of souvenir-hunting. The attic contained historic documents bearing the signatures "of Thomas Jefferson and George Washington, besides many other famous names . . . [and] as the house was only occupied by a poor family of tenants, our officers helped themselves to these literary mementos."[23]

The next day Sigel paused again, this time to rebuild the turnpike bridge over Cedar Creek. While the creek was fordable for infantry and cavalry, the bridge was necessary for wagon traffic and the maintenance of his supply line. It was a distinct oversight and evidence of poor staff work not to have ordered it rebuilt before the forward movement began. As a result, most of Sigel's infantry spent the day in camp or pounding the drill fields rather than marching south. At dark, noted Private Winters of the 1st West Virginia, "it commenced to rain . . . " beginning another round of precipitation that would plague the army for the next few days. During this pause Sigel also received the latest word of the much larger struggle going on east of the Blue Ridge between Grant and Lee.[24]

22 "Brother Israel," Camp near Cedar Creek VA, May 10, 1864, Andrew Powell Letters, AHEC.

23 Knight, *Valley Thunder,* 80; Eby, *Virginia Yankee,* 224.

24 Swiger, *Joshua Winters,* 106.

Federal dispatches forwarded from Martinsburg proved vague, informing Sigel only that the main armies had been locked in combat south of the Rappahannock River for several days. "The battles [were] indecisive," noted these missives, "but the advantage [was] with Gen'l Grant." Word among the Southerners was considerably different. An unidentified prisoner, captured near Berryville (just east of Winchester) the day before, boasted "that Grant had fallen back six miles with a loss of 8,000 killed and wounded." He did admit that the Rebels suffered as well, losing several generals in the fight, including "Longstreet wounded."[25]

This prisoner fell into Union hands as a result of Federal efforts to clear out Rebel partisans in the hills east of Winchester. Union patrols in the Berryville area found plenty of Rebels. A lieutenant of the 1st New York Cavalry reported that approximately 300 of Mosby's men were rumored to be gathering around the village, intent on striking Sigel's line of communications, or possibly even mount another attack on the B&O Railroad. The estimate of Mosby's strength was probably an exaggerated figure, but any party of Federals of less than company size was at risk: Of a 10-man courier detail sent out from Newtown on May 9, one was killed and six were captured after a running fight with what the three survivors estimated to be a party of 50 partisans.[26]

The 10th, had Sigel known it, was proving fateful to his campaign in other ways.

That same day, Crook elected to make for Meadow Bluff instead of Lewisburg. Crook, it will be recalled, grew discouraged upon discovering similar reports of Grant's "defeat," in captured Rebel telegrams at Dublin. Despite his victory at Cloyd's Mountain and the subsequent destruction (however temporary) of the New River Bridge, with this decision George Crook had effectively taken his command out of the rest of the campaign. Breckinridge's rear, though the Rebel general did not yet know it, was no longer threatened.

On May 11 Sigel's Yankees resumed their southward movement. The weather was mixed, warm but wet. In the van, the 21st New York Cavalry remembered making the march amidst a "very hard, driving rain," reaching Woodstock at about 2:00 p.m. and immediately establishing a

---

25 May 10, Campaign Journal, Sigel Papers WRHS.

26 Ibid.

picket line around the town. That rainfall must have been intermittent, for First Lt. Fabricus A. Cather of the 1st West Virginia Cavalry found the "weather pleasant and [only] inclining to rain," making it a "splendid day for marching."[27]

Colonel Thoburn's brigade followed the cavalry. There was a noticeable ratcheting up of tension as they marched, including an increase in bushwacking incidents; so much so that Thoburn stopped his column at Fisher's Hill, just beyond Strasburg, to order the men to load their weapons. This command struck the 12th West Virginia as ominous: "Those who had been under fire before, felt the gravity of the outlook," noted the 12th's regimental history. Lieutenant Cather recorded the presence of "150 Rebel cavalry hovering around our flanks & front," adding that "several of them [were] captured during the day." As the Federals neared Woodstock however, the Confederates declined to contest possession of the town.[28]

The Rebels directly opposing Sigel's advance were too desperately outnumbered to make a fight of it. They could do little more than harass the van and flanks of Sigel's force. After harrying Colonel Higgins's frightened Federals northward on the 10th, Imboden brought the 18th and 23rd Virginia Cavalry to the small hamlet of Mathias, West Virginia—25 miles west of Woodstock—where he was forced to lay over and rest his command through May 11. The Virginians, noted Lt. Julian Pratt, were simply to worn out to continue without rest, "having made a force march and running fight of ninety miles in forty-eight hours." Their absence left only Col. George H. Smith's 62nd Virginia Mounted Infantry, 550 strong, Capt. Sturgis Davis's small battalion of Marylanders, numbering 66; and Capt. John McClanahan's artillery battery to stand in Sigel's way. With Imboden and the bulk of the brigade absent, Smith and Davis chose to fall back slowly, forwarding reports of Federal action directly to General Breckinridge, who was by now established at Staunton and doing his best to hurry reinforcements northward.[29]

27 Bonnell, *Sabres in the Shenandoah,* 52; "Entry for May 11," Fabricus A. Cather Diary, West Virginia University, Morgantown WV.

28 Hewitt, *History of the Twelfth West Virginia,* 113; "Entry for May 11," Fabricus A. Cather Diary.

29 Julian Pratt Letter, VMI Archives; Davis's command included 26 of his own men and another 40 belonging to Major Harry Gilmor's Battalion, attached to Davis since

Smith and Davis dutifully reported Sigel's movement on the 9th, though they could offer few specifics. Captain Davis, for one, disputed Lieutenant Colonel Fitzsimmons's assertion that the Union cavalry was accomplishing nothing of note. "It is impossible to penetrate their lines," Davis complained. "They have large patrolling parties constantly in motion between their different posts. If you [Breckinridge] were familiar with the country, you would appreciate the difficulties of getting any certain information by scouting. . . ." Even worse, the near-constant rain negated another key Confederate advantage: "render[ing] observation from [Massanutten] Mountain impossible." With the Yankees on the move, things became a little clearer, and by the 11th both Davis and Smith reported Sigel's force at between 6,000 and 7,000 men, including "2,000 cavalry," further identifying 10 regiments of infantry and 28 cannon.[30]

Breckinridge reached Staunton on the night of May 8. Brigadier General Gabriel Wharton's troops were not expected to catch up until the 10th or 11th. The former vice president spent the ensuing two days trying to whip together a field force as best he could. He re-affirmed Imboden's earlier call-out of the local reserves, and on May 10 the Kentuckian sent a courier to Maj. Gen. Francis H. Smith, commandant of the Virginia Military Institute, informing Smith that the cadets would be needed for active service. Smith was unwell, but still wasted no time in turning out the students. The cadet battalion would be on the road by 7:00 a.m. the next morning, he replied, under the immediate command of Lt. Col. Scott Shipp. Numbering about 270 boys and young men, the battalion included four companies of infantry and a battery of two outdated six-pounder smoothbore cannon. Smith and a handful of the youngest cadets would stay behind, while another four companies of local reserves in the Lexington area would assemble at the Institute to help defend that place.[31]

Also in town was Maj. Harry Gilmor, still in arrest, awaiting a final decision, since his court of inquiry had already found Gilmor not guilty of the preferred charges. Breckinridge released Gilmor and sent him hurrying north. No one was sure whether Breckinridge had the authority

---

Gilmor's arrest.

30 *OR* 37, pt. 1, 729-730.

31 Ibid., 730.

to do so, but in this moment of crisis Breckinridge ignored any question of legality, what he needed now was manpower. He ordered Gilmor to gather his band of Confederate Marylanders as he went. The mission: "get in Sigel's rear, harass his supply trains and outposts, and do all I could to delay his march." Gilmor reached Mount Jackson on the night of May 11 and promptly informed an alarmed Captain Davis that he was resuming command of his battalion, which reduced Davis's own numbers by two thirds, to a mere 26 men. Davis's appeal was quickly overruled, and the dapper, formerly disgraced major resumed his role as bold partisan.[32]

At least some of Wharton's men reached Staunton on the 10th. John Schowen and his comrades in the 30th Virginia Battalion rolled into the rail depot that evening. They would have two extra days of rest waiting for the remainder of their brigade to arrive.[33]

Brigadier General John Echols's brigade was also struggling to reach Staunton, marching east from Lewisburg. Without the benefit of a railroad, Echols' 1,500 men faced a difficult slog through the mountains, having an especially hard time finding forage for their animals. The brigade staggered into Staunton on the 11th, five days after setting out from Camp Gauley West Virginia. Food and forage had been in short supply the whole way. They rested on May 12, taking spiritual sustenance by attending the local Presbyterian Church where, noted Sgt. William Mays of the 22nd Virginia, "we heard some fine sermons, delivered" (as Mays later mistakenly recalled) "by the Reverend Mr. Wilson. . . ."[34]

Last to arrive were the VMI cadets, mostly young men between the ages of 16 and 18, who tramped into town about midday on May 12. Cadet John Wise recalled the excitement that gripped the whole Institute, from the moment the long roll sounded at midnight on the 10th until "we marched into Staunton, not quite as fresh as when we started, but game and saucy, to the tune of 'The girl I left behind me.'" Echols's

---

32   Harry Gilmor, *Four Years in the Saddle* (London, 1866), 147.

33   Schowen, "Civil War Diary," 7.

34   Terry D. Lowry, *22nd Virginia Infantry* (Lynchburg, VA, 1988), 57. William Mays, *Four Years for Old Virginia* (Los Angeles, 1970). Mays was repeating a post-war myth that several old soldiers recalled, though it wasn't true. The Reverend Mr. Wilson was the father of future President Thomas Woodrow Wilson, but while Woodrow Wilson was indeed born in Staunton, the Wilson family had moved to Georgia in 1858.

and Wharton's veterans looked on these young men with a jaundiced eye, greeting them with the "taunting chorus 'Rock-a-bye Baby,' Which, Wise admitted, 'fill[ed] my soul with wrath.'"[35]

Breckinridge now faced a difficult choice; whether to continue north and face Sigel or turn back and deal with Crook. On May 11, another telegram from Robert E. Lee framed the dilemma nicely: "Just heard that Averell has cut Virginia and Tennessee Railroad at Dublin. It may be necessary for you to return to protect Lynchburg, &c. You must judge." Lee's earlier order to concentrate on Sigel was now apparently superseded, given the loss of the railroad. McCausland's men had already retained by Jenkins and come to grief at Cloyd's Mountain; they wouldn't be heading up to Staunton any time soon. Counting the cadets, Breckinridge would muster roughly 2,750 infantry by the close of May 12, plus some 500 men of the local reserves. Even adding in Imoboden's 1,400 men, this was a considerably smaller army than the Kentuckian hoped to assemble against Sigel's reported 8,000 troops; but the subtraction of McCausland's brigade could not be helped and no more support was forthcoming.[36]

Breckinridge decided to continue north. The next day he would march north to join Imboden. Southwest Virginia would have to fend for itself, and Breckinridge could only hope that Crook was going to retreat rather than press on down the Valley. It was a gamble, for Lee's army would be in serious distress if Staunton fell, and risk real disaster if Crook pressed on as far as Lynchburg, east of the Blue Ridge.

Sigel also faced decisions on May 11. His almost bloodless occupation of Woodstock yielded a substantial intelligence coup with the capture of several Confederate telegrams. From these Sigel learned that Breckinridge was in Staunton and that he had brought 4,000 troops north with him from Dublin Depot (this dispatch was dated May 5, before McCausland's retention.) It seemed that Breckinridge was also worried about all or part of Sigel's force turning east, either to join Grant or strike at Charlottesville, where Lee had another supply depot. One

35 John S. Wise, *Battle of New Market, Va. May 15th, 1864: An Address Repeated by John S. Wise, Esq., a Cadet in the Corps of 1864, Before the Professors, Officers and Cadets of the Virginia Military Institute, in the Hall of the Dialectic Society, May 13th, 1882* (Lexington, VA, 1882), 36-37.

36 *OR* 37, pt. 1, 728.

missive, dated May 10, stated that Lee was "driving [Grant] at every point." This last was worrisome, for it seemed to confirm the news Sigel had received earlier, about Grant retreating six miles.[37]

Based on similar news from captured telegrams, George Crook had already abandoned any thought of marching on Lexington, Staunton, or even heading for Lewisburg; he was in full retreat. Sigel, unaware of Crook's decision and worried about the outcome of Grant's fight, decided that he must do the opposite. In later years, Sigel would claim that "the unfavorable news relative to the great struggle between Grant and Lee could not fail to prompt me to energetic action." At the time he was not quite that emboldened. He would indeed continue to advance, but cautiously.[38]

On the afternoon of May 11, ensconced in the Cheney farmhouse just outside of Woodstock and with this new intelligence now in hand, Sigel outlined his intentions to his staff. The German informed the assembled officers that he "wished to take possession of New Market to secure the roads leading over the mountains east and west of that place." The road east "to Luray and Thornton's Gap," explained Sigel, "offered many advantages for a cavalry raid to Charlottesville . . . [while] Brock's Gap [to the west] . . . would have facilitated the opening of communication with Crook and resulted in a cooperation. . . ." New Market was 24 miles south of Woodstock, a long day's march. Imboden's full brigade, returned from the expedition against Higgins, was now positioned near Mount Jackson, 17 miles south of Woodstock. Imboden occupied Rude's Hill, an imposing height between Mount Jackson and New Market, prepared to resist any Union advance.[39]

In addition to the Rebels at Rude's Hill, enemy activity in the Luray Valley continued to pose a potential threat to the Union rear. Lacking the force to fully secure Front Royal, let alone send a parallel column southward on the east side of Massanutten, Sigel instead decided to send a flanking force of 300 cavalry to do the job, simultaneously pushing forward his own advanced guard as far as New Market. If successful, this movement would ensure that the Luray Valley was clear of Rebels and

37 Sigel, "Sigel in the Shenandoah Valley," 488.

38 Ibid.

39 Eby, *Virginia Yankee,* 224; Sigel Report, May 17, 1864, Sigel Papers. See Knight, *Valley Thunder,* 257-259, for a complete transcription.

allow the flanking column a quick means of escape westward through the New Market Gap if needed. It also entailed substantial risk, for Sigel was forced to repeatedly divide his small force into multiple columns, each exposed to piecemeal destruction if the Rebels were able to effectively coordinate against the various detachments. To Colonel Stother, Sigel's increasing tendency to fragment his command struck an ominous note.

Sigel's decisions on May 11 have been subject to criticism even ridicule; censure leveled both by observers at the time and by more recent historians. Imboden himself framed the nature of the debate when he denigrated Sigel's subsequent advance as "so slow and cautious," that ultimately it gave Breckinridge plenty of time to march north. The first historian to examine the campaign, Professor Edward Raymond Turner, followed Imboden's model: "The Federal movements had thus far been characterized," summarized Turner in 1912, "by uncertainty, slowness, and indecision." William C. Davis, who wrote a widely acclaimed history of the campaign in 1975, heaped outright scorn on Sigel for failing to dash forward: "And now, with the opportunity of a lifetime, one such as came to few generals in any war, he decided, was the perfect time to take root in Woodstock. After all," Davis mocked, "the men needed drilling." Historian Charles Knight, in his excellent 2010 study of the battle, drew the same conclusion: "Armed with this gift of knowing the enemy's strength and intentions, an energetic commander would likely have immediately set about destroying his opponent in detail. . . . Franz Sigel did no such thing." By doing so, Knight concluded, "Sigel was surrendering the initiative. . . ."[40]

Unfortunately, all these conclusions rest on a set of false assumptions. The first is that Imboden, contrary to all previous evidence, would suddenly stand and fight a pitched battle instead of simply retreating further south towards Staunton. Why would that happen? There was no strategic objective short of Staunton that would force Imboden to fight, and if Imboden refused action before reaching that place, all Sigel could do was keep chasing him, Federal strength dissipating with every step farther south. The idea that the Confederates were faced with defeat in

---

40 Imboden, "The Battle of New Market," 482; Edward Raymond Turner, *The New Market Campaign, May, 1864* (Richmond, VA, 1912), 9; Davis, *The Battle of New Market,* 55; Knight, *Valley Thunder,* 85.

detail simply isn't realistic, unless Imboden himself were taken with a sudden fit of incompetence.

The second was that Sigel could push south aggressively and maintain his strength. At Martinsburg, Sigel's force numbered nearly 8,000 men. By the time he got to Woodstock, his available numbers shrank to about 5,500 men. Higgins's disaster cost him 500 troops, and another 2,000 men were occupied in a daily struggle to keep his supply line open— roughly 1,000 troops for every 20 miles of road requiring protection and convoying. If that average held true, at New Market Sigel would have 4,500 men on hand, and at Harrisonburg, 3,500 or less. By the time he covered the whole 50 miles to Staunton, Sigel would be lucky to arrive with a battalion and a battery. Conversely, the Rebels would only grow stronger as they neared their supply depot and joined up their converging forces. At that point, it would be Sigel who was risking piecemeal destruction, not Imboden or Breckinridge.

The third mistake was in failing to remember Sigel's primary mission— to draw the Rebels away from Staunton so that Crook could seize it, or failing that, to form a juncture with Crook and bring overwhelming Union numbers against Staunton's defenders. By pushing Imboden rapidly up the valley, Sigel would be doing exactly the opposite: forcing the Rebels to concentrate their available forces at the vital point, not drawing the enemy away from it.

Far from surrendering the initiative or dithering in place, over the next few days Sigel adopted a perfectly sensible strategy aimed at drawing the Rebel army northward. His main camp remained at Woodstock, but he intended to send repeated probes and patrols as far south as New Market, giving every appearance of threat. If he failed to draw Breckinridge's main body out of Staunton, then he would go ahead and occupy New Market in strength, preparatory to the intended junction with Crook. Assuming that Crook was still in the game—and Sigel had no way yet of knowing he was not—Sigel's concept was sound strategy, and it worked exactly as intended.

CHAPTER 6

Skirmishing, May 12–14, 1864

To conduct the Luray expedition, General Sigel turned to Col. William H. Boyd. Boyd commanded the 21st Pennsylvania Cavalry, another six-month's regiment raised during the Gettysburg crisis and only re-organized as a three-year formation in January. Currently, the 21st was stationed at Harpers Ferry. Despite the regiment's limited field experience, Boyd himself was a seasoned veteran, having served with the 1st New York (Lincoln) Cavalry from the start of the war. In 1863, Boyd resigned his position as major in the 1st New York to recruit and ultimately command the newly raised Keystoners, who took the field early that fall. By the spring of 1864, Boyd knew the valley thoroughly, having waged anti-partisan warfare against Mosby's guerrillas for the past 10 months. On November 15, 1863, he'd even had a sharp fight with some of Imboden's people, under Rebel Col. (then a major) Robert White, at Rude's Hill.[1]

Not surprisingly, Boyd's credentials drew Sigel's attention. According to Lt. William H. Beach, Adjutant of the 1st New York: "Colonel Boyd . . . was directed, without his regiment, to report to General Sigel for special service. This was supposed to have been done at Sigel's request because of Boyd's acquaintance with the region, and his uniform success [there]." Boyd reached Winchester on May 8, taking charge of

1 http://www.shenandoah.stonesentinels.com/Mount_Jackson/A26-Cavalry_Engagement.php, accessed January 26, 2016.

a very mixed bag of cavalry oddments. His orders were to cover Sigel's flank around Berryville (seven miles east of Winchester) and to chase down Confederate partisans east of the Blue Ridge, keeping them from interfering with the flow of supplies up the Valley Turnpike.[2]

Now Sigel decided to send Boyd's ad-hoc command to Luray. The force included Capt. James H. Stevenson's Company C of the 1st New York Lincoln, "a troop from Cole's Maryland Battalion: another from the so called First New York Veteran Cavalry . . . and a squadron [two troops] from the Twenty First New York Cavalry." In addition, noted Adjutant Beach, small details from several other companies of the 1st New York Lincoln were also present. All told, this force amounted to between 250 and 300 men: more a patrol than an invasion force. Comprised of five companies drawn from four different regiments, all under the command of an officer unknown to almost everyone in the expedition, the ad-hoc battalion seemed destined for friction.[3]

On May 12 Boyd's battalion marched to Front Royal, amidst yet more driving rain. There they picked up Lt. Isaac D. Vermylia and Company H of the 1st New York (Lincoln), adding about 30 more sabers to the column. Vermylia had been separately pursuing some of Mosby's men. After detaching a party to escort prisoners (Rebel stragglers, apparently from Imboden's brigade) back to Winchester, and despite the incessant precipitation, Boyd led the column another 10 miles south, where they camped for the night.

On the 13th, Boyd's men headed for Luray, 14 miles distant. The morning's march brought action. Once again, partisans hovered just out of reach. Better mounted than the Federals, these Rebels "kept within a tantalizing distance ahead of the advance guard, defying every effort made to run them down." Provoked, Boyd turned snappish. "When told these Confederates had not been captured because they were too well mounted," noted Adjutant Beach, "he sneeringly remarked: '[That] is very strange.'" This implied rebuke, suggesting an unwillingness to close with the enemy if not quite insinuating outright cowardice, stung the New

---

2   William H. Beach, *The First New York (Lincoln) Cavalry* (New York: 1902), 318.

3   James H. Stevenson, *"Boots and Saddles": A History of the First Volunteer Cavalry of the War Known as the First New York (Lincoln) Cavalry, And Also as the Sabre Regiment, Its Organization, Campaigns, and Battles* (Harrisburg, PA: 1879), 260; Beach, *First New York*, 322.

Yorkers. Lieutenant Edwin New rapped out a challenge in return. "'You have a race horse, colonel. Suppose you and I try it.'" With that, Boyd and New recklessly spurred forward, finally overtaking of the enemy. New shot one of them before he could surrender, the others gave in more readily. These were not the only captures; by midday the Federals reached their objective, sweeping up at least one small Confederate supply train along the way, and destroying a quantity of stores and fodder stockpiled in the village of Luray.[4]

For the bulk of Sigel's army, the 12th passed quietly. His infantry spent the day foraging or preparing to march. Quiet did not mean comfortable, however. The constant rain saw to that. Charles H. Lynch of the 18th Connecticut had just come off picket that morning, after standing guard in a "severe rainstorm," and he was "wet through. Between the rain and the mud we are in misery. . . . What sleep we can get . . . doesn't amount to very much, as we must lie on the ground." In addition to weather induced delay, Sigel was also waiting for more troops to join the main body, as he called forward some of the force left behind to secure his flanks and rear. One of these commands was the 14th Pennsylvania Cavalry. After "breakfast & dinner at Front Royal," noted Cpl. Albert Artman, the 14th marched thirteen wearying miles to Strasburg, arriving at "10 at night and went into camp."[5]

Sigel's supply line now stretched 55 miles, running from Woodstock back to Martinsburg, every yard of it subject to attack. For the slow-moving supply trains, a round trip consumed most of a week's time. Wagons could travel safely only as part of heavily escorted convoys. Single vehicles and small detachments proved easy prey for the guerrillas. Every regiment was required to supply detachments for these escorts, each company taking their turn tramping back and forth along the Valley Turnpike. Additionally, the need to garrison Winchester, to protect the bridge at Cedar Creek, and picket other vital points along the way drained yet more manpower away from the main body. Probably a third of Sigel's entire strength was now occupied in securing this lifeline, greatly reducing his available combat power.

4   Beach, *First New York*, 323; Stevenson, "Boots and Saddles," 264.

5   Charles H. Lynch, *The Civil War Diary, 1862–1865, of Charles H. Lynch, 18th Connecticut Volunteers* (Hartford, CT: 1915), 58; "Entry for May 12," Albert Artman Diary, AHEC.

Mosby's men plunder Union sutlers' wagons, from Harper's Weekly. *Library of Congress*

Threats to the supply trains were constant, and creative. At Woodstock Sigel issued another order to reduce his army's excess baggage. In conjunction with this directive, the 116th Ohio regimental history recorded a remarkable incident. "Another order, allowing only one Sutler to a brigade, was issued, the rest being ordered to the rear. A note . . . [was] handed to the Division Quartermaster, purporting to come from the Chief Quartermaster . . . ordering a large train to the rear, with which were also to go the returned Sutlers' wagons. The train had started and was well out on the road *without a guard*, when the quartermaster discovered what had been done." In great haste the train was retrieved, but the rumor soon swept the camp that "Mosby and McNeil were in waiting for the train a few miles down the road."[6]

Whether or not this was a simple blunder or actually a clever Rebel ruse remains undetermined, but the incident certainly demonstrated how the partisan threat remained uppermost in everyone's mind. As if to underline the danger, On May 12 another column was attacked just outside Strasburg. Escorted by a mixed detachment of the 13th Pennsylvania and the 21st New York cavalries, this was a southbound train, heavily laden with rations and other supplies. An estimated 20 raiders under Capt. William Chapman of Mosby's 43rd Virginia Battalion struck the column, killing two Yankees and capturing four more before being driven off.[7]

Despite the miserable weather, not every Federal at Woodstock spent May 12 in camp. In keeping with his strategy of provocation, Sigel ordered other elements of the 21st New York Cavalry under command of Maj. Charles G. Otis out on a reconnaissance towards Mount Jackson.

6   Wildes, *One Hundred and Sixteenth Regiment,* 38.

7   Bonnell, *Sabres in the Shenandoah,* 53.

Sometime that afternoon, Otis's force drove in the Rebel pickets just north of that place, provoking a considerable response.

Major Gilmor, having re-asserted his authority over his Marylanders, was preparing that very afternoon to set out via the back valleys of Massanutten, intending to add his own effort to the ongoing attacks against Sigel's supply line. Gilmor was present at Mount Jackson when Otis's Federals arrived near 4:00 p.m. Gilmor recalled that "fifty or sixty" of his men "were feeding their horses, when I heard sharp firing at a short distance." Soon the Rebel pickets appeared, "retreating, but fighting as they fell back." Without hesitation, Gilmor ordered his men to mount and, moving in column of fours, trotted northward to join the fight. He soon bumped into Captain Davis, so recently the commander of these same men. "Davis rushed in, telling me it was useless to fight, as there were fully five hundred [Yankees] and I should lose every man."[8]

Gilmor hadn't ridden hard all the way from Staunton just to join a retreat. Ignoring Davis, he immediately charged into the teeth of Otis's advance, purportedly "to give Davis time to reform." How much time this bought Davis was arguable—it didn't take long before Gilmor discovered that Davis's assessment was accurate. The major immediately reversed course, with Union carbines "peppering us at every jump. They ran us handsomely for about two miles," admitted the bellicose Marylander, until the whole cavalcade thundered into the small hamlet of Hawkinstown, immediately north of Mount Jackson. Now the Federals were "pretty well strung out" thought Gilmor; he decided a riposte was in order. Wheeling about, he led his men in a fresh charge. Now the Yankees fell back, but Otis was prepared for just such a contingency. The Federal commander had dismounted a battalion about a half-mile back. As their comrades tore past, these men received Gilmor's renewed charge with a volley. Back again went the Marylanders, this time retreating to a point a mile south of Hawkinstown, with mounted Federals again in pursuit.

This second repulse marked the end of the action, though Gilmor, reckless to a fault, decided on one last show of bravado. While his men were retreating, he hid behind a house, and as the Federals approached he sprang out to discharge his revolver into the lead Yank. A second shot dropped the next man's mount. His sense of audacity satisfied, Gilmor took off. He might have gotten away clean from this escapade if he

8   Gilmor, *Four Years in the Saddle,* 148.

hadn't drawn up rein 50 yards away to fire again. Spotting him, a Union officer slid off his horse, grabbed a carbine from an enlisted man, and took aim. Gilmor turned his horse to ride away, "feeling a little mean that I had not kept front till he fired." As if to confirm his worries, the Union bullet hit Gilmor in the back, "two inches from the spine, on the upper part of the right hip bone." Gilmor's swagger had cost more than his own wound and a damaged sense of pride. Three of his men had turned with him when he stopped to fire the second time. Two of those were also shot down in this exchange.[9]

The running battle had been largely without point. His reconnaissance mission fulfilled, Otis elected to retreat and headed back to Woodstock. The Confederates re-established their original picket lines without further incident. Gilmor's wound turned out to be painful but not debilitating, though it did allow him to play the wounded hero at the home of a local sympathizer in nearby Mount Airy, where he spent the night. He was still determined to embark on his intended raiding mission the next day. Imboden, in a report to Breckinridge that night, speculated that the fight was a diversion designed "to get his cavalry in my rear tonight," a clear reference to Boyd's expedition. To counter that move Imboden "resolved to fall back three miles to New Market, and get in rear of the road by which he [Boyd] would turn my position." Otis's action also confirmed that there was a strong Rebel presence at Mount Jackson, one that would need more investigation the next morning.[10]

Back at Woodstock General Sigel also planned an active morning. At 7:00 a.m. Sigel ordered "two regiments of infantry, a battalion of cavalry, and a section of artillery" to move on Mount Jackson. Their mission was two-fold; to probe the Rebel defenses south of that town, confirming Major Otis's information of the previous afternoon, and to link up with Colonel Boyd's flanking column, expected to come over Massanutten Mountain from Luray sometime later that day.[11]

With substantial numbers of Rebels between the main Federal force and New Market, if left unsupported, Boyd could be riding into a trap. By occupying Mount Jackson with a strong advanced guard, Sigel could

---

9   Ibid., 149.

10   *OR* 37, pt. 1, 731.

11   Campaign Journal, Sigel Papers, WRHS.

offer Boyd that support, should he need it. As an added precaution, Sigel sent out Lt. Norman H. Meldrum and Company G of the 21st New York, reinforced by a detachment of the 20th Pennsylvania Cavalry, to find Boyd and warn him of the fact that the Federals did not yet control New Market or the pass over Massanutten. Meldrum's patrol—about 50 men—picked their way up the west face of Massanutten Mountain near Woodstock, and then descended into a small cleft atop the height called Fort Valley, which divided Massanutten's summit. Named after the colonial era settlement of Powell's Fort, Fort Valley was a narrow cove, the east and west crests of Massanutten framing it dramatically on both sides. Meldrum's party must have lost considerable time in both scaling the mountain and in finding their way through the sparsely settled cove, for his men would spend the night in Fort Valley, having failed to either reach Luray or locate Boyd.[12]

Sigel selected Colonel Augustus Moor to lead the Mount Jackson probe. In doing so, he evidenced another bad habit: that of assigning regiments to missions without regard for the chain of command. Instead of drawing entirely on men from his own brigade, Moor was given only his own 28th Ohio, supplemented by the 12th West Virginia from Colonel Thoburn's command. The artillery was a section of Captain Carlin's Battery D, 1st West Virginia Battery, while Maj. Timothy Quinn of the 1st New York Lincoln led the cavalry component. When Quinn departed Woodstock, his force amounted to only 50 men, but he was supposed to link up with another 250 troopers en route. The whole force amounted to roughly 1,400 men; 1,000 infantry, two cannon, and, once Quinn had his full complement, about 300 cavalry. Their instructions, noted one of Carlin's gunners, "were to go above Edenburg and wait for Colonel Boyd, who with his cavalry had gone up the Luray Valley. . . ."[13]

The small hamlet of Edinburg lay just a mile or so north of the equally minor village of Hawkinstown, which in turn was a mile north of the only slightly larger town of Mount Jackson. Sigel intended for Moor to establish an outlying picket at Edinburg, halting there with

12 Gilmor, *Four Years in the Saddle,* 149. Bonnell, *Sabres in the Shenandoah,* 54; Stevenson, "Boots and Saddles," 269; Davis, *The Battle of New Market,* 65, all rely on Gilmor's account of Meldrum's patrol.

13 Sigel, "Sigel in the Shenandoah Valley," 488; Phillips, *Wheeling's Finest,* 41. Sigel estimated the mounted force at 500 men, but as will be seen, it was much less.

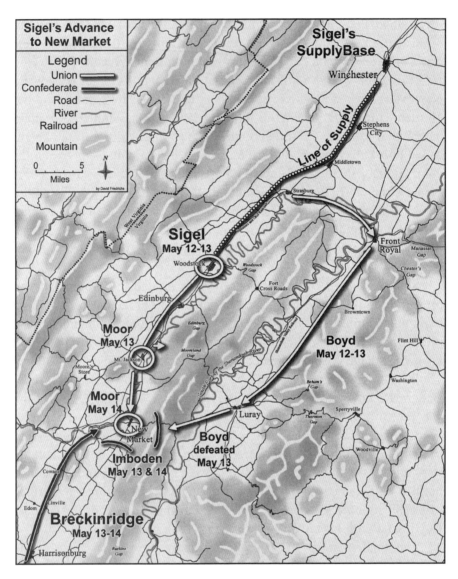

the infantry while Quinn's cavalry pushed on to Mount Jackson. Moor reached Edinburg at about 4:00 p.m., meeting no Rebels along the way. Once here, however, everyone could hear sounds of fighting; the rumble of "artillery at New Market, but [we] did not know . . . what caused it." As intended, Quinn now pressed on alone. Unfortunately for the mission, the other 250 cavalrymen had not yet shown up, leaving Quinn with just his initial 50 troopers. Quinn later reported that "on approaching

Mount Jackson . . . I heard the report of guns to the left [east] of New Market. I went about two and a half miles beyond Mount Jackson" as far as the bridge over the North Fork of the Shenandoah River, just short of Rude's Hill. Here Quinn discovered that he could go no farther. A full Confederate regiment, the 62nd Virginia Infantry, barred the way south. "As I could not accomplish the object for which I was sent (to communicate with Colonel Boyd)," wrote Quinn, "I returned."[14]

While headed back north, the missing 250 cavalrymen finally caught up, but it was too late to do anything but return to Edinburg for the night. Quinn reported his findings to Moor. Moor in turn sent a courier back to Sigel, informing the army commander that while Quinn's trip was opposed by some "enemy in front making a show . . . [they] were not believed to be in force." This was a curious conclusion, ignoring the presence of the entire 62nd Virginia at Rude's Hill, and it is not known whether the opinion was Quinn's take on the afternoon's ride or if Moor discounted Quinn's findings. In any case, having decided that the threat to the south was minimal, Moor elected to leave the 12th West Virginia and Quinn's cavalry battalion at Edinburg while he and the 28th Ohio returned to the main camp at Woodstock.[15]

Moor seemed to have forgotten about Colonel Boyd. Also left unresolved was the issue of the overheard cannon fire. In fact, that distant artillery rumbling marked Boyd's arrival in New Market. Unlike Moor's expedition, Boyd met with plenty of opposition. Much more than he could handle, as it turned out: he met with disaster.

Boyd's 300 men left Luray about midday on the 13th, crossing the South Fork of the Shenandoah River a little west of town and then ascending the road to New Market Gap. Massanutten Mountain narrows here to a single ridge, with Fort Valley's southern apex beginning just a few miles farther north along the spine of the mountain. Once Boyd's column crested the ridge the Federals were presented with a wide view of New Market and the rest of the Shenandoah Valley spread out below. They were also visible to anyone watching the gap.

One of the first to spot the Federal column was "young Davey Crabill," a 16-year-old private in the 18th Virginia Cavalry. Along with

14 Phillips, *Wheeling's Finest*, 41, *OR* 37, pt. 1, 74.

15 *OR* 37, pt. 1, 74; Entry for May 13, Campaign Journal, Sigel Papers, WRHS.

the rest of his company, Crabill had been sent to picket the Luray Road. Excited now, Crabill "shouted, 'Lieutenant, lieutenant, come out here. Sir, I see men riding through the Gap.'" Plenty of others saw them, too. Charles O'Farrell of the 23rd Virginia Cavalry remembered that "a Federal regiment was discovered on top of the mountain, four miles distant." Fascinated, O'Farrell watched as "there they halted for a few minutes and then commenced to descend the mountain, coming directly towards us. The movement was a great surprise . . ." Imboden, with plenty of time to react while the Yankees picked their way down the west face of the mountain, left Colonel Smith's 62nd Virginia Infantry to watch Moor and took the rest of the brigade to confront this new threat.[16]

That pause O'Farrell witnessed was due to a debate within the Federal ranks. Captain Stevenson and Lieutenant New of the 1st New York Lincoln, leading the column, halted when they saw "a large body of troops marching up the Valley Pike, from Mount Jackson to New Market." Stevenson was sure they were Rebels, but when Boyd rode up, the colonel insisted they must be Sigel's advanced guard. Lieutenant Beach, also present, was clearly nonplussed. He noted that the troops in question were "leading" their advance with a train of wagons and a herd of cattle, pointing out "how absurd it would be for Sigel to place his wagon train between his army and the enemy." Besides, added Beach, "our army had no herd of cattle." Boyd would hear none of it, certain that they had to be Sigel's men.[17]

"To settle the question," Lieutenant New volunteered to take a couple of men and ride forward on a quick scout. At the western foot of the mountain the Luray Road crossed Smith Creek. Here, New encountered Rebel pickets, doubtless Private Crabill and his comrades. They opened fire, and New hurried rearward. He didn't get far. Boyd had already decided not to wait, starting down the mountain with the rest of the command.[18]

Stevenson recalled that Boyd, though "a little staggered" by the sight before him, "concluded to proceed, [again] observing that they must be Sigel's troops. They soon encountered Lieutenant New, returning.

---

16   Woodward, *Defender of the Valley*, 107; O'Farrell, *Forty Years*, 94.

17   Stevenson, "Boots and Saddles," 264-265; Beach, *First New York Lincoln Cavalry*, 324.

18   Beach, *First New York Lincoln Cavalry*, 324.

The lieutenant's information, however, failed to clarify matters. Yes, the pickets had fired on him," said New, but he also related that "they were dressed in our uniform," leaving Boyd to conclude that "they were [simply] some of Sigel's men who had not been informed of our approach." The column pressed on. As if to further cloud the matter, this time the pickets retreated without shooting.[19]

Boyd had fewer than 300 men. Imboden's strength, even absent the 62nd, numbered about 930 troopers and 93 artillerymen. As if outmatching the Federals three times over wasn't advantage enough, the Rebels also had warning enough to arrange an ambush. To Stevenson, Beach, and everyone but Boyd, disaster now seemed imminent. We held a little "Pow Wow," recalled Stevenson, and at last some caution prevailed. Instead of pressing on directly towards the town and all those unknown troops on the turnpike, the Federals decided to cross the creek, turn north, and try and slip in behind the regiment they observed earlier.[20]

That decision came too late. Imboden was ready to attack. While Boyd's men were still filing across the bridge, the woods around them erupted with fire and Rebels. "Now we've got the d—d Yankees! Give 'em h--l!"[21]

Caught unprepared, the outnumbered Federals stood no chance. The column soon collapsed into chaos. "We pitched directly at them," recalled O'Farrell, "but after firing a few shots as we approached them, they wheeled about and struck pell-mell, every fellow for himself. . . ." Circumstances only grew worse for the Federals when the 18th Virginia joined in, sent by Imboden to outflank Boyd's column from the south and cut off any Yankee retreat up the mountain.[22]

If Boyd lacked judgment, he at least possessed considerable personal courage, a trait which did much to redeem him in Stevenson's eyes. "A body of the enemy [18th Virginia] was discovered coming down through a cut in the bluff," noted Stevenson, to charge us in flank. My advance guard charged upon them and drove them back. While only a temporary

19 Stevenson, "Boots and Saddles," 265.

20 Berkley Report, May 16, 1864, Sigel Papers, WRHS; Stevenson, "Boots and Saddles," 265.

21 Stevenson, "Boots and Saddles," 265.

22 O'Farrell, *Forty Years,* 95.

check, this bought enough time for Boyd to try and arrange a stand. He "sent some men to open a gap in a fence to his rear" and create a path of escape that way. It was not to be. "The firing was so hot from the bluff, and a shell bursting over us at that moment, the men under Boyd gave way, notwithstanding his example of coolness and courage." Boyd now ordered Stevenson to try and get to the head of the column and rally it farther back. But that same fence now presented a dangerous obstacle.[23]

It was here that "the rebels brought up their artillery to the bank of the creek . . . and opened on [us] . . . with grape and canister." The shelling "demoralizing the men very much," lamented Stevenson, "and those of our regiment were the only ones I could control. The others dashed on as if pursued by furies." Now it was Stevenson's turn to try to "let down [the] fence, but the others crowded up in such numbers as to retard the work and delay the retreat." Stevenson himself was nearly captured here, now afoot with an unsteady saddle on a wild-eyed mount, saved only by the quick-thinking of a carbine-wielding private who grabbed hold of his reins in one hand and dropping a looming Confederate at the same time.[24]

The Federals never managed to reform. Confederate Lieut. James Potts of the 18th recounted that "[we] drove them into Massanutten Mountains, capturing nearly the entire detachment." Those Federals who did get away did so mainly on foot, many of them forced to abandon mounts and equipment as they scrambled up the rugged slopes behind them, eventually making their way back to Woodstock. Boyd, Stevenson, and a few others managed to remain mounted, but were entirely at a loss about what to do next. Stevenson recalled that Boyd, "who had behaved splendidly in the fight, now seemed very much discouraged, [saying] he would rather have been killed than to have had such a misfortune."[25]

The action cost Boyd 125 casualties, most of them captures, or nearly half of his command. These prisoners were marched into New Market, where they spent a miserable night, denied shelter and huddled in the rain. New Yorker Charles Peterson recorded that the poorly equipped

23 Stevenson, "Boots and Saddles," 266.

24 Beach, *First New York Lincoln Cavalry,* 326; Stevenson, "Boots and Saddles," 266-267.

25 J. N. Potts, "Who Fired the First Gun at New Market?" *Confederate Veteran*, vol. 17, no. 9 (September 1909), 453; Stevenson, *"Boots and Saddles,"* 267.

Rebels, "villains" in his eyes, "took the blankets, rubbers, overcoats, and in many cases the hats and coats of the prisoners." Those Federals who managed to evade capture were scattered across the top of Massanutten and throughout Fort Valley. They faced rough going, trying to return to their own lines. Some of them never would. One such was Cpl. Robert Cowan of the 1st New York Veteran. Swept from his horse by the force of the swollen waters of Passage Creek in Fort Valley, Cowen drowned. His body was discovered when a local farmer, Andrew Coverstone, noticed a strange horse, still wearing saddle and bridle, cropping grass in the pasture with his own livestock. When he located Cowan's body, Coverstone buried the unfortunate soldier, eventually sending the corporal's watch off to New York in hopes of it finding its way to his family. Coverstone never heard another word about the dead man. Not until 1993 would Cowan's remains be discovered, changing his status from "missing" to "killed in action."[26]

Unfortunately, all these losses were unnecessary. Boyd's men suffered because of Boyd's own recklessness, coupled with Moor's strange inertia. If Boyd had simply halted atop the mountain, Imboden would not have been able to send troops up after him, given the presence of Moor at Edinburg; nor could Imboden have remained north of New Market with enemy cavalry perched in the Gap waiting to turn his flank or strike at his rear. Instead, Imboden would likely have done what he told Breckinridge he intended to do all along: retreat to a point south of New Market to avoid just such a threat. Alternatively, Moor's force alone was roughly equal to Imboden's whole strength, and if Moor had only pressed forward more aggressively Imboden could never have diverted two thirds of his command to strike Boyd while leaving only 500 men to oppose Moor. In either circumstance, with Imboden's men deployed on one of the hills south of New Market, Boyd's column could have easily slipped down the Gap Road and linked up with Moor's force. The responsibility for the day's disaster rested mostly with Boyd, but Moor's inaction certainly contributed. It would not be the last curious decision Moor would make in this campaign.

By now it was obvious that Sigel had plenty of reason to be dissatisfied with his cavalry, who were proving to be no match for

---

26 Beach, *First New York Lincoln Cavalry*, 331; Bonnell, *Sabres in the Shenandoah*, 201-202.

Imboden's veterans. Out of the approximately 3,000 troopers assembled at Martinsburg a fortnight ago, roughly 1,400 of those men had already been—one way or the other—removed from the campaign. While sending the first 600 of them back to Martinsburg on May 5 to guard the B&O was probably necessary, the remaining losses were hardly unavoidable. Colonel Higgins took 500 men off into West Virginia on May 6, only to be ambushed by Imboden at Lost Gap, and then had ridden right out of the campaign in panicked flight back to Cumberland. Now another force was shattered, 300 more men entrusted to the reckless Colonel Boyd. Even those of Boyd's column that avoided outright capture lost their weapons, equipment, and even most of their mounts. They were effectively *hors-de-combat* for the foreseeable future.

The remaining 1,600 blue troopers were now needed for a multiplicity of tasks. Many were of necessity tasked with convoying the various supply trains back and forth to Martinsburg, enduring constant sniping along the way. More were needed to lead the way south, for both reconnaissance purposes and to screen Sigel's own main body. Troops also had to be assigned to guard that portion of the supply and baggage train that accompanied Sigel's main body, for those wagons contained not only Sigel's own provisions, but the re-supply Crook's men would need once the two columns joined. What Sigel really needed was a solid division of veteran cavalry, well-led and proven in combat. Unfortunately, so, too, did others: those troopers were all serving with the Army of the Potomac, or sent off under Averell to join Crook. Sigel simply had to make do with what was left, and that force had so far proved inadequate.

By contrast, Imboden and his men were performing well. Not only had Imboden so far blunted or shattered two Federal expeditions, but he was also keeping Breckinridge well informed. May 13 was no exception. One dispatch, sent at 4:00 p.m., noted Moor's limited advance and the appearance of Boyd's flanking force, easily visible from the telegraph office in New Market itself. A follow-up wire trumpeted the triumph over Boyd: "Imboden killed several, took some prisoners, and scattered the residue in the mountain." Despite this success, Imboden was still wary, informing the Kentuckian that "my advance is at Rude's Hill. I will make a stand here against his cavalry, but if he gets up his infantry and artillery before reinforcements reach me I shall be forced to retire. Lacey Spring [ten miles south of New Market] . . . is the next position in which we should have any advantage of ground. By what hour can I expect support here?"[27]

Back in Staunton, Breckinridge remained committed to his chosen course, despite a series of ominous telegrams emanating from both Richmond and the troops back in southwest Virginia, opposing Crook. On the night of May 12, a disturbing missive reached Secretary of War Seddon. It was sent by Robert L. Preston, one of Salem Virginia's most prominent citizens, who warned that "unless reinforcements are sent to Colonel McCausland at once, the Virginia and Tennessee railroad from Dublin to Lynchburg is at the mercy of the enemy." This alarming news triggered a response from Gen. Braxton Bragg in his capacity as President Davis's military advisor, instructed Breckinridge to immediately send a brigade of infantry to Lynchburg, unless he had "instructions from General Lee to conflict" with that order. Given Lee's own instruction that "you must judge," Breckinridge felt authorized to ignore Bragg's directive, correctly grasping that to obey would simply have his limited infantry force uselessly shuttling back and forth, defending nothing, guaranteeing defeat on both fronts. McCausland would have to fend for himself. Breckinridge remained unswervingly focused on Sigel.

New Market was 50 miles north of Staunton. Hard marching would be required to cover that distance quickly. Accordingly, at 6:00 a.m. on May 13, Breckinridge's 3,500 troops filed north, headed first for Mount Crawford, 20 miles down the Valley. The day's trek proved difficult, conducted in yet another driving rain that had so far characterized the campaign. VMI Cadet Beverly Stanard recalled that unlike the tramp to Staunton on the 11th, where "the roads were very good but were quite dusty," now "the roads were awful *perfect loblolly all* the way and we had to wade through like *hogs*." To cap off the day's misery, thunderstorms lashed the camps that night; lightning struck amid the tents of the 23rd Virginia Infantry, injuring 11 men. There were other ramifications of the long march and miserable conditions: Echols's brigade suffered a rash of desertions. Both the 22nd Virginia and the 23rd battalion recorded a surprising number of absentees during the movement; 17 men from the 23rd alone.[28]

27 *OR* 37, pt. 1, 733.

28 Davis, *Breckinridge*, 417; Beverly Stanard, with John G. Barrett and Robert K. Turner, Jr. eds. *Letters of a New Market Cadet* (Chapel Hill, NC: 1961), 61; J. L. Scott,

Echols was also having personal difficulties. Despite his imposing size—he stood six feet, four inches tall and weighed two hundred and 60 pounds—Echols was not a hale man. He had already resigned his commission once, in June of 1863, citing ill health, but was soon reinstated. He was often unwell thereafter. He was ill again just before arriving in Staunton. He remained with his command, but only in a limited capacity.[29]

Roused again early on the 14th, Breckinridge's little army headed for Lacey Spring, the site of Imboden's next advantageous defensive position. This day's march required another 18 miles, and while it still rained intermittently, Cadet Wise's attention was not on the weather. Instead, he noted, "at short intervals along the valley pike . . . carriages and carts and wagons blocked the way, laden with household goods and people fleeing from the hostile advance." More alarming was the appearance of the occasional "haggard trooper of Imboden, who dispirited by long skirmishing against overwhelming force, gave gloomy enough reports of the power and the numbers of the enemy." Echols' and Wharton's veterans probably ignored these last, knowing them for the stragglers and laggards that every action produced, but the cadets had no such battle-wise experience to call upon.[30]

Breckinridge rode ahead, reaching Lacey Spring at noon. There he met with John Imboden, who had come south upon news of the Kentuckian's approach. The two discussed their options over lunch, with Imboden reporting that all had been quiet at New Market when he left that morning. Breckinridge's troops, still on the road, would not all be up until evening, and couldn't push on to New Market until the next morning. During this council, a courier from Colonel Smith arrived, who commanded at New Market in Imboden's absence. "Sigel's cavalry, 2,500 strong, had reached Rude's Hill and . . .Colonel [George W.] Imboden [John's brother] was falling back skirmishing. . . ." To Smith, this looked like more than just another probe, and as if to underscore that point, even as the courier delivered his message Imboden and Breckinridge could hear the boom of cannon in the distance. Imboden immediately

23rd Battalion Virginia Infantry (Lynchburg, VA: 1991), 27.

29   Terry Lowry, *26th Battalion Virginia Infantry* (Lynchburg, VA: 1991), 37

30   Wise, *New Market*, 39-40.

mounted, preparing to return to the front. Breckinridge ordered him to hold New Market "at all hazards" until at least nightfall, "and then fall back four miles. . . ."[31]

Perhaps worried about all the recent Confederate activity around New Market, first thing on the morning of May 14, Moor dispatched Maj. Horace Kellogg and the 123rd Ohio (approximately 400 bayonets) south to Edinburg, with orders to reinforce the 12th West Virginia. The 123rd departed immediately, taking three hours to cover the distance. Why Moor simply didn't leave the veteran 28th Ohio at Edinburg in the first place, he never explained. In hindsight, it would have been smart to do so.[32]

Had Franz Sigel been aware of Breckinridge's movements, the German would have been pleased. Sigel was determined to keep Confederate attention fixed on himself, the better to let Crook's column move freely. For that reason, the Union commander decided to send an even stronger probe south towards New Market on May 14.

At 9:00 a.m. Colonel Moor was once again summoned to General Stahel's headquarters tent, where he found Sigel, Stahel and Sullivan in conference. Sigel wanted Colonel Moor to lead this second probe. This time Moor's expedition was to be much stronger, comprised "of three regiments of infantry, 1,000 cavalry, and six pieces of artillery. . . ." His orders were to "feel the position and strength of the rebels . . . reported to be on Rude's Hill."[33]

Once again, troops were assigned to this mission without regard for chain of command. For this trip, Moor was given two regiments from Thoburn's brigade, the 1st West Virginia and the 34th Massachusetts, and would pick up the 123rd Ohio from his own brigade once he reached Edinburg. This was a mystifying decision. Three of Moor's regiments— the 18th Connecticut, 28th and 116th Ohio—were to remain behind, presumably with Thoburn, while in the meantime, three of Thoburn's four regiments—the 34th Massachusetts, 1st and 12th West Virginia— would be operating with Moor.

31 Imboden, "The Battle of New Market," 482.

32 Entry for September 14, Leander Coe Diary, Dorothy Ringle Papers, BGSU.

33 Agustus Moor campaign account, Moor Papers, Henrich Rattermann Collection, University of Illinois; OR 37, pt. 1, 79.

Similarly, instead of just sending a complete battery, this time the accompanying artillery included two sections (four guns) of Capt. Alonzo Snow's Battery B, Maryland light artillery, and two guns from Capt. Chatham T. Ewing's battery G, 1st West Virginia. For the cavalry, General Stahel assigned Colonel John E. Wyncoop's Second Brigade, reduced by so many detachments to a force of only about 300 men. Wyncoop would be bolstered by Major Quinn's ad-hoc battalion of 550 more troopers, also still at Edinburg.

According to Moor's later recollection, Sigel intended to follow with the remaining force, assuring the Ohio colonel "that by 5 o'clock next morning the whole army would be up with me." Here Moor also made a startling request, which was, he claimed, denied. He "asked for scouts or [a] topographical map of the Valley as I was a perfect stranger there, but could not be furnished with either!" This exclamation was surprising on two counts. First, Moor seemed to believe that Sigel intended to bring the whole army up to New Market, which was incorrect; and second, Moor was hardly a stranger to the area, having been at least as far as Edinburg only the day before. Additionally, he would also have Quinn's force at hand. Among Sigel's whole force, Moor and Quinn were probably the two Federal officers most familiar with the area south of Woodstock.[34]

If Moor was confused about Sigel's intentions, he was likely not alone. Sigel's dispositions on the afternoon of the 14th reflect a certain confusion across the Union chain of command, nowhere more evident than among the ranks of the cavalry. General Julius Stahel was by now serving as Sigel's chief of staff, while simultaneously retaining command of the much-reduced cavalry division. To fill in, Colonel Robert F. Taylor of the 1st New York (Veteran) Cavalry served as the day-to-day head of the cavalry, a duty he had held intermittently prior to Stahel's arrival, and now continued when the need arose. New Market was 20 miles distant, too far away for Sigel to personally manage affairs from his main headquarters at Woodstock, and too far to the front for Sigel to go and take charge of what amounted to a reconnaissance in force. Stahel should have been the obvious choice to command this advanced guard. He commanded the cavalry division, he ranked Moor, and he had Sigel's confidence; all important qualities for such a critical post.[35]

---

34 Moor campaign account, Moor Papers.

35 Oddly enough, Taylor was not the ranking colonel in the cavalry division. Colonel William Tibbets, who led the First Brigade, ranked Taylor, but did not automatically

Colonel David M. Strother, of Sigel's Staff.
Library of Congress

Observing from the vantage of headquarters, David Strother was greatly bothered by the increasing dispersal of Sigel's small army. Strother fretted over "sending detachments of his force so far from the main body as to be destroyed in detail. . . ." Already, two such detachments—Higgins and Boyd—had come to just such grief. Sigel, thought Strother, now "court[ed] destruction . . . in the case of Moor's brigade."[36]

Moor's column left Woodstock at 11:00 a.m. The weather was again cloudy and rainy. The pace was fast. Colonel Wells noted that his 34th Massachusetts made 21 miles in 7 hours, "with but ten minutes' halt" for rest. Moor recollected that Colonel Wyncoop caught up to him on the march, and was immediately dispatched forward to Edinburg to find and support Quinn.[37]

Maj. Timothy Quinn chose not to wait for Wyncoop or Moor before moving on New Market. Quinn already received reinforcements early that morning; another cavalry battalion of roughly 300 men. This force was Maj. Charles Otis's battalion of the 21st New York, which had skirmished for control of Mount Jackson on the 12th. Captain Michael Auer of the 15th New York recalled that on the morning of the 14th, he was commanding a 75-man detachment from his regiment when he reported to Otis for the day's orders. Otis "was then partaking of an appetizing breakfast," recollected Auer, "and without inviting me to partake, he in a very few words directed me to move up the pike and see

move up to divisional command in Stahel's stead. This odd arrangement likely had much to do with Stahel's efforts to hold both positions at once, leaving Taylor serving more as an administrative head rather than exercising full command.

36 Eby, *Virginia Yankee*, 224.

37 *OR* 37, pt. 1, 79, 83.

what I could find." Auer would also remember with some disdain that this was "the last I saw" of Otis. Auer complied, though in his recollection he thought he did so alone. Writing in 1911, Auer's memory failed him. All of Otis's men joined Quinn in this movement. Also present were at least some members of the 14th Pennsylvania Cavalry. Keystoner Albert Altman noted in his diary that he "left camp [from Woodstock] at 4 o'clock this morning . . . went to Mount Jackson their engaged the enemy and drove them . . . as far as New Market . . . all this was dun in a drenching rain."[38]

After organizing these new additions to his expanded command, Quinn rode through Mount Jackson without opposition, and soon halted at the bridge across the Shenandoah, the floor of which had been removed. There they saw Confederates on Rude's Hill, but not in strength sufficient to deter Quinn, who had his men quickly repair the bridge. Quinn now had between 450 and 500 Federal horsemen with him, having left strong flank guards along the march route, but he took care to conceal his full complement from the Confederates. Initially he sent forward only a 50-man detachment under command of Lieutenant Cameron of the 15th New York, to skirmish with the Rebel pickets at the foot of the hill. When Cameron handily pushed the Rebels back, Quinn reinforced him with another 60 men (Auer's force, who noted that "my first encounter with the Confederate Cavalry was on the heights about one and a half miles south of Mount Jackson") and soon Rude's Hill was in Union hands. Encouraged by this success, Quinn crossed the rest of his battalion and began to drive south.[39]

A running fight developed. A small force of Confederate horse attempted a charge, only to be rebuffed by Quinn's greater strength. The Federals continued to push for another two miles. One section of McClanahan's Virginia Battery, deployed at the north end of New Market, saw Quinn coming and opened fire on the Federals, but the Rebel guns did not loiter long. It had not been Imboden's intention to fight for the village, but instead fall back to the rise of Shirley's Hill, the next defensible height to the south. Colonel Smith executed that plan well, withdrawing slowly, that retreat punctuated with frequent counter-attacks.[40]

38 Michael Auer Letter, May 23 1911, New Market Collection, VMI; Entry for May 14th, Altman Diary, AHEC.

39 *OR* 37, pt. 1, 74, 79.

40 Ibid.

Quinn reported that he made first contact with the Rebels at about 1:00 p.m., and the skirmishing lasted until nearly 5:00 p.m. Confederate Lieutenant Potts of the 18th Virginia Cavalry was not nearly so precise when recalled the day's events, but he admitted that Quinn's Federals "gave us a very hard afternoon's work."[41]

Sometime during this fighting Colonel Wyncoop and his 300 men arrived. Wyncoop's force consisted of 170 men from the 20th Pennsylvania, commanded by Maj. Robert W. Douglas, and 130 men of the 15th New York, led by Maj. Henry Roessle. Wyncoop reached Edinburg about 2:00 p.m., and, in response to the clearly audible "heavy firing" that marked Quinn's engagement, rode on at once towards New Market. Arriving on the scene close to 3:00 p.m., he found himself in the middle of an active fight. Wyncoop reported that he arrived just as Quinn retiring before one of those Rebel counter-attacks, and Wyncoop promptly ordered Major Douglas's 20th Pennsylvania Battalion to charge and clear the town. Douglas did so, pushing forward to the foot of Shirley's Hill, followed by the rest of the Federal cavalry. Here, noted Wyncoop, they found more Rebels, including another gun of McClanahan's battery, barking away. Wyncoop ordered Captain Ewing of Battery G to unlimber and return fire.[42]

Imboden was now present. He found little to criticize. Colonel Smith had handled the fight with skill, delaying the Federals for several hours with little loss. Imboden found that Smith deployed the whole brigade across the pike and atop Shirley's Hill, with the 62nd Virginia dismounted and formed in a single rank instead of the usual two-rank formation, an effort to deceive the Federals into magnifying Confederate numbers. Rebel cavalry were positioned on both flanks. McClanahan's guns had a commanding view of the town and valley from atop the hill. When Imboden reached McClanahan's position he realized the action was over for the day: "from what I saw I felt no apprehension of any attempt to dislodge us this evening."[43]

Imboden did spot Union infantry moving up to support the cavalry, a movement which he interpreted as Sigel arriving with the bulk of the

41 Potts, "Who Fired the First Gun at New Market?" 453.

42 Wyncoop Report, May 17th, Moor papers.

43 Imboden, *Battle of New Market,* 482.

Federal army. Accordingly, he sent a courier southward with that news, who reached Breckinridge at Lacey Springs about 9:00 p.m.[44]

Imboden's first assessment was correct; the action had concluded for the day. Realizing he was now outnumbered, Wyncoop broke off and sent for Moor, who was already nearly on the scene. Once he arrived, Moor deployed his three infantry regiments across the floor of the valley and ordered the rest of the Union cannon to unlimber and return McClanahan's fire. This resulted in a prolonged artillery duel, noisy but not especially damaging to either side. For green troops, however, the shelling was impressive enough. A member of the 34th Massachusetts recalled the scene:

"We soon came near the town which is situated in a hollow with high hills to the north and south. The Confederates had their battery planted on the hill south of the town, and we had two planted on north side of the town. The Col. then moved the regiment around and under the hill in rear of the battery so as to support it in case it was charged upon; he then went up on top of the hill to take a look at the rebels. I followed him up a short distance and heard him direct the Adjutant to send us around to watch the ridge in front of our battery and notify him if any force appeared in front of our guns. I volunteered for the job—he gave me my instructions and went back over the hill—I could see the flash of the enemy's guns and then hear the shell come whizzing along—if it was coming near me, down I would go to my face and there lie until it either passed or exploded. While in this position several burst near me and several pieces came as near as I wished to see them—one particular one I could hear coming directly towards me—and I was almost certain I was hit—down I went, flat on my face. I heard the Colonel laughing behind me, but I had a chance to turn it in a few moments—the particular shell that I was dodging struck the ground in a direct line about two rods in front of me and burst; how the mud flew—one piece of shell came so near me that I rolled over and picked it up. I put it in my pocket and have it now. The Col. stood laughing in which I heartily joined him but in another moment we saw the flash of the rebel gun. We stood waiting and listening for the shell. Finally it came. I saw it burst in the air in front of us. I glanced at the Colonel—down he went—thinks I to myself, 'Follow suit or you may be trumped,' and again I ran my nose into the ground like a regular porker."[45]

44 Breckinridge Report, New Market Collection, VMI.

45 "In the field at Cedar Creek," May 17, 1864, *Northampton Free Press,* June 7, 1864.

The artillery duel continued until dark. Aside from one adjustment to his battle line to more fully cover the front of Imboden's force, Moor ordered his infantry to spend the night in place, "In perfect order of battle without fires." Twice during the night Rebels attempted to probe the Union position, and twice the Union line erupted in infantry volleys, but neither effort turned into a serious engagement. Instead Imboden withdrew, as per Breckinridge's orders, sometime after midnight. The only substantial damage inflicted was to McClanahan's Battery, which had two of their six guns damaged or disabled by the Union shelling.[46]

Sometime in the afternoon of the 14th, Franz Sigel received word that Breckinridge was close to uniting with Imboden at New Market. Word of Breckinridge's proximity was first relayed by Moor, who undoubtedly got wind of it from prisoners captured during the day. Imboden attributed the information leak to a "Negro from beyond Lacey Springs who had made his way down Smith Creek," and who witnessed Breckinridge's columns pass by. Fortunately, thought Imboden, "He . . . exaggerated [Breckinridge's] numbers, [and] this false information would naturally have caused General Sigel to advance with great caution."[47]

Moor's advance guard numbered somewhere between 1,200 and 1,500 infantry. Wyncoop added another 800–900 cavalry; in all there were perhaps as many as 2,500 Federals at New Market, nearly half of Sigel's available combat power. To support Moor, Sigel ordered most of his other troops to Mount Jackson, including the 18th Connecticut, 28th Ohio, 116th Ohio, and at least one battery of artillery. There they joined the 12th West Virginia, with the Nutmeggers of the 18th relieving the 12th on picket.[48]

The constant rain and slow progress of the supply convoys, however, meant that a substantial force had to be left at Woodstock to safeguard those trains. This task fell to the Keystoners of the 22nd Pennsylvania Cavalry and Campbell's 54th Pennsylvania Infantry. The 22nd's history noted that Sigel's initial "orders to march early . . . were countermanded,

46 *OR* 37, pt. 1, 80; Imboden, *Battle of New Market,* 482; Robert J. Driver, *The Staunton Artillery—McClanahan's Battery* (Lynchburg, 1988), 88.

47 Imboden, *Battle of New Market,* 482.

48 Walker, *Eighteenth Regiment Conn. Volunteers,* 217, Wildes, *Record of the One Hundred and Sixteenth Regiment,* 38.

waiting for the arrival of the supply train. It had rained hard the previous night and was threatening to continue."[49]

Charles Lynch was one of those Connecticut men detailed to go on picket at Edinburg that night. He also recalled a difficult night. "Posted in the woods about one mile from headquarters," he noted in his diary. "Hot, muggy weather. We are very anxious about the marrow, as we listen to the heavy artillery firing. We are about 50 miles from Harpers Ferry, our base of supplies, with no prospect for re-enforcements, if needed. Report comes that our cavalry are putting up a hard fight at New Market. . . ."[50]

---

49 Samuel Clarke Farrar, *The Twenty-Second Pennsylvania Cavalry and the Ringgold Battalion 1861–1865* (Pittsburgh: 1911), 221; "Entry for May 14," Jacob Cohn diary, VPI.

50 Lynch, *Diary,* 59.

CHAPTER 7

Commencement—Morning, May 15, 1864

ohn C. Breckinridge was determined to fight. With threats from two directions, he couldn't afford any delay. His only hope of defending his department effectively lay in winning a quick decision over Sigel and then turning to face the danger still posed (as far as he knew) by Crook. When Imboden's latest dispatch arrived at Lacey Spring, informing the former vice president that there was now a strong Federal presence at New Market, Breckinridge determined to act immediately. "I gave orders for the command to march at 1 a.m. with the intention of attacking the Enemy early in the morning." The Kentuckian was as good as his word: the column moved out on time, as ordered, and at a furious pace. "We marched very fast until daybreak," recalled Private Schowen of the 30th Virginia, in Echols's brigade. Fellow Private G. W. Dunford of the 51st Virginia, one of Wharton's men, concurred: "We break camp early," Dunford recalled. "A battle is expected. . . . We hurry forward on a forced march, and sometimes at double-quick."[1]

The entire arena of what would soon be the battlefield of New Market was a narrow corridor of valley floor, two miles wide by roughly seven miles in length. The North Fork of the Shenandoah River formed the western boundary. The eastern limit was defined by Smith Creek, running along the base of Massanutten Mountain. The town of New

---

1   Breckinridge Report, New Market Collection, VMI; Schowen, *Diary*, 7; G. W. Dunford Letter, New Market Collection, VMI.

Market was a crossroads settlement of about 1,000 souls, a village that was much longer on its north-south axis than it was wide, and roughly centered between the two watercourses. Four main heights dominated the scene, named, in order from south to north: Shirley's Hill, Manor's Hill, Bushong Hill, and finally, the much-contested Rude's Hill.[2]

Colonel Moor's defensive line began somewhere near the south end of town and ran west towards the Shenandoah, at the northern foot of Shirley's Hill. As noted, the Federals spent a difficult night, marked by the fire of jittery pickets and periodic full volleys from the sleepless infantry line. Some of this shooting was provoked by small parties of probing Confederates sent forward at Imboden's orders. Much of it, however, was clearly the product of nerves. Federal accounts described repulsing what seemed to the inexperienced Federals to be several full-scale Rebel attacks: "The picket line commenced firing," noted a member of the 34th Massachusetts, and "the shots grew faster . . . until suddenly came two terrific volleys, the flash of the guns . . . and the singing of the minnies through the trees leading us to think a whole regiment was right upon us. Colonel Wells came up on his feet . . . shouting 'Up boys,'" but the Rebels seemed to have vanished.[3]

Moor's line remained in the valley between Shirley's and Manor's Hills through the night. Sunrise on Sunday, May 15 came at 4:59 a.m., with first light brightening the gloom about an hour earlier. Taking no chances, Colonel Moor had the troops stirring at 3:00 a.m. His deployments remained essentially unchanged, with the 1st West Virginia in line near St. Mathews Church, the 123rd Ohio on their right, and the 34th Massachusetts in reserve on Manor Hill. Snow's Maryland Artillery was stationed in St. Matthews' graveyard, supporting the West Virginians, while the section of Ewing's Battery remained atop Manor Hill behind the 34th. Moor's frontage stretched no more than three quarters of a mile. With no Rebels in sight and no attack immediately apparent, Moor ordered his pickets out. These included three companies of the 34th Massachusetts, one of them led by Captain George Thompson, who noted that "we moved forward to occupy a hill [Shirley's] where the enemy's battery was posted the day before." Thompson and his men met no opposition on the hill, but he

---

2   Knight, *Valley Thunder*, 105-108.

3   Ibid., 109.

A wartime image of Brigadier General John D. Imboden. *Miller's Photographic History of the Civil War*

"soon saw the enemies skirmishers advancing . . . [and] our cavalry went out to meet them."[4]

Imboden was also up at 3:00 a.m., awakened by Breckinridge. The Kentuckian oversaw his command's departure from Lacey Spring and then rode on ahead to find Imboden. Now Breckinridge informed the brigadier that the Rebel main body would be on the scene by sunrise, giving the Confederate force a combined strength of approximately 5,300. As the morning lightened, (with visibility still limited by the overcast and yet more promised rain) Imboden ordered the 18th Virginia Cavalry forward to cover the arrival of Breckinridge's infantry and contest the Federal effort to occupy Shirley's Hill. Picket firing soon erupted. Initially Captain Thompson planned to contest the height, but then he observed what he thought was a second Rebel regiment deploying at the foot of Shirley's Hill in support of the 18th. Now heavily outnumbered, he noted, "we fell back."[5]

Despite the imminent arrival of the Confederate army, most of the Federals present spent a quiet if wet morning. While their comrades skirmished with the Virginians, the remainder of the 34th stacked arms shortly after daylight and sought breakfast, since the regimental wagons had come forward. Company D even managed to pitch a cook tent, and "got some good fires going to try and warm up." At 7:00 a.m. some of Moor's scouts reported in, bearing the first word that the Rebels were approaching in force. Dutifully, Moor sent word to Sigel informing

---

4   "Entry for May 15th" George M. Thompson Diary, AHEC.

5   Breckinridge Report, New Market Collection, VMI; Imboden, "The Battle of New Market," 482; Delauter, *18th Virginia Cavalry,* 19. Thompson Diary, AHEC. This figure includes the 4750 effectives of Wharton, Echols, Imboden and the VMI Cadets; plus approximately 500 local reserves who were present but ultimately did not enter the fight.

the Union commander that "Breckinridge [has] joined Imboden, which report was corroborated by the citizens and by pickets stationed on the hilltops"; but although this should have been alarming news, Moor seemed strangely unworried. Breckinridge was reported to be bringing 4,000 men, and Imboden's strength was estimated at between 2,000 and 3,000; 6,000–7,000 men all told, according to Federal estimates. Yet Moor had less than 2,500 troops immediately at hand. Outnumbered at least 2.5 to 1, if the Confederates attacked immediately, Moor would be in grave trouble.[6]

Even worse, both of Moor's flanks remained vulnerable. At the point where Moor drew up his line, the distance between Smith's Creek and the North Fork ran nearly two miles. His three infantry regiments could only cover the distance between the town and the slope of Manor Hill. This left his cavalry to cover the flanks, with most of them concentrated on the Union right between the 34th Massachusetts and the Shenandoah. Moor placed almost no force to cover his left, between the town and Smith Creek. If Rebels were to slip around the town to the east they could easily outflank the 1st West Virginia and seize control of the Valley Pike, thereby severing Moor's only line of retreat. A much better position was available a half-mile to the rear, atop Bushong Hill. Here could be found the same open, sloping fields of fire as atop Manor Hill, but fortuitous inward bends by both the Shenandoah's North Fork and Smith Creek narrowed the distance between the two watercourses to about a mile. This made for a more manageable frontage, given Moor's limited infantry strength, and provided secure flanks.

If Moor pondered any of these factors, he made no mention of them, then or later. Instead, Moor remained seemingly complacent concerning both the approach of a much larger Confederate army and about his own dismal choice of terrain. He made no adjustments to his deployments and gave no thought to retreat.

At about 8:00 a.m., Major Theodore Lang and an escort party rode up. Lang, of the 6th West Virginia Cavalry, was currently serving on Sigel's staff. Previously he had been part of Averell's military family. Sigel ordered Lang to depart army headquarters at 4:00 a.m. that morning to "ascertain the extent of the skirmishing between Colonel Moor and the

---

6   "In the field at Cedar Creek," May 17, 1864, *Northampton Free Press,* June 7, 1864; *OR* 37, pt. 1, 80.

Colonel Augustus Moor. *Scott Patchen*

enemy . . . ." Lang was to then keep Sigel continuously updated via the dozen well-mounted couriers who accompanied him for that purpose. Once Moor brought Lang up to speed concerning Breckinridge's arrival, the major immediately noticed what Moor had so far failed to grasp—the Union line's vulnerable flanks. While Lang admitted that Moor seemed well-positioned against a frontal assault, if the Rebels outnumbered him heavily—which, by all reports, they now did—Moor would face disaster. Lang "at once dispatched a courier . . . requesting [Sigel] to bring forward his entire force, and to make no delay, as we would soon certainly have a battle." This message would have a profound impact on the course of the day's events.[7]

Now it was the Rebels' turn to summit Shirley's Hill. Wharton's brigade held the Rebel left, deploying the 30th Virginia Battalion as skirmishers across the little army's front and placing the 51st Virginia's 680 men in battle line on the southern slopes of the hill, below the crest and out of sight of the enemy. Breckinridge borrowed the 62nd Virginia from Imboden and placed them on the 51st's right, between the hill and the town's southern edge. The remainder of Imboden's brigade, the 18th and the 23rd Virginia Cavalry regiments, remained horsed and positioned farther to the east. Echols deployed his three units in two supporting lines behind the 51st Virginia. The army's second line included the 22nd Virginia on the left and the 23rd Virginia Battalion on the right, with Col. George M. Edgar's 26th Battalion forming a third line behind them.

---

7   Lang, *Loyal West Virginia*, 113; Theodore F. Lang, "Personal Recollections of the Battle of New Market," VMI. Lang recalled that "General Sigel did not believe that there was much of a force in front of Colonel Moor," but Moor had already reported Breckinridge's arrival to Sigel the night before.

The Cadets were placed as a final reserve behind Edgar's battalion. This deployment kept virtually all of Breckinridge's force concealed from the Federals, and out of the line of fire of Moor's cannon.[8]

One of the more curious additions to the Confederate battle line in this army of nearly all Virginians was Company A of the 1st Missouri Cavalry, led by Captain Charles A. Woodson. Company A was recruited from Missourians who had been previously captured earlier in the war and exchanged in Richmond. Instead of being sent back west to rejoin their comrades, Woodson, who desired to remain in Virginia, managed to secure permission to recruit some of those exchanged men into an independent force. His company numbered 62 men, and usually served alongside the 62nd; that is where they fell on the morning of May 15, between the 62nd and 51st Virginia. Smith's 62nd was further strengthened by the dismounted elements of the both the 18th and 23rd Virginia cavalries, formed into least three ad-hoc companies of men whose horses were either unserviceable for combat or lacked mounts altogether. All told, these additional troops probably raised Smith's fighting strength to just over 700 muskets.[9]

Deploying for battle ate up a great deal of time. Because of the rain the fields and side lanes were little better than bogs. "The ploughed fields [were] almost miry," recalled VMI Cadet Capt. Benjamin A. Colonna, "so that to march across [them] even at slow time was hard work, and at double quick, exhausting." This slow pace annoyed Breckinridge, who at one point verbally fretted: "Why don't Echols come up? He is the slowest fellow!" In fact, Echols was actually so ill by this point that he relinquished formal command to his senior colonel, the 22nd Virginia's George S. Patton; it was all Echols could do to try and keep up with the brigade. Still, he followed along doggedly. Echols had no intention of letting his men go into the fight without him.[10]

---

8   John A. Porter Letter Extracts, New Market Collection, VMI; Schowen, *Diary,* 7.

9   Knight, *Valley Thunder*, 277-283, 291-295. Knight has an excellent sketch of Company A's origins and service, as well as great detail concerning the 23rd's deployment.

10   B. A. Colonna Letter, April 14, 1909, New Market Collection, VMI; George H. Smith Letter, March 16, 1906, Edgar papers, University of North Carolina; Knight, *Valley Thunder,* 121.

Brigadier General John Echols. Miller,
Photographic History of the Civil War

While their troops struggled through the muck, Breckinridge and Imboden both rode to the crown of Shirley's Hill, now cleared of the enemy. From here both men had a fine view of the surrounding terrain and could examine Moor's dispositions in detail. Imboden timed this reconnaissance at "about an hour after daybreak . . ." So far, the only fighting was "a desultory cavalry skirmish . . . in and around the town." Imboden also remembered that Breckinridge needed "only a few words of explanation from me" to grasp the situation. "He remarked after five minutes study of the scene, 'We can attack and whip them here, and I'll do it.'" Imboden later recalled that this seemed to galvanize the Kentuckian into action, claiming that Breckinridge immediately "sent orders at once for all the troops to advance at once. . . ."[11]

Writing for publication in the 1880s, Imboden was waxing dramatic. In reality, several hours elapsed between the initial Confederate deployment and Breckinridge's subsequent decision to attack. Once atop Shirley's Hill, Breckinridge abruptly changed strategies. Up until this moment, the Rebel general had been determined to strike the first blow; to attack at the first opportunity offered. Now, however, he suddenly decided to try and provoke Sigel (whom both Imboden and Breckinridge believed was in personal command) into assuming the offensive.

With that in mind, Breckinridge ordered his troops to begin defensive preparations. He directed the 12 guns of Chapman's, Jackson's and the Cadet batteries to take up positions atop the height. According to Col. George Smith of the 62nd Virginia, Breckinridge also ordered his infantry to fortify their line "as well as we could with fence rails, etc." Colonel Edgar corroborated Smith's recollections, noting that "Breckinridge took

11 Imboden, "The Battle of New Market," 483.

up a defensive position, choosing the best ground available: [which] afforded a pretty good position, being flanked by wooded hills, from which an approaching column . . . would have received a deadly fire." This was all well and good, but someone would have to lure the Yankees into playing along. To do so, Breckinridge "ordered Imboden forward to charge the enemy and then retreat, hoping thus to lure them into a pursuit. Imboden tried out this ruse repeatedly, each time in vain."[12]

The Confederate infantry did not simply remain quietly in position while Imboden executed his bluff. Colonel Edgar recalled several changes of position, each involving a fair amount of marching and counter-marching during this period. Edgar surmised that this shifting about was also a clever ruse, designed to fool the Federals into believing that Breckinridge's army was even stronger than supposed. Breckinridge biographer William C. Davis agreed, finding this to be "an old but artful deception . . . [that] worked admirably. He set his regiments to marching and countermarching on and around Shirley's Hill, hoping to create the illusion of greater numbers. . . ." If so, however, the effort worked at cross-purposes. If Breckinridge really intended to lure the Federals into a foolhardy assault, he should want to give an impression of weakness, not greater strength.[13]

In fact, Breckinridge did take pains to conceal his initial deployments from Union eyes, noting that "Wharton's Brigade" moved up "under cover of a wood," and of course holding his infantry in position behind Shirley's Hill. The marching and counter-marching was likely merely the by-product of a difficult deployment, not representative of some deeper game on Breckinridge's part.[14]

However, the general's sudden reversal from an offensive to a defensive mindset was curious, and potentially a disaster for Confederate fortunes. Why was Breckinridge willing to pass the initiative back to Sigel at this critical moment? Breckinridge never explained this decision. Perhaps he thought that all of Sigel's army was already on the field, but if so then Imboden's reconnaissance work and intelligence-gathering failed him at the worst possible moment. Never would the odds better favor an

---

12 George H. Smith Letter, March 7, 1896; and George M. Edgar Letter, February 18, 1896, New Market Collection, VMI; Turner, *New Market,* 25.

13 Davis, *Breckinridge,* 419-420.

14 Breckinridge Report, VMI.

immediate Confederate attack. Waiting only gave the Federals time to either reinforce or withdraw, falling back to the more defensible positions of Bushong Hill, Rude's Hill, or even all the way to Mount Jackson. Any of those options could only lessen Breckinridge's chances of achieving an immediate knock-out blow. It is possible that Breckinridge decided that the miry state of the ground favored defense over offense, but again, he never explained his thinking.

Why hesitate when time was of such importance? After all, how long could Breckinridge afford to dawdle with Sigel before Crook's column fell upon Staunton and the critical supplies stored there? For as of that morning, Breckinridge had no knowledge that Crook had turned back or ceased to be a threat to his rear.

Fortunately for Breckinridge, the news from the south was about to improve, but only slightly. By the afternoon of May 14, Colonel McCausland was reporting that Crook's force had "left the immediate line of this railroad," and also that "Averell's command . . . [was] scattered . . . in the mountains," driven off before they could do any damage to the salt works. However, McCausland still regarded this reprieve as only temporary. He was working with Generals Morgan and Jones "to concoct a plan, but" as he gloomily admitted, "the whole of us cannot stop Crook."[15]

This was somewhat cheering news, since it meant that the threat from the south was at least momentarily abated, but Breckinridge had yet to learn any of this information early on the morning of the 15th. McCausland's telegrams wouldn't be received at Harrisonburg until 9:45 that morning, and it would take any courier several more hours to find Breckinridge near New Market. Hence, when Breckinridge decided to await Sigel's attack at dawn, as far as he knew the threat to Staunton loomed as large as ever.

For the next few hours the battle of New Market continued in much the same manner as the fight the night before concluded; marked only by skirmishing and a largely bloodless artillery duel. Breckinridge's artillery was commanded by Maj. William McLaughlin, a 34-year old Virginia lawyer from Lexington who first enlisted as a second lieutenant in the Rockbridge Artillery, serving on Echols's staff since the summer of 1862. When McLaughlin opened fire, his 12 guns augmented by some

15   *OR* 37, pt. 1, 735-736.

of McClanahan's pieces, the Union artillery replied in kind. The Rebels deployed at least 14 guns in this action, six of Chapman's Battery, four from Jackson's, two outdated six-pounders from VMI, and at least two of McClanahan's guns. Moor still had only six cannon with which to return fire.

Out in no-man's land, the 30th Virginia had front row seats for this action. "We filed out in [an] open field," recalled John Schowen, "and deployed as skirmishers. . . . I could see the Yankee skirmishers very distinctly. We moved square across the field toward the enemy. Presently our artillery got in position . . . and commenced shelling Yankees, and the Yankee Battery commenced firing on us. We were ordered to lie down. And they shelled us furiously." Caught in the middle of this barrage, "I thought I would not live another minute," he confessed. For a time, the 30th was taking fire from both sides. "We were so far in advance of the line," noted Captain R. C. Hoffman, commanding Company E of Schowen's regiment, "that our own artillery . . . commenced to shell us, thinking we were the enemy's skirmishers, and we had to send back to stop it. . . ."[16]

Despite the intensity of the bombardment, actual casualties were few. Amid the ranks of the 34th Massachusetts, the worst damage done was in interrupting breakfast and scattering the men trying to warm themselves in front of the fires. Company D's correspondent noted that those fires "were hardly going when the sharp report of artillery, and the shrieking and bursting of shells were heard. All this time shells had been bursting around us but providentially no one was injured." Bay-Stater Henry Brockway noted in his diary that he "got up . . . about daylight and got breakfast. The fight recommensed this AM about 10 o'clock (between the artillery). . . ."[17]

The cannonade proved similarly disruptive to the men of the 123rd Ohio, who bizarrely had begun to establish a regular camp that morning, as if no enemy were present at all. "We drew a few rations at breakfast," wrote Cpl. Leander Coe, "and the[n] pitched tents expecting to remain but no sooner was it done then the enemy opened their conan [cannon]

16 Schowen, *Diary,* 7; Edgar, "Battle of New Market, May 15th, 1864," Edgar papers, UNC.

17 "In the field at Cedar Creek," May 17, 1864, *Northampton Free Press,* June 7, 1864; "Entry for May 15th," Henry Brockway Diary, University of Iowa.

on us and we were ordered to strike tents immedietly." The Confederate gunners delighted in catching so many Yankees unawares. "As soon as we were in position we opened on the enemy, and I think that was the first intimation they had that we were near them. We fired right into their camp and I think spoiled their breakfast," chortled Charles Warner, serving one of Jackson's pieces.[18]

New Market's civilian residents now found themselves in the middle of this shell storm. With a Union battery planted in St. Matthews churchyard at the north end of town, the 18th Virginia's skirmishers holding the south end of the village, and Rebel artillery arrayed on the heights above, artillery shells from both sides now flew over the settlement, sometimes dropping into the streets. Citizens scrambled to hide in cellars, under floorboards, or crowded into the few structures they felt were safest, including the Soxman house at the south end of town.[19]

Moor's action—or rather inaction—that morning remained inexplicable. He well knew that Breckinridge's main force was within striking distance, if not already present. He reported that very fact to Sigel the previous evening. He struck an equally alert note that morning when he roused his men before dawn and prepared to receive an attack, but when that attack did not occur he seems to have relaxed his guard completely. Mystifyingly, Moor allowed his men to begin pitching camp in the very face of the enemy, erecting those tents that proved such a tempting target for the Rebel gunners. At 7:00 a.m. his cavalry patrols confirmed Breckinridge's presence, a point underscored by the enemy cannon fire which erupted shortly thereafter. This fire coincided with Major Lang's arrival, who immediately sent word to Sigel that a battle was in the offing. Despite Lang's attempt to place a positive spin on Moor's chosen position, Moor's nearest support was at Mount Jackson, some miles and several hours away. Outnumbered and beyond support, Moor's decision to stand pat was foolhardy. But that is exactly what he did, his troops deployed in a thinly sketched defensive line strung between the town and the river, waiting for the Rebels to make the next move. If Breckinridge's decision to await an attack abruptly surrendered

18 "Entry for May 15th," Leander Coe Diary, BGSU; Charles Warner, "Who Fired the First Gun at New Market?" *Confederate Veteran,* vol. 17, no. 5 (May 1909), 237.

19 Knight, *Valley Thunder,* 129.

the initiative to the Federal army that morning, Moor was trying just as determinedly to pass on the honor.

While Breckinridge was deploying, Moor could have easily retreated to either Bushong or Rude's Hill. As noted, Bushong Hill had the same open fields of fire as Manor's Hill, along with more secure flanks, but Rude's Hill was an even better choice. It was a position that Imboden, for one, considered one of the strongest in the entire Shenandoah Valley. It was also much closer to Mount Jackson and possible reinforcements. Instead, Moor simply elected to wait.[20]

Meanwhile, back at Woodstock, Franz Sigel spent a difficult, nearly sleepless night. One officer "characterized the general 'to be as restless as a chained hyena'" as he scanned each dispatch and report. He had reason to be worried. His army was divided into three parts, the whole separated by 20 miles' distance. Moor and 2,500 troops—about 45% of Sigel's entire complement—held New Market. 700 more men (the 18th Connecticut and two batteries) were at Edinberg. The 28th Ohio, 116th Ohio, 54th Pennsylvania, 12th West Virginia and Dupont's Battery B of the 5th US were all still at Woodstock, also 2,500 strong. Most of Sigel's cavalry was with Moor, and of course each infantry regiment still had sizeable numbers of detached men escorting those supply convoys or positioned to guard Sigel's line of communications across the department. This divided posture was a classic recipe for military disaster, and as Sigel now knew, Breckinridge was present with his full force.[21]

The one heartening bit of news came when a wire from General Kelley arrived sometime before midnight, informing the German that "General Crook is in Lewisburg." If true, this meant that a junction with Crook was still possible, or, alternatively, Crook could still strike at Staunton before Breckinridge could return to defend the place. This latest news provided an added incentive for Sigel to maintain as threatening a posture as possible. Unfortunately, the reality was that Crook was nowhere near Lewisburg. Neither was he marching on Staunton or moving to affect a junction with Sigel's column. Though Sigel had no way of knowing it at the time, Kelley's information was in error. Crook was still struggling to

20 Imboden, "The Battle of New Market," 482.

21 Knight, *Valley Thunder,* 114; Michael Gardner Letter, May 17, 1864, Sigel Papers, WRHS; *OR* 37, pt. 1, 455. The guns at Edinberg belonged to Von Kleiser's 30th New York Battery, plus a section each from Ewing and Snow's batteries.

cross the rain-swollen Greenbrier, and from there, headed for Meadow Bridge. Sigel was supporting a chimera.[22]

Nonetheless, the bantam German stuck to his plan, resolving to concentrate his best available strength at Mount Jackson. Accordingly, Sigel ordered that "the troops will be ready to march to-morrow morning [May 15] at five o'clock. They will be prepared for action. . . ." As for Moor, Sigel added, "the troops now in front will remain in their present positions until information from them is received and further orders sent to them." In the meantime, Moor would be reinforced. At 2:00 a.m., four companies of the 12th West Virginia were rousted out and sent to Edinburg, ordered to replace the 18th Connecticut, who in turn received a 3:00 a.m. order to move to New Market come the dawn.[23]

By 6:00 a.m. Sigel departed Woodstock, headed for Mount Jackson, the 54th Pennsylvania and 12th West Virginia leading. The van reached Edinburg by 8:00 a.m., where the 12th picked up their four picket companies, and everyone pressed on to Mount Jackson. The leading elements of the main column reached that hamlet between 10:00 and 11:00 a.m., pausing only long enough to eat dinner. The 28th and 116th Ohio made worse time, stuck as they were guarding Sigel's supply train of over 200 wagons. They did not reach Mount Jackson until "the middle of the afternoon."[24]

Sigel, Stahel and their staffs rode on ahead, leaving Sullivan to supervise the march column. Strother noted an "absurd" contretemps as Sigel departed the Cheney house that morning. Just before departing, Sigel discovered "he had lost a favorite brandy flask and was accusing everyone he met of stealing it." Running about half-dressed in agitation, Sigel vowed "By Got, I vill catch dot dam tief." Mistress Cheney was much offended by the accusations, but there was little time to do a proper search. Sigel rode out, the flask gone for good.[25]

At Edinburg Strother noted another unsettling sight. "The shops and houses [were] full of unarmed stragglers from Boyd's command." No

---

22 *OR* 37, pt. 1, 458.

23 Hewitt, *Twelfth West Virginia*, 106-107; *OR* 37, pt. 1, 81, 454.

24 "Entry for May 15," Jacob Cohn Diary, VPI; Wildes, *Record of the One Hundred and Sixteenth*, 87. These wagons included the extra supplies needed for Crook's command and could not be left unsecured.

25 Eby, *Virginia Yankee*, 224. Strother's disdain for Sigel is obvious.

one had thought to collect them and march them back to camp in any organized fashion, suggesting both a grievous lapse in staff work and demoralization among the men. No one thought to do anything about it now, either. The morning cannonade at New Market was now clearly audible to the command party, and they rode on.[26]

The exact sequence of several subsequent events remains unclear, largely because of conflicting memories by the participants involved, which in turn reflects the muddled state of Sigel's own intentions at this time. As Sigel rode south, he began receiving a steady stream of couriers from Lang, each of which alternated between alarming and encouraging. The first, informing of Sigel of Breckinridge's presence and the likelihood of battle, was soon amplified by a second that stated The Rebels had a "skirmish line across the entire valley" and suggested that Sigel "push forward his entire command at a double-quick."[27]

The 18th Connecticut and their supporting artillery were already nearly on the scene, having headed south per Sigel's earlier orders, but New Market was still not where Franz Sigel wanted to fight. As Sigel would recount, "I immediately sent orders for [Moor] to return to Mount Jackson . . " This retreat order was prompted by Lang's dispatches, each of which strongly suggested that Moor was badly outmatched. To orchestrate the intended retreat, Sigel now dispatched Julius Stahel to take personal command, intending Stahel to use the cavalry already present "to cover the retreat of Moor, and retard the movement of the enemy." Stahel immediately galloped off. Sigel proceeded at a more measured pace, reaching Mount Jackson at about 10:00 a.m.[28]

While en route, Sigel received three more couriers from Lang, all conveying a rising sense of urgency. Lang sent one dispatch (his third of the day) when he spotted Wharton's infantry deploying, and almost immediately thereafter, sent another when he saw Echols's Confederates moving into position. Then, as the artillery opened in earnest, Lang "became impatient because neither General Sigel nor his troops had come to the front. I . . . sent a fifth messenger and urged more positively than before our critical situation, and went so far as to overstep my position

26   Ibid., 225

27   Lang, *Loyal West Virginia*, 113.

28   Hewitt, *Twelfth West Virginia*, 111; Sigel, "Sigel in the Shenandoah," 488.

as A. D. C. to say to General Sigel that he must bring up his entire force
. . . otherwise he would be too late."[29]

Lang was clearly becoming overwrought. While the major did not
specify the exact timing of this batch of dispatches, he noted that they
were all sent off before Stahel's arrival, and thus, all early in the morning.
It was simply impossible for Sigel's force to have reached New Market
within that time frame, and Lang certainly should have known that, having
just come from Woodstock himself. His rising agitation—which by the
fifth dispatched was bordering on panic—was affecting his judgment.

The 18th Connecticut reached New Market sometime after 9:00 a.m.,
after a gruelingly fast march of 15 miles. Major Henry Peale reported
that the 18th mustered only seven companies present, with a strength of
about 420 men. The three remaining companies were still far to the rear.[30]

Peale's numbers were almost much less. When he received Sigel's
pre-dawn instruction to head for New Market, Peale was in such haste to
comply that he completely forgot to call in his own pickets at Edinburg,
leaving nearly 200 Nutmeggers behind. Those men only discovered their
abandonment by accident. Sometime near dawn, noted Private Lynch, "it
is past time for the relief to show up." A detail sent to discover why soon
returned with alarming news: "the regiment had left for parts unknown."
Finally, some Federal cavalry pickets informed the bewildered New
Englanders that their "regiment left in the night, going up the valley
towards New Market." Lieutenant Robert Kerr, the senior officer present,
followed suit immediately, setting a torrid pace. "Kerr kept urging us
on," said Lynch, but "duty having been so severe, and the lack of rations
for the past few days, we were near used up." Nearly exhausted, they
eventually found Peale and the rest of the regiment making coffee and
trying to bolt down a bit of breakfast. Before anyone could finish that
meal, however, Colonel Moor posted them in the line.[31]

---

29 Lang, *Loyal West Virginia*, 113-114.

30 *OR* 37, pt. 1, 81. Major Peale gives the arrival time as 11:00 a.m., but this is
probably too late, given the amount of pre-battle maneuvering the 18th was involved
in and the length of time they waited for the Rebels to attack. The reported strength of
the 18th Connecticut was 599 officers and men, but with three companies absent their
actual combat strength was closer to 420, less the additional stragglers shed during
the ensuing forced march.

31 Lynch, *Diary*, 59-60.

Major General Julius Stahel. *Library of Congress*

In addition to Peale's 400 infantrymen, Moor was happy to see the arrival of additional artillery, given the nature of the fighting so far. Ewing's and Snow's detached sections of artillery rejoined their batteries, adding their weight of metal to the artillery duel. Moor deployed the 18th on his right flank, replacing the 34th Massachusetts, whom he pulled back to the Rice house. The men in the ranks found these movements pointless and tiring. Repeated orders "during the forenoon," complained William Clark of the 34th, kept "us in motion almost constantly from one point to another [until] at last, a satisfactory position having been reached, we lie down on our arms. . . ." Moor also posted von Kleiser's battery here, alongside the Bay-staters, both units forming a reserve and rallying point.[32]

Stahel now arrived and assumed command. His appearance, however, did not trigger the expected withdrawal, as Sigel ordered and expected. Why that disengagement did not occur remains unclear. Stahel never explained his thinking. Perhaps Moor, heartened by Breckinridge's relative inaction, persuaded Stahel that it would be better to bring up the whole army and fight where they were rather than risk a retreat in the face of a larger foe. Perhaps the ever-belligerent Lang convinced Stahel that a retreat was too perilous, though Lang never described any such discussion. Interestingly, writing in 1891, Sigel suggested that the movement was indeed initiated, but "executed so slowly and the distance from Mount Jackson to New Market was comparatively so great" that it never progressed very far. Perhaps Sigel, relying on second-hand testimony for this part of the battle, confused Moor's decision to bring the 34th Massachusetts back to the Rice house with some sort of larger retreat.

After an hour of waiting at Mount Jackson, Sigel grew impatient with the lack of either news or result and headed for New Market himself.[33]

Stahel did make one significant decision, which unfortunately would greatly complicate and confuse the Federal cavalry situation, not to mention any postwar attempt to understand the role played by the Union horse on May 15. Upon his arrival, Stahel assumed personal command of all the cavalry, ordering both Tibbets and Wyncoop to join his staff, instead of retaining command of their brigades. This move certainly rankled Tibbets, who, when informed of this change, snapped: "I [will] be damned if I [will] serve on [your] staff . . . I want my brigade!" This unfortunate decision is, from a military standpoint, inexplicable. Stahel was already serving as both Sigel's chief of staff and as cavalry division commander, not to mention the fact that he now commanded the entire advance guard, since he was senior to Moor. Superseding both his brigade commanders and assuming their duties as well was a gross blunder. Instead of providing overall direction, Stahel would spend the rest of the battle micro-managing Union cavalry battalions and companies.[34]

At about 11:00 a.m., having digested the contents of at least two more of Lang's dispatches, Sigel departed Mount Jackson. It was a six-mile ride to New Market. Within a few minutes of setting forth, he got further information, all of it seemingly positive. First came Captain Alexander of Moor's staff, who reported that Moor's "troops were in an excellent position and that I should come to their assistance."[35]

Next came another report from Lang, along with an encounter with Capt. Carl Heintz of Stahel's staff. Lang's most recent note confirmed Moor's assessment of the Union position, adding the endorsement that the men "were eager for the fight." Heintz amplified that sentiment, informing Sigel that "Breckinridge was in force in our front, and that 'if I would send two batteries they would be of excellent use.'" Together, this stream of reports suggested that neither Moor nor Stahel were now thinking of retreat. Sigel's spirits were buoyed with optimism: the numbers between the two armies were about equal, reasoned the German, "and from what had happened the day before I thought the advantage was

---

33 *OR* 37, pt. 1, 80; Hewitt, *Twelfth West Virginia*, 111.

34 Wyncoop Report, Moor Papers; Knight, *Valley Thunder*, 163.

35 Sigel Letter of August 19, 1891, quoted in Hewitt, *Twelfth West Virginia*, 111.

on our side." Abruptly, Sigel modified his plan. Instead of bringing the whole Union army together at Mount Jackson, he would push all his troops forward to fight on the ground chosen by Stahel, Moor and Lang. Though for him the terrain was sight unseen, Sigel was now committed to battle at New Market.[36]

Franz Sigel was not the only one growing impatient. For six hours, John C. Breckinridge had been trying to induce the Federals to attack. They refused every bait. Atop Shirley's Hill, he must have witnessed the arrival of the 18th Connecticut and supporting cannon. How many more Federals would arrive before battle was joined? Captain J. W. Parsons, commanding company A of the 18th Virginia, reported to Imboden on Shirley's Hill as the morning waned. "General Breckinridge and his staff were there too." Parsons recalled, impressed with his new commander's martial demeanor: "I think he was the handsomest man I ever saw. General B. looked over the country carefully, took out his watch, and said [to Imboden] 'General, we shall have to attack them. It's now eleven o'clock, and we can't wait any longer for them to attack us. Call in that cavalry skirmish line.'" Colonel Edgar of the 26th Battalion recalled the same electrifying moment. Breckinridge, "after hours of weary waiting . . . [said] in a confident tone: 'Well, I have offered him the gage of battle and he has declined it, I shall meet him on his own ground.'" More prosaically, Breckinridge simply wrote in his report that "the enemy showing no disposition to assume the offensive[,] I made preparations for immediate attack."[37]

Given the rain and the mud, "immediate" was a relative term. To strengthen his left, Breckinridge now ordered Echols to detach the 477 men of Colonel Edgar's 26th Virginia Battalion and move them up into a supporting position behind the 51st. This movement reduced his third line to only the Cadets, Captain Davis's very small (26 man) Maryland Battalion, and 44 more men of Captain William Hart's Company E of the 3rd Confederate Engineers; 297 troops all told, most of them the young men from the Virginia Military Institute. While the 26th was shifting position, Breckinridge rode back to the Cadet Battalion, where he told

---

36 Sigel, "Sigel in the Shenandoah Valley," 488.

37 J. W. Parsons, "Capture of a Battery at New Market," *Confederate Veteran,* vol. 17, no. 3 (March 1909), 119; Edgar, "Battle of New Market, May 15th, 1864," Edgar papers, UNC; Breckinridge Report, VMI.

Lieutenant Colonel Shipp that "he did not wish to put the Cadets in if he could avoid it, but should occasion require it, he would use them very freely." Then, addressing the VMI contingent as a whole, Breckinridge continued on in the same vein. "Young gentlemen, I hope there will be no occasion to use you, but if there is, I trust you will do your duty." Cadet John C. Howard was taken aback by Breckinridge's pronouncement. "The instant thought in my mind was: 'what do you mean by that?' Here we are, a part of the second [actually, the third] line, and if it advances we will have to advance with it."[38]

Breckinridge also directed Imboden's two mounted regiments to move through the town and, with the rest of McClanahan's Battery, advance north along the west bank of Smith Creek to threaten Moor's left. Much of the area northeast of the town up to Smith Creek was "a low swampy area," wooded, made even muckier by all the rainfall. As Imboden's skirmishers picked their way through this morass, they reported seeing "a large body of enemy cavalry in the open fields beyond." Instead of trying to drive off that cavalry and get in behind the 1st West Virginia Infantry's left flank along the Valley Pike, Imboden instead decided to cross Smith Creek and working his way up the east bank, turning his flanking effort into a larger turning movement that might envelop the whole Federal line. He quickly dispatched a courier back to Breckinridge, requesting permission to do just that. Securing the Kentuckian's approval for the move, however, and then actually executing that movement would take time.[39]

During the morning artillery duel, Brig. Gen. Gabriel Wharton made profitable use of his time. On foot, (Breckinridge had ordered all infantry brigade and regimental officers to dismount) Wharton stole forward to examine the Federal line and the ground he would have to traverse to reach it. The most exposed portion of his advance would be in descending the north slope of Shirley's Hill, bereft of cover. Between Shirley's and Manor Hills, however, a ravine drained by a small stream dipped low enough to shelter his men from Federal fire atop Manor Hill. Accordingly, when the time came, Wharton ordered the 51st Virginia to

38   Edgar Report, August 8, 1864, Edgar papers, UNC; Knight, *Valley Thunder,* 122, 246-247; *OR* 37, pt. 1, 89; John Clarke Howard, "Recollections of New Market," *Confederate Veteran,* vol. 34, no. 2 (February 1926), 59.

39   Delauter, *18th Virginia Cavalry,* 19.

"rush down that slope without regard to order" pausing to reform once back under cover. Edgar's men and the cadets, Wharton noted, "were to conform their movements to mine."[40]

Before that advance could begin Breckinridge wanted his skirmishers to drive in their Federal counterparts. This task fell to the 306 men of Lieutenant Colonel Clark's 30th Virginia Sharpshooters, who were relieved to finally be doing something besides hugging the ground amid an artillery barrage. "Finally," noted Private Schowen, "the line of [battle] was brought up and we chased the Yankees back." This fighting drew blood almost immediately. Among the Federal pickets were companies A and B of the 18th Connecticut, who suffered several casualties in the ravine between the hills before falling back to the main line. Among those was Captain William Spaulding, commanding company B, mortally wounded in the abdomen. Following on the 30th Virginia's heels, by 11:30 a.m. the Confederate front line, 1,400 bayonets strong, stepped off, descending the north slope of Shirley's Hill towards the smaller Union line opposing them.[41]

The Confederate second and third lines followed. Suddenly, it looked to Moor's men like their entire viewshed was swarming with Rebels. "When the enemy came into view the situation was appalling," noted the 18th Connecticut's regimental history. "The Union line consisted of only about one thousand two hundred men, while the enemy numbered seven thousand men, advancing in three compact lines of battle." Even given the regimental history's exaggeration, Moor's line was obviously badly overmatched.[42]

Sigel arrived just in time to witness this movement. It was probably about 11:15 a.m. when he and his staff trotted over the North Fork bridge near Rude's Hill. Sight of the river's state made Colonel Strother "uneasy." The waterway was at flood stage and not easily fordable; if the Rebels hadn't already burned the bridge it was only because "they were ready for us and confident."[43]

---

40   Knight, *Valley Thunder,* 134.

41   Schowen, *Diary,* 7; December 13, 1910 Letter, C. H. Richmond, New Market Collection, VMI.

42   Walker, *Eighteenth Regiment,* 221. Actual Rebel numbers were closer to 3,000.

43   Eby, *Virginia Yankee,* 225.

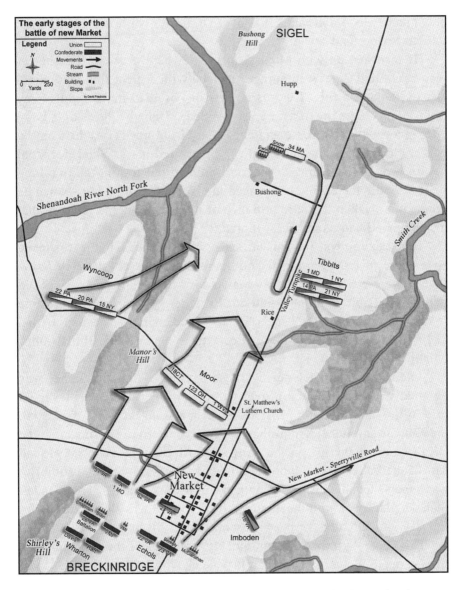

From atop Rude's Hill the morning's artillery duel was both more audible and now just barely visible, with smoke rising in the distance. After a brief, assessing pause the party cantered on. A few minutes more brought them to Dr. Rice's house, where they found the 34th Massachusetts and von Kleiser's guns waiting patiently in line. Here someone told Sigel that Breckinridge's strength now stood at 10,000 men of all arms. Sigel likely knew this to be an exaggeration, but by how much? He told his staff to wait at Dr. Rice's while he rode forward to locate Moor and Stahel.[44]

He also met up with Major Lang somewhere near the Rice home, who noted that Sigel's entourage "arrived with a great flourish." Sigel chastised Lang a bit. "He was at first disposed to make light of my frequent messages; he told me I was excited," Stung by the charge, Lang later recorded—with some hauteur—that "I did not get excited on the battlefield." If anyone had a right to be excited it was Sigel, for what he saw was an unfolding disaster. "I pointed out to him the two long lines of battle the enemy had placed in his front," said Lang, "when he seemed to awaken to the importance of his situation, and realized that his command had its match or more."[45]

The situation was indeed serious, even precarious, but it was made so because of Lang's, Moor's and Stahel's actions, not those of Franz Sigel. There was no time to lay blame now, however, and so Sigel did the only sensible thing he could do: He ordered Moor's advanced line to fall back slowly to Dr. Rice's. He also sped couriers back up the road to find Sullivan and urge that officer "to bring forward all his troops without delay."[46]

And what of Stahel during these events? After all, Stahel was nominally in command until Sigel arrived, but seems to have played no role in this next decision. In fact, Sigel made no mention of meeting the Hungarian. Stahel had probably already moved off to supervise the cavalry, now gathering on the army's left, in the relatively flat ground east of the Valley Pike. Once Sigel reached the field, Stahel's authority was superseded, but his role remained confused. As cavalry commander, Stahel's place was with the mounted force, but he was also Sigel's chief of staff, and should have been present to brief his boss.

The Federal pullback began quickly, well before the main infantry lines came to blows. Connecticut Private Calvin Richmond of the 18th, out on that skirmish line as a member of Company B, recalled that "as soon as the Confederate support came in sight we were ordered to fall back." The Union cannon focused their attention on the Rebel infantry,

44 Entry for May 15, Campaign Journal, Sigel Papers, WRHS.

45 Lang, *Loyal West Virginia,* 114.

46 Sigel, "Sigel in the Shenandoah Valley," 489.

but Wharton's earlier instructions now paid off, at least for the 51st and 62nd Virginia. They dashed down the hill without loss, shells screeching overhead while they ran to mostly plough up the slope behind them. The support lines were not so lucky, especially the cadets. "By the time the second line reached the same ground," noted VMI's Colonel Shipp, "the Yankee gunners had gotten the exact range and their fire began to tell on our line with fearful accuracy." With pride, Shipp further reported, though "great gaps were made through the ranks . . . the cadet, true to his discipline, would close in . . . to fill the interval and push steadily forward." The cadets' ordeal was made worse by the fact that unlike Wharton's veterans, who broke formation and ran down the open slope, the cadets kept formation and descended much less speed, and more precision.[47]

Cadet John Howard could clearly see the shells furrowing the ground as the 51st crested the ridge ahead of them. When Shipp ordered the VMI battalion to step off, Howard braced himself for what was coming. On the right flank, the boy suddenly wondered, "very absurd[ly] . . . if from my position on almost the extreme right I looked down the battalion I was any more likely to get hit than if I looked in front. Anyhow, I looked: and while looking, the first shell exploded in front." Howard saw several people go down, including Captain A. G. Hill, commanding company C, in "about the center of the battalion . . . Captain Hill fell like a log."[48]

Cadet Corporal J. S. Wise and at least one other member of Company D also fell here. Once at the foot of the hill and under cover of the ravine, Shipp halted the battalion to reform, at the same time ordering them to shed blankets and any other excess baggage. Here also Cadet Frank Preston witnessed the alarming sight of officers from Edgar's 26th Virginia, halted ahead of them in the hollow, chivvying skulkers back into ranks "at the point of their pistols."[49]

Watching from afar, Colonel Wells of the 34th Massachusetts watched as those same three lines "with much yelling, advanced upon [Shirley's] Hill only to find it empty." Wells mistakenly attributed this movement to

---

47 December 13, 1910 Letter, C. H. Richmond, New Market Collection, VMI; *OR* 37, pt. 1, 90.

48 Howard, "Recollections of New Market," 89.

49 "The V. M. I. Cadets at the Battle of New Market," *The Bivouac Banner*, vol. 3, no 1 (Spring 2004) online journal at http://www.bivouacbooks.com/bbv3i1s4.htm.

the fact that his own skirmishers had been up there earlier, leaving the Rebels to assume it was still defended, but of course Wharton already knew he would not have to fight for Shirley's Hill. Still Wells was not very far off when he stated that "This maneuvering gave us two or three hours' time, in which General Sigel, with a part of the remainder of the army, arrived on the field." The "maneuvering" referred to the retreat from Manor Hill, for once Moor's three regiments fell back from that advanced line, the battle reached another impasse.[50]

Initially the Union retreat was conducted in surprisingly good order, considering the relative inexperience of the troops and the fact that no one seemed willing to try and undertake any such movement previously. Corporal Powell of the 123rd Ohio attributed it to Sigel's own skills: "Sigel is famous for fighting in retreat," bragged Powell, writing home three days later, "and justly so, I think." A member of the 1st West Virginia Infantry noted that it was "after 12 o'clock n. when we were pressed back by overpowering numbers. . . . A short time was occupied getting our batteries and troops in position after we were forced back."[51]

Only Ewing's Battery had a narrow scrape, for here Wharton's tactics proved successful. "The ground in front of us was very uneven," noted one of Ewing's gunners, "giving the enemy considerable protection as they advanced. . . . On our right and within thirty yards of our battery was a skirt of woods from which we received a terrible fire as we retired. . . ." Despite this near-run-thing, the battery extricated itself and was soon planted east of the Valley Pike, a little to the north of von Keiser's New Yorkers, having joined the cavalry massing in that area. By all appearances, with this successful disengagement the first round of the match had gone to Sigel, escaping without serious loss from the trap Moor's (and Stahel's) incaution had allowed Breckinridge to finally spring.[52]

50 *OR* 37, pt. 1, 83.

51 "Dear Friends at Home," May 18, 1864, Powell Letters, Hayes Library; Phillips, *Wheeling's Finest*, 39.

52 Phillips, *Wheeling's Finest*, 41.

CHAPTER 8

Climax—Afternoon, May 15, 1864

nfortunately for Franz Sigel, the Union retreat, which began so well, didn't end the same way. A strange, collective confusion now seemed grip the Federals. When the 18th Connecticut and 123rd Ohio reached the Rice house both regiments halted as per their instructions, filing into a farm lane that ran due west off the turnpike. The 123rd Ohio fell in on Von Kleiser's immediate right, with the 18th extending the 123rd's right in turn. Major Henry Peale of the 18th thought that his men had traded a strong location for a very inferior one. "The new position . . . was most unfortunate for its efficiency," he lamented, "being in a lane backed by barns and two rows of fence." The mire made things much worse, for here "the men stood knee deep in mud." To further complicate matters, with the buildings and fences blocking any escape directly to their rear, in a pinch "nothing but a flank movement could extricate the regiment" should there be a need for additional retreat. Veteran troops would likely have immediately dismantled the fences to free up maneuvering room, but this seems not to have occurred to Peale. Perhaps he didn't think he had sufficient time, for the Rebels were pressing forward aggressively. To cope with the Confederate skirmishers, Major Peale also reinforced his own skirmish screen, leaving only four companies—a mere 200 men—in the 18th's battle line.[1]

---

1   *OR* 37, pt. 1, 82.

The Nutmeggers' morale was now uncertain. Their first retreat had been arduous. The cloying mud sucked shoes right off the men's feet, leaving some of them barefoot in the quagmire. Private James Haggerty of company I later recalled how Sgt. James G. Spencer waved "the flag, signal fashion, at the advancing Confederates. He had lost one of his shoes in crossing the field. 'Jim' [Haggerty] said, 'you ought to get a shoe somewhere.' 'We won't need any shoes when this thing is over, is my opinion,'" Spencer grimly retorted. The sergeant had reason to be pessimistic. It quickly became obvious that the 18th and 123rd were holding their position all alone, far ahead of the rest of the Union army. Two other regiments which should have been present here, were nowhere around.[2]

When they reached the Rice house, the 1st West Virginia failed to fall in with the 18th and 123rd. Even worse, the 34th Massachusetts, already in position at the Rice house, picked up and left! Both the West Virginians and the 34th Massachusetts kept retreating, moving an additional 1,200 yards, all the way past the Bushong farm and up the slope of Bushong Hill. There they met their brigade commander, Colonel Thoburn, just arriving on the field with Capt. John Carlin's Battery D of the 1st West Virginia Light Artillery in tow. Thoburn's remaining infantry, the 12th West Virginia and 54th Pennsylvania, were not far behind. Thoburn decided to form his newly-reunited brigade right where he was, atop Bushong Hill. He made no effort to move forward to support the 18th and 123rd.

Thoburn planted Carlin's cannon on the Federal right, at the highest part of the hill, where the battery's left was protected by a high bluff overlooking the North Fork of the Shenandoah. It was an excellent position that could not easily be outflanked, allowing Carlin's guns a broad field of fire to the south and southeast. Colonel Wells's Bay-Staters fell in on Carlin's left, facing south, with the 1st West Virginia extending that line eastward towards the Valley Pike. Snow's Maryland Battery, trailing the 1st West Virginia, squeezed into position between Carlin's guns and the 34th's infantry line. The 54th and 12th West Virginia filled out the new line as they came up, with the 54th extending the 1st West Virginia's right, and the 12th taking up a reserve position behind the guns and the 34th. When fully formed, Thoburn's line numbered 1,900 infantry and 12

2   James Haggerty Letter, June 3, 1914, New Market Collection, VMI.

Colonel Joseph Thoburn. *Library of Congress*

cannon. Thoburn's decision to form on Bushing Hill, however, created an entirely new battle line much too far to the north to properly support Moor's regiments. The separation made no sense, and a disaster was in the offing. How did this state of affairs come to pass?

Was this staggered positioning intentional on Sigel's part? The German never said so, or indeed never really made it clear that he understood that there even *were* two separate positions. "Colonel Moor was ordered to form on the left of Thoburn," wrote Sigel in the 1880s, "but unfortunately only two of his regiments . . . came into line on the right and left of Von Kleiser's Battery, and a short distance in advance of Thoburn's line." This "short distance" was actually three-quarters of a mile. Either Sigel failed to understand where Moor was now deployed, or Moor failed to understand that Sigel wanted him arrayed much farther back and on Thoburn's left. Either way, Moor's two regiments were dangerously exposed.[3]

By now, if anyone was overwrought, it was Sigel. Colonel Strother described the agitated German thusly: "[He] seemed in a state of excitement and rode here and there with Stahel and Moor, all jabbering in German. In his excitement he seemed to forget his English entirely, and the purely American portion of his staff were totally useless to him." The Irish-born Colonel Thoburn must not have fared much better in divining Sigel's intentions. Moor's own comments reflect his anger at the blunder. "The . . . 1st Va. & 34th Mass. were again detached from my command to march to the rear and hunt up their Brigade at the very commencement of the Battle" he fumed, "leaving me [only] two small regiments to form line of battle." To Strother, at least, the problem was

---

3   Sigel, "Sigel in the Shenandoah Valley," 489.

obvious. "Von Kleiser's battery . . . [was] too far advanced I think for the support of the main line." Sigel had now taken personal control of the field, and his first important decision produced chaos.[4]

Thanks to Breckinridge's earlier decision to remain on the defensive, Moor's foolhardy stand on Manor Hill through the morning produced no adverse consequences. This new blunder would not go similarly unremarked. Breckinridge was through with waiting.

The Confederates took some time to restore order among their ranks before stepping off against the Rice house line. They also found that maneuvering of any sort was very difficult in the mud, reducing movements to a crawl, and so it was probably sometime after 1:30 p.m. when the Confederates finally advanced *en masse*. Part of this delay resulted when Wharton lengthened his line by moving Edgar's 26th Virginia up and to the left, extending his line on the 51st's flank, before putting the whole line in motion. With the North Fork bending away westward here, there was ample room to do so, and the prospect of flanking the 18th Connecticut was tempting.

This renewed sight of advancing Confederates, their lines overlapping both flanks of Moor's position and backed with ample reserves, unnerved those Federals upon whom this blow was about to land. "We were drawn up," remembered Cpl. Edmund P. Snyder of the 123rd, "without any particular reference to strategic advantage. . . . To stand out in the open . . . and await the oncoming enemy is the hardest part of a battle. It is nerve-wracking and fear-inspiring." Instead, noted Snyder, "I have always believed that had we been ordered to charge the lines of the enemy as soon as they came into sight we would have run right over them."[5]

Fellow Buckeye Corporal Powell was for a time more optimistic, noting that "our artillery did good service . . . in slaughtering the rebs . . . pouring the canister into them at short range, opening their lines at each shot" but, as the 123rd's regimental historian grimly noted, "not checking them for an instant." Corporal Henry S. Clapp recalled that Major Kellogg, sensing the 123rd's restiveness, rode out in front of the regiment moments before Wharton's line closed and "told us in very few words that he expected every man to do his duty. The prospect ahead

---

4   Eby, *Virginia Yankee*, 226; Moor report, Moor Papers.

5   Edmund P. Snyder, *Autobiography of a Soldier of the Civil War* (Privately Printed: 1915), 12.

of us was not encouraging, and the [Major] wisely thought that a little advice of the 'stand pat' order was needed."[6]

The 30th Virginia Sharpshooters sent their Union counterparts tumbling back to Moor's main line, with the Confederates in hot pursuit. Some part of the 30th now quickly reformed and joined the advance, falling in between the 51st and 62nd. Other sharpshooters helped clear the northern end of the town of lingering Federals. In this latter effort they were aided by additional men from Colonel Patton's 22nd Virginia Infantry, led by newly promoted Second Lt. Joseph A. Brown of Company H. The rest of Patton's men and Lieutenant Colonel Derrick's 23rd Virginia Infantry Battalion held their formation in Breckinridge's support line, roughly 1,000 bayonets strong and quite visible to Moor's Federals.[7]

It was now clear to Moor's troops that standing pat was not a sensible option. This fact was obvious to the men of the 18th and 123rd, even if Sigel, Moor, and Stahel all seemed oblivious to unfolding disaster. Colonel Smith's augmented 62nd Virginia advanced directly toward the 123rd Ohio. In that waiting blue line, Corporal Clapp recalled that Major Kellogg ordered the 123rd to fire a single volley and break for the rear. More contemporary observations note that the Buckeyes lingered a bit longer. "As they came up," wrote Powell, "we commenced firing and fired about a half dozen volleys," all of which failed to check Smith's advance.[8]

Corporal Snyder remembered that his "Captain [Dwight Kellogg] . . . happened to be right behind me shouting and urging the boys to 'give 'em--sugar!'" Snyder fired three times when he was struck with what felt like "a red-hot stone." At first Snyder was confused, perhaps a little stunned by the blow. Captain Kellogg "saw that I wasn't acting right, and excitedly said 'Don't you see you are hit? Get back! get back! as quick as God will let you!'" Wounded in the groin, Snyder stumbled for the rear. Within a few minutes, his twin brother Edwin took a similar injury. Within a few

6   "Dear Friends at Home," May 18th, 1864, Powell Letters, Hayes Library; Keyes, *123rd Ohio*, 55; Henry S. Clapp, *Sketches of Army Life in the Sixties, and "The mansion in the spring": A Civil War story of the Shenandoah* (Newark, OH: 1910), 16. Powell was probably referring to the shelling that struck the cadets.

7   Joseph Alleine Brown, *The Memoirs of a Confederate Soldier* (Abingdon, VA: 1940), 33.

8   Clapp, *Sketches of Army Life*, 16; "Dear Friends at Home," May 18th, 1864, Powell Letters, Hayes Library.

more minutes, the rest of the regiment was scrambling rearward as Major Kellogg ordered a general retreat.[9]

The same scene was playing in the ranks of the 18th Connecticut, facing off against the Virginians of the 51st and Edgar's 26th Battalion. Nutmegger James Haggerty watched with growing alarm as the 18th's own skirmishers fell back around the regiment's right flank to reform. That movement triggered a burst of cheering in the Rebel ranks, begun at the urgings of the gray-clad officers. Haggerty recalled one particularly striking Confederate, mounted on a white horse, who trooped the line of enemy regiments, provoking wild excitement as he stopped before each unit. "I thought of Napoleon in Egypt addressing his veterans under the shadow of the pyramids," said Haggerty, and took aim at the man, but decided against taking the shot. The Confederates didn't wait long. As the main Rebel line advanced, they flushed several cattle. "A small herd of 8 or 10 cows came charging along our line of battle," Haggerty recalled. "At first I thought it was a cavalry charge . . . until I saw them rush by with tails straight in the air. Following the cows came a large black Newfoundland dog."[10]

By now the 18th was fully engaged, paying no attention to farm animals. "The line fired several volleys," reported Major Peale, "when, it being apparent that . . . the enemy greatly outnumbered [us] . . . and that [a] further stay . . . was worse than useless. . . . [T]he commander of the regiment on [the] left . . . gave the order to retreat, which movement was followed by the 18th." Private Lynch was blazing away when he heard Peale shout "by the right of companies, to the rear in column."[11]

That order was much easier to issue than to execute. Trapped by the fences bordering the farm lane, The Nutmeggers soon lost cohesion. "As we fell back we took the lane to the right of the house," recalled Haggerty, which "became terribly crowded and the Confederate batteries took full advantage of that fact." Haggerty found himself momentarily behind Peale, and for a second was more afraid of a kick from Peale's

---

9   Snyder, *Autobiography,* 13.

10   James Haggerty to Colonna, June 3, 1914, New Market Collection, VMI Archives. Haggerty's recollections are similar to those of other veterans in many different battles, in that he recalled seeing the enemy general (probably Breckinridge) and that he almost shot him, but some other sense stayed his hand.

11   *OR* 37, pt. 1, 82; Lynch, *Diary,* 60.

horse than from the shelling; "I knew the horse," he quipped. Once the mob pushed through the lane, Peale and the other officers tried to rally the 18th, but without success. "Considerable confusion prevailed."[12]

At this point in the conflict, though their actual losses were relatively modest by the severe standards of Civil War combat, both the 123rd and the 18th were effectively destroyed as military formations. The 18th had about 350 men engaged; losing 56 killed wounded or missing. The 123rd numbered roughly 420, suffering 86 total casualties.[13]

While their losses were not to be sneered at, the endemic lack of officers was the more telling problem. Confused and leaderless, the men of both regiments bolted for the supposed security of the support line atop Bushong Hill, three quarters of a mile distant. Once there, however, few stopped. Panic had set in. Most kept going as far as Rude's Hill. "It was impossible to collect and rally our Reg't or the 18th either," admitted Corporal Powell, until well to the rear. Even there, only "about 100 of us [the Ohioans] rallied around our major and our flag," and by the time they did, it was too late to return to the fight. Some portion of the 18th fared a little better, rallying with Peale behind the 1st West Virginia; but only a handful.[14]

Moor was rendered furious by this turn of events. Later he would fume that "of course" his two small regiments "were overrun literally at once by overwhelming numbers of the enemy whose attack was spirited, well led & conducted." This remark was a jibe obviously aimed at Sigel, but it just as easily could have been leveled at Moor himself, since it was the fate he had been courting since before dawn.[15]

This abrupt retreat and subsequent disintegration on the part of the blue-clad infantry line left von Kleiser's guns dangerously exposed. The 30th New York Battery had already taken a pounding. Earlier, when von Kleiser unlimbered in front of the Rice house, his six Napoleons became the focus of virtually all the available Rebel artillery. At least 10 Confederate pieces directed their fire at the New Yorkers, all of them three-inch ordnance rifles which out-ranged von Kleiser's own

---

12 Haggerty Letter, VMI.

13 *Tiffin Weekly Tribune*, June 2, 1863, gives the 123rd's casualties.

14 Powell Letter, Hayes Library.

15 Moor report, Moor Papers.

weapons. This fire was effective, reported the German, noting that "the right wheel of [one] piece having been entirely knocked off, while in position soon after the commencement of the battle . . ." With no time to fix the carriage while under such a punishing fire, that cannon was hurriedly dispatched rearward, (though it was not through causing von Kleiser problems) leaving the other five guns to carry on the fight.[16]

To further complicate von Kleiser's precarious situation, Rebel shells were now also coming in from his right-rear. That fire came from McClanahan's guns, deployed on "a little hill" east of and overlooking Smith Creek several hundred yards to the northeast of Dr. Rice's home. With the mounted portion of his brigade and McClanahan's four guns, General Imboden was moving northward up the east side of the creek, seeking a crossing that would allow them to outflank the Union position, when a "few stray shots" from Ewing's Battery G landing among the Rebels. Those shots were un-aimed, since Imboden's men were concealed by a belt of timber, but when Imboden rode forward through those trees to investigate he came upon a target too tempting to ignore. "I was rewarded by the discovery of Sigel's entire cavalry force," Imboden exulted, "massed in very close order in the fields" below. A little "less than one thousand yards" distant, Stahel's force was "massed in column, close order, squadron front, giving our gunners a target of whole acres of men and horses."[17]

Imboden hurriedly brought up McClanahan, who managed to unlimber without being noticed, and whose fire, once commenced, caught the Yankees completely by surprise. Lieutenant Colonel Charles Fitzsimmons, commanding the 21st New York Cavalry, was already unhappy, viewing the position of Tibbets' brigade as wholly unsatisfactory. "The ground in front [of us] . . . was . . . steep and impractical" for horsemen. Mounted cavalry could not effectively charge the advancing Rebels here. Quoting a respected tactician of the day, Fitzsimmons further noted that "cavalry, unless posted where an advance can be made, is almost certain to break for the rear. This instance proved [the] . . . assertion correct; set up as a conspicuous target for Breckinridge's well-served artillery, the long line of troopers soon assumed a very irregular formation, uniform in nothing

---

16   http://newmarketbattle.blogspot.com/2010/07/alfred-von-kleisers-other-gun-lost-at. html, accessed June 5, 2013

17   Imboden, "Battle of New Market," 483.

but a general scrambling towards the rear." As the cavalry thundered back in a mob, McClanahan turned his attention to von Kleiser. Now it was the Union battery's turn to beat a precipitous retreat, scrambling for safety up the Valley Turnpike until they were intercepted by Sigel, who personally placed them on Bushong Hill.[18]

New York Sgt. Asa Noble of the 21st was experiencing his first full-out battle, and while he found it confusing, his courage did not fail him. On May 17, Noble wrote home to the Oswego *Times*, describing his piece of this action: "I thought I should be awfully frightened, but I was not in the least. The line of cavalry consisting of the 1st, 21st and 1st Veteran N. Y. regiments, and some cavalry from Pennsylvania, Col. Tibbets intended to have charged the [Rebel] line when it came into view . . . but the 1st Veteran broke for the rear, all the other regiments followed in quick succession with the exception of the 21st, which was the last to leave the ground." The 21st, bragged Noble, "marched by fours in good order to the rear the 1st Va. (Union) infantry. . . ." Here Noble lost his own "good order." Overwhelmed by curiosity to see more of the battle, Noble admitted that "wishing to see how our infantry received [the rebel attack] I lingered behind."[19]

This might have been the perfect moment for Breckinridge to commit his cavalry, if any were to be had, but Imboden and all the available mounted men were on the wrong side of the creek. They were completely unable to follow up McClanahan's startling success or capitalize on Moor's rout. Despite the ongoing heavy rains, Imboden chose instead to work his mounted force farther northward along the east bank of the creek, optimistic that some sort of crossing might be had further downstream.

Sigel's greatest flaw as a general was his inability to react effectively to the ebb and flow of battle. Operationally, Sigel had performed well in the run up to New Market, accomplishing all he was supposed to in drawing Confederate attention away from Crook and simultaneously preventing Breckinridge from reinforcing Lee. Even his decision to give battle at Mount Jackson was sound. He could have easily assembled his army there on the morning of the 15th, forcing Breckinridge to come look for him. Moor's, and subsequently Stahel's, refusal or inability to

18 Fitzsimmons, "Sigel's Fight," 63-64; Henry A. du Pont, *The Battle of Newmarket, Virginia* (Washington, D. C.: 1923), 26.

19 "Dear Friends at Home," *Oswego Times,* June 16, 1864.

execute the intended retreat, however, forced a series of rapidly changing circumstances upon the German, and Franz Sigel never reacted well to rapid change. This flaw manifested itself as early as 1861, at the battle of Wilson's Creek, where Sigel executed a masterful flank march to arrive exactly where and when he promised he would; but after an initially successful assault, a Rebel counter-attack threw Sigel's green force into a panic. Unable to restore order, Sigel ultimately fled the field with his beaten men in wild rout. In moments of crisis Sigel flailed about incoherently, and while no one doubted his physical courage, many had reason to doubt his grasp of a situation. His inability to either order Moor's men back to the Bushong Hill line or to properly support them at the Rice house was a perfect example of how Sigel could lose control of a situation at the worst possible moment. The next phase of the battle would only see more of the same.

Now a new line of Union regiments awaited the next blow atop Bushong Hill. This line was much stronger, soon to number four regiments and studded with 21 cannon. As noted earlier, this new position was also geographically superior to Moor's line on Manor Hill. The inward loops of both watercourses meant that here, both Union flanks were reasonably secure. Carlin's and Snow's batteries, 12 guns in all, were well-sited to sweep their fire laterally in front of the Union infantry line. Though initially the line included only the 34th Massachusetts and the 1st West Virginia, with the West Virginians' flank resting a couple of hundred yards short of the Valley Turnpike in a cedar grove, it was growing in strength. Even while Moor's line was collapsing into chaos, Thoburn's force was being fleshed out.

First came four more guns of Captain Ewing's Battery G, 1st West Virginia Artillery, who dropped trails astride the pike, to the left of the 1st West Virginia. Sigel placed von Kleiser's five remaining guns on the forward slope between and just ahead of the 34th and 1st. To ensure that no Rebels worked their way along the river bank and up the bluff to assail Carlin's and Snow's gunners, Colonel Wells of the 34th detached Company C and sent them into the woods on the right, and also ordered Company G forward about 200 yards as skirmishers.[20]

Even better, Thoburn's own 12th West Virginia and the 54th Pennsylvania had just arrived on the scene as Moor's line was overrun.

---

20 Lincoln, *Thirty-Fourth Massachusetts,* 281-282.

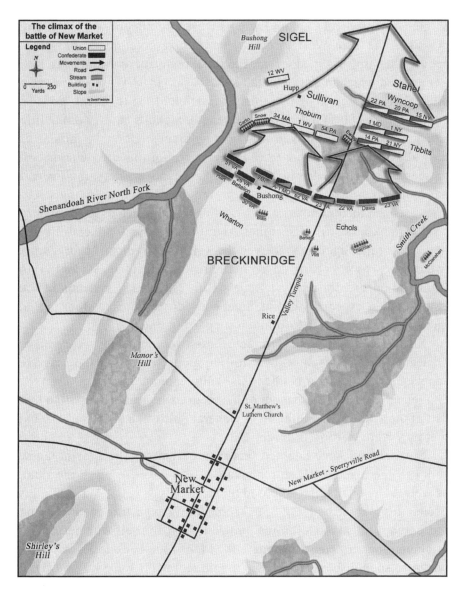

"When we came up," noted the 12th's Surgeon, Alexander Neil, "all exhausted & drenched with rain to the skin, the cannons were belching forth their music like the crashing of a thousand thunders . . . the heavens were literally blackened with shells and canister."[21]

Sigel immediately sent Col. Jacob Campbell's Pennsylvanians forward into line on the 1st West Virginia's left filling a gap between the West

---

21 Duncan, *Alexander Neil*, 29.

Virginia infantry and Captain Ewing's West Virginia gunners straddling the pike. The 12th West Virginia went into reserve, about 200 yards behind Thoburn's right, alongside the small fragment of the rallying 18th Connecticut which managed to halt at Peale's urgings. These Nutmeggers probably amounted to no more than a fraction of the regiment, perhaps 30 to 40 men, at best a company's strength. Stahel's cavalry did a little better. They were still tasked with holding Sigel's left on the far side of the Valley Pike, though how steady they were for this task remained to be seen. After being driven off by McClanahan's artillery, the Federal horsemen reformed, still mounted, in the open fields to Ewing's left. They retained their numbers and formation, but the lack of solid infantry on that flank was still Sigel's most significant tactical vulnerability.[22]

At this time Sigel also received the welcome word that Moor's other two regiments were nearly up. A courier reported that the 28th and 116th Ohio had apparently reached Rude's Hill. The steady veterans of the 28th would be especially useful. Sigel hurriedly dispatched Moor to find them and rush them forward into a supporting line.[23]

Sigel was misinformed. In fact, those two commands were still at or near Mount Jackson, slowly toiling along, escorting the massive supply train. Sigel later blamed this faulty communication on Capt. R. G. Prendergast, the commander of his escort, who had just reported that "all of the artillery and infantry of General Sullivan had arrived . . . and that they were waiting for orders."[24]

Sigel should have doubted this report from the first, for he knew full well the distance those regiments had to cover to reach the field, as well as the difficulties imposed by the supply wagons, but again, his excitability got the better of him. Momentarily expecting Moor to bring those troops up on the left, Sigel turned to busy himself with personally arranging matters atop Bushong Hill. Moor rode back to Rude's Hill, where he soon discovered the truth: both regiments were still at Mount Jackson. Dispatching a staff officer to bring them up as quickly as possible, Moor set about trying to rally the fragments of the 18th and

---

22 *OR* 37, pt. 1, 86.

23 Ibid., 80

24 Sigel, "Sigel in the Shenandoah Valley," 489.

123rd he found there. It would be close to 4:00 p.m. before the 28th and 116th could even reach Rude's Hill. By then the battle would be decided.

The 12th West Virginia was a large formation, made even stronger by the fact that unlike most Union regiments on the field, all 10 companies were present. Their combat strength was probably around 650 officers and men. Initially Colonel Curtis placed his regiment in line a couple of hundred yards behind Thoburn's main position, but within a few minutes Sigel marched them up the hill to a position only 60 yards behind the 34th Massachusetts. Once there, companies A and B of the 12th were detached and sent to join C Company of the 34th to aid in holding the wooded bluff leading down to the river. All this happened quickly, and while Sigel was fussing with his deployments, The Confederate advance continued unabated.[25]

The 51st and 62nd Virginia continued to anchor the center of Breckinridge's line, temporarily dividing as they passed the Bushong house and outbuildings. As they moved, one part of the reformed 30th Sharpshooters fell in between these two larger two commands, though with at least half of their men deployed as skirmishers on the east side of the turnpike, the sharpshooters' frontage was likely quite small. The 26th Virginia Battalion, formerly on the 51st's left, found itself advancing down into and then along a ravine known locally as Indian Hollow, which led down to the river bank as it bent eastward, forcing Colonel Edgar's men out of the front line. "I found it necessary," noted Edgar, "to throw my battalion in rear of the regiment on [our] right," meaning that once again the Rebels were advancing in multiple lines of attack. Colonel Smith, at the head of the 62nd Virginia, remembered that "our advance was unchecked until we arrived opposite the northern fence of Bouchong's yard, at which point the troops on my left . . . halted."[26]

That fence marked the northern border of the Bushong orchard, and beyond it a large stretch of open ground rising towards Bushong Hill, now bristling with Federal cannon. The 51st and the 30th Virginia

25 Hewitt, *Twelfth West Virginia,* 108; Knight, *Valley Thunder,* 250. See chapter 3. The strength of the 12th West Virginia is an estimate. The regiment numbered 675 the year before, at Winchester. Davis, *The Battle of New* Market, gives their strength as 949 and Knight follows suit, though the latter notes that figure is probably too high.

26 Report, Edgar Papers, UNC; Edgar, "Battle of New Market," Edgar Papers, UNC. Note that Edgar's report and his post-war manuscript, "Battle of New Market," are different. Edgar's postwar account is longer and more detailed.

sharpshooters fell into a line running from the Bushong house leftward to the steadily rising bluff fronting the river, with the 51st's right draped over that bluff, and thus at least partly obscured from the Union line atop the hill. Smith's 62nd (still augmented by the Missourians and the dismounted elements of the 23rd Cavalry) extended that line eastward from the farmhouse to the turnpike. Somewhat behind and to Smith's right, still moving up (formed *en echelon*) were Colonel Patton's 22nd Virginia Regiment and Lt. Col. Clarence Derrick's 23rd Virginia Infantry Battalion. Men of 51st estimated the distance from their line near the Bushong house to the Federal position as about 250 yards. Smith placed the distance at a slightly longer 300 yards. As the Confederates swept through and around the Bushong farm, the Union line erupted in fire.

Lieutenant Colonel Lincoln of the 34th Massachusetts remembered the moment clearly. First had come panicked Federals from the routed 18th and 123rd, "some of them running through and over our lines. . . ." Beyond them Lincoln could see that "the advance of the Rebels . . . was steady and continued." With the enemy in full view, no skirmish line was needed, so Colonel Wells hurriedly recalled Company G, who scrambled back to reform behind the main line. "Our front fire was heavy," exulted Wells, "and the artillery had an enfilading fire, under which their first line went down." Given their elevation, one Massachusetts boy now had a dramatic view of the action. "We could see all three rebel lines as they came on—as soon as they appeared in sight they opened fire, we replied from our batteries, and from where I was I could see the shells mow them down by scores. As soon as they came within range our boys opened with killing effect. . . . [T]he first rebel line melted away." This first check was heartening, but almost immediately the Bay-Staters discovered a new problem: they were taking fire from their immediate rear.[27]

This fire came from some members of the 12th West Virginia, in line just a short distance behind the 34th, who also started shooting as the Rebels hove into view. Lieutenant Colonel Lincoln, posted behind the 34th's right, watched in shock as the West Virginians broke ranks and "opened fire over the heads of our men, causing [our] first casualties of the day. . . ." Lincoln rushed back to put a halt to things before that fire demoralized his own troops, where he found Sigel embarked on

---

27   Lincoln, *Thirty-Fourth Massachusetts*, 282; *OR* 37, pt. 1, 84; Anonymous, "In the field at Cedar Creek," May 17, 1864, *Northampton Free Press*, June 7, 1864.

the same course. The 12th, recalled Sigel, "was very well drilled in the manual of arms, but . . . deficient in battalion drill. . . . This created considerable trouble at the beginning of the fight, when they left their position in reserve, came forward, and fired over the heads of the 34th Massachusetts." "Gen. Sigel rode up to the eight companies of the 12th," recalled Lieutenant Hewitt, "and ordered it into column by division." With officers and NCOs chivvying the West Virginians back into ranks, the new formation was soon achieved, though not, admitted Sigel, without "difficulty." From there, the 12th was ordered to lie down, where perhaps they would be less inclined to break ranks and wage independent (if indiscriminate) warfare.[28]

Despite the sudden roiling of confusion on the Union right, Sigel's line still delivered an accurate, deadly fire into the oncoming Rebel formations. The 30th Sharpshooters and the right wing of the 51st, along Bushong fence, bore the brunt. The 51st's left was still covered by ground sloping toward the river. Wharton was there personally, trying to find a way around the Union right, and for the moment remained unaware of the difficulties now facing the center of his brigade.

Those difficulties were mounting. Fire from three Union batteries played on the Confederate line, with von Kleiser's five guns shooting dead ahead while Carlin's and Snow's 10 pieces delivered an angled fire sweeping in from the Rebel left. Most of the 800 muskets in the ranks of the 34th and 1st West Virginia also stung the 51st and 30th. Virginia Capt. Daniel Bruce commanded Company A of the 51st. "We were on level land in a wheat field, where the growing grain was about knee high. The Yankees were in a meadow . . . with no protection on either side. . . . Our regiment lay down and the Yankees stood up. We . . . fired as fast as we could load for one hour and fifteen minutes, according to a man who was not in the battle and noted the time." While it must have seemed like an eternity to Captain Bruce, this firefight probably really lasted only a few minutes before the intensity of the Union fire began to break up the Rebel formation. First went the 30th, falling back in some disorder. Bruce, from his position in the center of the 51st's line, next noted that the "four companies . . . on our right gave way one at a

---

28 Lincoln, *Thirty-Fourth Massachusetts,* 282; Hewitt, *Twelfth West Virginia,* 108, 114.

time, slowly falling back; they dropped down to try and stay under the shot and shell . . . that seemed to keep the air blue."[29]

This was an alarming development, especially when Bruce implored the company immediately on his right to hold firm, only to watch them give back in turn. Lieutenant Colonel Wolfe was off on another part of the field, perhaps with Wharton still trying to figure out how to storm the hill, leaving Bruce on his own. "The time had come for no foolishness; at least half our command was giving way." Feeling he faced certain slaughter if he stayed, Bruce followed suit, falling back across the Bushong fence, through the farmyard, and into the field of new corn south of the house, so recently churned to "loblolly" by the 51st during their previous advance.[30]

Over on the left, the rest of the 51st now crested the rise, to view a quickly deteriorating situation. In Company B, Pvt. George Dunford found the spectacle daunting. Dunford could see down the length of the Confederate line off to the east and also "the enemy, seemingly three or four to our one, so also is their battery immediately in front. . . . Here we halted and gave them a grand salute, but to stay here meant annihilation for us. It was too warm a place, for the enemy received us royally."[31]

Colonel Edgar, still struggling to find a place where he could get his battalion into action, sent Capt. Edmund Read of Company B, the 26th Battalion (Read was a man of many hats that day; he had charge of the battalion's skirmishers and was also acting as Edgar's second-in-command) over to Wharton for orders. Wharton, focused on trying to flank the Union artillery from under the bluff, relayed instructions for "Edgar to move by the right flank and go to the assistance of the center . . . [then] hotly engaged."[32]

Though the 51st halted, stymied, Colonel Smith and his 62nd continued their advance. With every step northward, however, Smith's left was farther exposed to Union enfilade fire, especially once Carlin's and Snow's gunners turned their attention to this new target, so perfectly

---

29 D. H. Bruce, "Battle of New Market, VA," *Confederate Veteran,* vol. 15, no. 12 (December, 1907), 553.

30 Ibid.

31 G. W. Dunford, "As a Private Saw New Market Fight," unknown clipping, 1906, New Market File, VMI.

32 *Staunton Spectator*, May 20, 1904.

presented. "On they came without wavering," marveled one Union gunner, "closing up the gaps . . . and yelling like demons. The order is passed for two second fuses. The next moment there is a demand along the line for canister, and the men work with a will. . . ."[33]

Smith's line pushed perhaps a hundred yards farther north, facing the right of the 1st West Virginia and the entire 54th Pennsylvania, until Colonel Smith realized that his regiment was making this movement all alone. Not only had the 51st faltered on Smith's left, but 22nd and 23rd Virginia infantries on his right were also not keeping up. As a result, the 62nd was chewed to pieces. Smith recalled that he led his men over a "slight elevation" in the grain field, but upon "reaching the depression beyond came under the close concentrated artillery and infantry fire of the Federal line, losing in a very few minutes over two hundred men." The entire color guard fell, killed or wounded. On the regimental left, the attached Missourians took an especially fearful pounding: Only six of the original 62 enlisted men in the company would emerge unscathed at the end of the day. Given these fearful circumstances, Smith had little choice but to retire his butchered command and reform under cover of more sheltered ground in the lee of the Bushong house.[34]

While Wharton's attack faltered, over on the Union left a different drama was unfolding. So far, the Union cavalry had contributed little to the fight besides a confused, disorderly retreat. Now they stood, massed east of the turnpike, watching the action swell and rage over on the Union right. Directly to their front, however, the Confederates were lagging. Stahel decided that the moment was ripe for a counter-stroke. He ordered his entire force—roughly 1,000 sabers—forward in a massed charge.

The Union troopers were currently positioned on the reverse slope of the Bushong Hill ridgeline. They were near the Strayer farm, their formation further screened by the cedar grove that also concealed the left half of the 54th Pennsylvania just across the pike. At the southern end of that grove another wet-weather drainage cut its way down to Smith Creek, amounting to a small ravine, and given the weather, that drainage was certainly a running creek today. The only way the cavalry could

---

33   *Wheeling Intelligencer,* May 23, 1864.

34   G. W. Smith, "More on the Battle of New Market," *Confederate Veteran,* vol. 16, no. 11 (November, 1908), 570. 80% of Smith's losses for the entire battle fell here, in this first push forward.

cross this stream was via the stone bridge on the Valley Pike. Thus, to close with the enemy the Yankees would have to form column of fours, ride through the grove, funnel across the ravine via the bridge, and then re-deploy for a charge in full view of the 22nd Virginia, 23rd Virginia Battalion, and the Rebel artillery.

To oppose this effort, the Confederates massed 12 cannon: Capt. George B. Chapman's six guns, the two outdated six-pounder smoothbores from VMI under Cadet Capt. Collier Minge, and McClanahan's four guns on the hill across Smith Creek. McClanahan's crews had the chance to repeat their enfilading fire success against these same Federal troopers as they came forward. Chapman, trailed by Cadet Minge, was moving north behind Echols's infantry, trying to find positions from which to assail Sigel's main line. Chapman had been in position just west of the town, engaging Moor's Rice house line, and subsequently advanced when those Federals bolted rearward. Chapman leapfrogged three of his guns northward to their current position, a rise east of the turnpike, and roughly 800 yards southeast of the Bushong farm, covering them with the half-battery left behind. Once here, Chapman summoned his remaining three guns forward. Minge's two pieces went into position on Chapman's left, closer to (but still east of) the pike. Only Jackson's Battery, four guns commanded on this field by Lt. Randolph Blain, was not on the scene, having followed Wharton's advance and dropped trail somewhere behind the right wing of the 51st Virginia, nearer the Bushong outbuildings.[35]

The charge turned into calamity right at the start. Even in trying to form up, noted Jacob Lester of the 1st New York (Veteran) Cavalry, "horses got stuck in the mud and fell over each other and in a moment we were mired up like a flock of sheep." With such terrible footing, the Confederate right had plenty of time to prepare a response. Most of the Federal troopers were aimed to strike Lieutenant Colonel Derrick's 23rd Battalion, but at least some of Stahel's force funneled straight down the turnpike and across the stone bridge towards Patton's 22nd Virginia. Breckinridge, who had spotted the movement, rode over to Chapman and ordered the gunner to "double Shot" his pieces "with canister."[36]

---

35 Henderson Reid to George Edgar, June 12th, 1908, Edgar Papers, UNC.

36 Knight, *Valley Thunder,* 164; J. Stoddard Johnson, "Sketch of Operations," New Market File, VMI.

Derrick's response to this charge displayed an impressive amount of sangfroid. He did not recall his own left wing, apparently drawn out as a skirmish line; instead he ordered them to form fours, back to back. While this was the doctrinal response for skirmishers caught out in the open by cavalry, it was only to be used if they could not get to any other cover. As such it was a tactic of last resort. Fortunately for these skirmishers, those Federal horsemen never reached them.

While his left was scrambling into fours, Derrick wheeled his battalion's right wing to rake the opposing cavalry's left flank.[37]

Simultaneously, Patton wheeled the 22nd Virginia to savage the Union troopers' right, and within minutes the Federals found themselves caught in a deadly crossfire. Confederate cannon and muskets belched fire from the front and both flanks, shattering Stahel's intended charge at the outset, and the cavalry broke for the rear. Milling about, some of those Federals had to pass under the very muzzles of the Virginia 22nd to escape. Several of these, noted Sgt. William Mays of the 22nd, rode "right into the midst of our ranks and through our line. As their leader passed, nearly running me down, I fired at him hurriedly at a distance that could not have been much more than twelve inches. In my haste and excitement, and as he was riding at top speed. I missed. The charge from my gun went through his cloak, which was streaming out behind, and set it on fire."[38]

"We were whipped before we commenced fighting," Col. Robert F. Taylor of the 1st New York Veteran complained angrily only two days after the fact. "My cavalry behaved gallantly," he insisted, despite the carnage and the folly of the attack. "Capt[ain John J.] Carter had two horses shot under him . . ." the last when "a shell passed through [the animal's] neck and exploded, pieces of it striking [Carter] in [the] face; the concussion so completely paralyzed him that for several hours he was unconscious and unable to speak." In the charge, Taylor "lost 14 men and a great number of horses."[39]

37 Scott, *23rd Battalion Virginia Infantry*, 29.

38 William Mays Recollections, Lake Forest College.

39 R. F. Taylor to Wife, Camp near Strasburg Va., May 17, 1864, online auction catalogue, http://www.mqamericana.com/Col_Taylor_1st_NY_Vet_Cv.html, accessed April 18, 2010. Captain John Joyce Carter survived, and in 1897 would be awarded

Colonel William B. Tibbits. *Library of Congress*

In fact, all the regiments involved lost more horses than men. The 21st New York Cavalry also reported 14 casualties—2 men killed and 12 wounded—but lost no less than 68 of the 165 horses who made the charge. John E. Mattoon, another trooper in the 21st, was one of those abruptly de-horsed. "Got licked like thunder," Mattoon noted dolefully, "I had my old horse shot out from under me so I had to foot it back to . . . Mount Jackson." Thoroughly disgusted, Colonel Tibbets termed the charge "a disaster." It was all of that.[40]

This time the Union cavalry would not reform. They were now out of the battle for good. One Federal wrote mockingly that Stahel, apparently bewildered and overwhelmed by this disaster, rode west to find the army commander. Upon reaching Sigel the befuddled Hungarian wailed, "Mein Gott, General Sigel! Vare ish mein Cavalrie!"[41]

Sigel might have been unaware that Stahel was about to commit an offensive blunder, but he was nevertheless also thinking of a counter-attack. So far, Union commander had spent all his time on the Federal right, "chained" there, as he described it, "by a circumstance that is unpleasant to record." A few minutes earlier the German started to ride

the Congressional Medal of Honor for action at Antietam, while a Lieutenant with the 33rd New York Infantry, a two years' regiment.

40 "Letter from Major Jennings," *Troy Daily Times*, May 26, 1864; Robert Bruce Donald, *Manhood and Patriotic Awakening in the Civil War. The John E. Mattoon Letters, 1859–1866* (Lanham, MD: 2008), 27; Davis, *New Market*, 126.

41 Davis, *New Market*, 126. Davis's source for this quote is unclear, but it appears to come second-hand from the Diary of Charles Halpine, an Irish immigrant, Union army officer, and prolific wartime author and correspondent. Halpine was not present at New Market. Instead he served on the staff of General David Hunter, who would soon supersede Sigel.

towards the left when he discovered that the 12th West Virginia "quickly rose from the ground and followed me, as if by command." Nonplussed, Sigel immediately reversed course and brought the 12th back into position behind the Union guns, but now the Union commander feared to leave, lest the troops here give way completely. This circumstance meant that with his view eastward limited by the intrusion of the cedars, Sigel knew nothing of Stahel's attack and repulse. From his location near the 12th West Virginia, that which he could see to his immediate front all seemed encouraging. The Confederate attack was faltering, with the enemy's first line (the 51st and 30th Virginia) breaking, and the 62nd took a terrible loss in the open field before also falling back. To any professionally trained soldier, this was the moment for a counter-attack. Accordingly, Sigel ordered Colonel Thoburn to charge.[42]

Despite Sigel's concerns over the reliability of the 12th, the rest of the Federal front line had been steady enough when holding their own ground. They were loading and firing into the enemy ranks as rapidly as any veterans. Advancing proved another thing entirely.

Colonel Wells had watched with growing satisfaction as the enemy first slowed, then fell into disordered retreat. "Their fire ceased to be effective," Wells reported. "A cheer ran along our line, and the first success was ours. I gave the order to 'cease firing.'" Then an apparently excited Colonel Thoburn "rode along the lines telling the men to 'prepare to charge.' He rode by me shouting some order I could not catch, and went to the regiment on my left. . . ." Suddenly that regiment, the 1st West Virginia, lurched forward in the attack, and any question Wells had about what Thoburn intended him to do next was resolved.[43]

The 1st was Thoburn's own command, now led by Lt. Col. Joseph Weddle, and was easily the most experienced Union regiment then in the fight. They were also the smallest, numbering only about 350 officers and men; but they certainly advanced with alacrity. Too quickly, in fact, for they were up and moving almost as soon as Thoburn ordered them to, before Wells and the 34th could grasp what was happening; or indeed, even before Thoburn could ride on to alert the 54th Pennsylvania. Carlin's gunners, watching from atop the hill on the right, watched with growing

---

42 Sigel, "Sigel in the Shenandoah Valley," 489.

43 *OR* 37, pt. 1, 84.

alarm as the attack miscued. "Our infantry raised up, and the command was 'charge.' They moved forward, but slowly—not like men who go for victory or death. . . ." To the artillerists, it seemed as if "the 1st Va. [was] the only regiment that charged. . . ."[44]

The Confederates might be checked, but they were far from routed. As historian Charles Knight pointed out, luck was breaking in Breckinridge's favor on that rainy afternoon, for the collapse of the Confederate line occurred at precisely the place where Confederate reserves were best situated to deal with any such crisis and led by an officer perspicacious enough to immediately understand what to do.[45]

Lieutenant Colonel George Edgar and his 26th Virginia Battalion, 477 strong, had previously moved up behind the 51st as per Wharton's orders. As Wolfe's 51st Virginia began to fall back, said Colonel Edgar, "I at once ordered my battalion forward to its support." Almost immediately, routed 51st'ers swarmed through the 26th's formation. "Do not let those men break your ranks," barked Edgar to Capt. Thomas C. Morton of Company F, growling for Morton to "shoot them if they will not halt." Edgar's line was not sufficient to fill the whole space occupied by the 51st, but alongside Edgar's men on their right, the rest of the gap was also soon to be filled.[46]

Major Charles Semple was an Irish immigrant and a capable staff officer. He helped raise a company for service in the Confederate 2nd Kentucky in 1861, caught John C. Breckinridge's eye in the retreat from Corinth after the battle of Shiloh, and been serving on Breckinridge's staff since the battle of Murfreesboro, 17 months previously. While Breckinridge was supervising the repulse of Stahel, Semple witnessed the beginning of the rupture on the Rebel left. Riding hard, Semple found his boss and offered up the only remedy available; the V. M. I. Cadets must go into the line. Breckinridge hesitated, worried both that he would be sacrificing children, and that they might not stand the test. They would stand, insisted Semple. "Breckinridge then gave the word. 'Charlie, bring up the boys—and God forgive me the order!'"[47]

The four companies of cadets, numbering about 225 muskets, were currently positioned south of the Bushong house near Jackson's Battery.

44 Phillips, *Wheeling's Finest*, 36.

45 Knight, *Valley Thunder*, 160.

46 Edgar Report, Edgar Papers, UNC; Thomas C. Morton to Edgar, 1906 letter, Edgar papers, UNC.

47 Ed Porter Thompson, *History of the Orphan Brigade,* (Louisville: 1898), 453.

A postwar image of the Bushong House, from the southeast corner. Turner, *The New Market Campaign*

They had suffered their first casualties coming down Shirley Hill and a few more in the subsequent minutes, as artillery thundered all around them, but they had yet to face the full fury of a Union infantry line blazing with musketry. Lieutenant Colonel Shipp led them through the farmyard, the battalion breaking formation to surge around the house, two companies passing to each side, reforming in the orchard beyond. They did so at about the same time as the Federal attack was getting under way. The rain was coming down heavily now, complicating movement for both sides.

The Union 1st Virginia was now advancing all alone into the field north of that same orchard, directly opposite the cadet line. The West Virginians' regimental history recorded that "the First was . . . ordered to move forward to receive the charge [of the enemy] and when . . . within a distance of one hundred yards a volley . . . was given with marked effect." They drew attention from all along the Confederate line. Rebel return fire proved "overlapping and enfilading [so] the order was given to fall back. . . ." In that retreat, it was grudgingly admitted (with some understatement) that the 1st West Virginia "was for a short time thrown into confusion."[48]

The West Virginians' retreat came at the worst possible time for Colonel Wells and the 34th Massachusetts, who were just starting

---

48 Charles J. Rawling, *History of the First Regiment Virginia Infantry,* online at http://www.lindapages.com/wvcw/1wvi/1wvi-20.htm, accessed July 1, 2013.

Colonel George D. Wells. *Library of Congress*

their own forward movement. "The regiment on my left . . . turned and went back, complained the frustrated Wells" leaving the 34th rushing alone into the enemy's line. "Among the Bay-Staters, discipline broke down almost immediately, converting what should have been a steady advance into an impetuous rush—this was their first-ever charge on a real battlefield, after all." I shouted at them to halt, "lamented Wells," but could not make a single man hear or heed me. "Only an" intervening fence "slowed the men long enough for the blue-blood colonel to" run along the lines, and seizing the color bearer by the shoulder, hold him fast as the only way of stopping the regiment. "The first line of the enemy gave way," noted Capt. George Thompson of Company D, and "we were just over the fence [when] the order came to halt & fall back."[49]

Wells managed to restore some measure of order but now discovered that it was his regiment's turn to face the fire of an entire Confederate battle line all alone. Within mere minutes the 34th fell back, slowly, struggling to remain in line, only to be picked apart by rebel musketry. "The continuous cheering of the enemy shows that they fully appreciate their advantage," remembered William Clark, and "we now begin to feel seriously the effect of the heavy fire."[50]

Determined to preserve order, Wells directed the regiment to turn about and march back to their original position in "common time"—a stultifying pace suited for drill fields, not combat. That decision cost the regiment heavily. By the time the 34th retraced their steps back to

49 *OR* 37, pt. 1, 84; "Entry for May 15," George W. Thompson Diary, AHEC.

50 Clark, *The Soldier's Offering,* 31-32.

their starting point, about-faced, and resumed firing, Wells recalled that the field in front of him "was sadly strewn with our fallen." The cost of that slow retreat was staggering. The 34th lost 215 men during the battle, more than 40% of their initial complement, and most of them fell in this movement.[51]

The slaughter was not yet done. The 54th Pennsylvania was also going forward. Col. Jacob Campbell apparently never saw Thoburn or received any orders to charge; but when the 1st West Virginia lurched into their advance Campbell decided he had better follow suit. The 54th's portion of the line, closest to the turnpike, was at a lower elevation than that of the 1st or 34th; in addition, the same cedar grove that hindered the Union cavalry advance provided additional cover for the Pennsylvanians. From here, the Pennsylvanians could see little of the main fight off to their right, a problem only exacerbated by the heavy firing. "The smoke was so thick I could see nothing in front," admitted one Keystoner. Unwittingly, the 54th was marching into a deadly trap.[52]

The 54th numbered 566 officers and men, a strong force, and had they confronted only the now-battered 62nd Virginia they might have prevailed. The 62nd was short almost 200 men from their own earlier foray, plus the inevitable stragglers, and now probably numbered close to 400 men. The Virginians were also still trying to recover their own composure. However, with Stahel's cavalry shattered and Ewing's Federal battery cleared off, Colonel Patton now needed something else to do. Patton, exercising brigade command due to Echols' indisposition, moved the 22nd and 23rd Virginia northward east of the Valley Pike. Realizing that the 54th Pennsylvania's left flank was now dangerously exposed, Patton and wheeled the 550 men of the 22nd to take advantage of that fact. The result was devastating.[53]

Bereft of support on either flank, the 54th's advance stalled well short of the 62nd Virginia's front. The Pennsylvanians' charge began well, with "alacrity and spirit," but as Campbell's line crested the little rise and emerged at the edge of the cedars, instead of impetuously flinging themselves at the enemy, the 54th halted and began to exchange

---

51 *OR* 37, pt. 1, 84; Knight, *Valley Thunder*, 180-181.

52 *OR* 37, pt. 1, 86; Bennett, "Four Years with the Fifty-Fourth," 31.

53 Confederate losses from the cavalry fight had been minimal.

volleys with the 62nd. Here, noted Campbell, "a rapid, vigorous, and, as I believe, effective fire was for some time kept up on the enemy. . . ."[54]

The decision to stop and engage in a static firefight was a serious blunder, one Campbell did not explain. The fact that he was wholly unsupported on his left, and that the 1st West Virginia had already given way to his right, probably had a lot to do with his decision to halt. Remaining in that spot, exchanging repeated volleys with an enemy line that overlapped the Pennsylvanians' front on both flanks is less explicable. Campbell's hesitation only let additional Confederate troops maneuver to take advantage of his exposed position.

And maneuver they did. Colonel Patton's Virginians delivered a crippling flanking fire into the 54th's naked left. Then things grew even grimmer for the 54th. "The enemy," Campbell reported, "pressed forward his right . . . and was rapidly flanking me in that direction . . . when it was called to my attention that the regiment on my right . . . [the 1st West Virginia] had given way." Rebels from the left wing of the 62nd Virginia were now advancing into this gap as well, threatening to completely surround the Keystoners. With the disaster now apparent, Campbell ordered a retreat.[55]

The Pennsylvanians gave ground stubbornly, halting to check pursuit via well-delivered volleys at least twice; and though they also paid a heavy price (174 killed, wounded or missing, plus at least 30 more slightly wounded who stayed in ranks) they did not break. Their repulse, however, marked the turning point in the battle of New Market. Victory was now out of Sigel's grasp. All that was left to do was to save the army from annihilation.

54   *OR* 37, pt. 1, 86.

55   Ibid.

CHAPTER 9

Conclusion—Late Afternoon, May 15, 1864

ith the rout of his cavalry, the repulse of his infantry counterattack, and with his only remaining fresh troops still a couple of miles short of the field, Franz Sigel had shot his offensive bolt. Though Sigel's army was stronger overall, poor deployment and inept troop handling meant that the Federals now could no longer win this battle. This did not mean, however, that a Confederate triumph was assured. The Yankees were wavering, but some formations were still effective. Could the Rebels make one final effort to crush Sigel once and for all?

They could. That effort began on the Union right, still anchored on the high bluff of Bushong Hill.

When the Federal line advanced, Carlin's and Snow's artillery both ceased fire. The gun crews had a panoramic view as each Union regiment—the 1st West Virginia, then the 34th Massachusetts, and finally the 54th Pennsylvania—was first checked and then driven rearward. At least some of the infantry, noted one of Carlin's West Virginia gunners, did so "in a perfect panic." As the cannoneers leapt back to their guns and prepared to re-engage, however, they discovered a new threat coming from their right.[1]

The bluff bordering the river was too steep for artillery to fire immediately down the slope. To cover this blind spot (dead ground, in military parlance) Sigel posted an ad-hoc battalion comprised of two

---

1 *Wheeling Daily Intelligencer,* May 21, 1864.

companies of the 12th West Virginia and one drawn from the Massachusetts 34th, probably 180 men all told, as a flank guard. These men were stationed to the artillery's right-rear. Who commanded this force, what happened to them, or even where exactly they were positioned remains unclear. Observing the Union position, Confederate brigade commander John Wharton realized that the bluff offered him an opportunity. By working their way along the river, Rebel infantry could approach that deadly gun line from the flank, and under cover.

Colonel Edgar's 26th Virginia Battalion had already plugged the gap left by the 51st Virginia's retreat and subsequently rebuffed the 34th Massachusetts, but Edgar's circumstances were not without complications. Some of Edgar's people were intermingled with men of the 51st, and at least a portion of the 26th's line lay draped over the crest leading down to the river on the right, enmeshed in woods and out of Edgar's direct view or control.

As noted previously, Edgar sent Capt. Edmund S. Read of the 26th to go hunt up Wharton, seeking orders, which resulted in the bulk of the 26th plugging the gap left by the 51st. That accomplished, now Edgar sent Read to find Wharton a second time, relaying updated information. "Capt. Reid of Edgar's battalion," noted Wharton, "ran up to me and said that Col. Edgar's battalion was cut off by the bluff, at the same time saying that there were some Federals down the bluff." Wharton's next decision was potentially fraught with danger. He now ordered Read to take personal charge of that cut-off portion of the 26th and drive forward. Once Read had driven off those Yankees below the crest, he and his half-battalion were to climb that slope and assail the right flank of Carlin's battery. The danger lay in Wharton intention to split the 26th while under a galling fire. That movement, if misunderstood, could lead to the sudden collapse and rout of the entire 26th Virginia, duplicating the crisis brought on when the 51st broke. Instead, the maneuver worked as planned. "As my battalion advanced," Edgar reported, "a portion was detached to dislodge a flanking party of the enemy that had taken position in the cliffs near the river."[2]

Curiously, Read's own account of this incident, though accurate enough in most particulars, strikes a false note concerning Wharton's

---

2   Gabriel C. Wharton, "Forty Years Ago," *Staunton Spectator and Vindicator*, May 20, 1904; Edgar Report, Edgar Papers, UNC.

Brigadier General Gabriel C. Wharton.

Miller, *Photographic History of the Civil War*

personal behavior. While moving through the timber below the bluff, Read "claimed he spotted General Wharton hiding behind a tree to his left, yelling 'Charge, Read, charge—for God's sake!'" Read, who in the words of one contemporary was "a man of strong prejudices," took affront at what he considered to be this example of cowardice on Wharton's part.[3]

Read was almost certainly mistaken about Wharton's actions here. Wharton had a clear purpose in mind; one that precluded accompanying Reed and his fellow 26th Virginians into a headlong rush forward with just a few companies. Instead, the brigadier was now trying to get his whole line re-engaged. "With the idea to take that battery [Carlin's] and thus turn their right flank, I placed myself on the left company of the 51st [Virginia]," explained the brigadier. He had grasped at the outset that the bluff was the key to Sigel's line, and was he was now attempting to re-ignite the 51st's advance in support of Read's effort.[4]

Federal opposition below the bluff all but melted away. Sigel's ad-hoc combined battalion of men drawn from the 34th Massachusetts and 12th West Virginia, tasked with holding the flank here, now broke at the first onslaught. Read exulted that "on gaining the top of the hill the enemy's sharpshooters at once fled from their position . . . I had

3   Lowry, *26th Battalion*, 39. Read's accusation appears to stem from a vigorous post-war dispute between the 26th Virginia and the 51st Virginia about the capture of three of Carlin's cannon. Wharton supported the 51st's claim. Historian Charles Knight, in *Valley Thunder,* 197, believes that Read was trying to discredit Wharton to bolster the 26th's competing claim.

4   Wharton, *Staunton Spectator*, May 20, 1904.

completely overlapped the enemy's right flank." Delighted with his easy success, Read noted that "I [now] half-wheeled, fired, and we rushed the guns." Carlin's cannoneers proved game enough for the fight. They sprang to their tubes, pivoting to engage Read's Rebels, now appearing on the crest. Carlin might have held on, given sufficient support, for the climb up the bluff left the Confederates in considerable disorder, more a jumbled mass than a battle line. However, one West Virginia gunner now noticed another problem: "Snow's battery on our left limbers to the rear and retires." The Union center was suddenly giving way.[5]

Snow's Marylanders knew nothing of Wharton's flank movement, but they were plenty unsettled by the earlier repulse of the abortive Union infantry assault. Artillery Private John J. Gray recollected that the 1st West Virginia Infantry refused to rally after their failed charge. Even 31 years later, Gray vividly remembered how "an officer of the 34th Mass . . . call[ed] to the crowds of infantry as they went to the rear . . . but the response was 'To ___ with the 34th; we are going across the bridge.'" Gray, focused on the crisis to his front, went so far as to insist that "there was no flank movement made by the rebels. If they had made a flank movement they would have taken us sure, as not more than a thin skirmish line stayed to support us." Gray, of course, was mistaken, but the collapse of the infantry line flummoxed him, driving all other aspects of the fight from his consciousness.[6]

Snow's Marylanders were not reacting to Reed's flank movement; as Gray's account proved, they couldn't even see it occurring. Instead their attention was riveted on the Rebel center, where Col. Edgar and his half of the 26th Virginia—along with Col. Scott Shipp's VMI battalion—were now also advancing from the vicinity of the Bushong orchard, converting Wharton's flanking effort into a general advance. This movement so alarmed the Federals that it induced Lt. Lucius A. C. Gerry (who commanded the battery while Snow was serving as Sigel's chief of artillery) to order his guns away. Perhaps Gerry lost his nerve, fearing to lose the pieces now under his charge. Or perhaps Snow ordered him to leave, since both the 1st West Virginia and the infantry support over the bluff had apparently abandoned them. Neither man made a report of

---

5   Read to Edgar, March 29, 1906, Edgar Papers; Knight, *Valley Thunder*, 189.

6   John J. Gray, "New Market," *National Tribune*, March 14, 1895. In that article Gray is incorrectly identified as a member of Battery B, 1st Pennsylvania Light Artillery, but his service records place him as a member of Snow's Battery B, 1st Maryland Light Artillery.

Lieutenant Colonel Scott Shipp, wounded in the Bushong orchard. *Library of Congress*

their actions on May 15. In his diary, Snow recorded only that "the battery . . . retired slowly and sullenly feeling [we] were made to retire without cause." Their departure, however sullen, was another blow to the morale of the fast-crumbling Union line.[7]

To further complicate matters, Sigel's reserve regiment now balked. The 12th West Virginia, fragile reed that it was, remained Sigel's last uncommitted infantry formation. When Carlin's and Snow's batteries were first threatened, Sigel returned to the West Virginians and "immediately ordered two companies of the 12th . . . to advance and protect the pieces, but to my surprise, there was no disposition to advance; in fact, in spite of entreaties and reproaches, the men could not be moved an inch!"[8]

Colonel Edgar's report is also unclear on the exact nature of his advance. He reported that in order "to cooperate with and protect the detachment referred to, the Battalion was thrown further forward during *the pursuit* [emphasis added] than the rest of the line." Edgar's account of the engagement compressed a great deal. In fact, most of the Confederate accounts describing this stage of the fight conflate their various tactical movements, the final charge, and the breaking of the last Union line as a single event. Almost certainly because he fell, wounded in the Bushong orchard just before that advance began, Col. Scott Shipp's description of the VMI Cadets' participation embraced only two terse sentences: "Our line took a position behind a line of fence. A brisk fusillade ensued; a shout, a rush, and the day was won."[9]

---

7   Daniel Carol Toomey and Charles Albert Earp, *Marylanders in Blue: The Artillery and the Cavalry* (Baltimore: 1999), 40.

8   Sigel, "Sigel in the Shenandoah Valley," 489.

9   Edgar Report, Edgar Papers, UNC; *OR* 37, pt. 1, 91.

Captain D. H. Bruce of the 51st Virginia offered a bit more detail. Bruce managed to rally his company of the 51st back in the "loblolly field" when Cpl. John Wampler called for Bruce's attention. "Captain, the Yankees are running on the left." Looking around, "I saw some two or three hundred yards off, Derrick's Battalion [actually, the 26th Virginia] going toward the enemy. I gave the command, 'Attention!' which brought my company to their feet; then I told them to 'Forward! Double-quick! Charge!' My company and the whole left raised that old Rebel yell, and at them we went." Bruce's line, upon which a number of other 51st'ers rallied, reached the open field north of the orchard in time to see that the Federals "had their horses to the artillery and were starting [away.] I gave the command to 'Fire left oblique into that artillery!'"[10]

Snow's Marylanders were already limbered and departing, fast disappearing out of sight behind the crest of Bushong Hill. They suffered only a few casualties in both men and livestock. By contrast, Carlin's West Virginians were just starting to pull out when Bruce's fire struck.

Sigel had already ordered Carlin to retreat by section from the right, a command that was now hopelessly out of date. The hail of Confederate musketry converted Carlin's retreat into an ordeal. Retiring from the left, the No. 1 gun managed to limber and depart, though the driver was shot and killed. No. 2 escaped without loss, though two of the horses "were skipped with balls, making their hair fly." The No. 3 piece had three horses cut down while limbering. The surviving team managed to move the gun a short distance before the dead animals snared the harness; it would fall into Rebel hands. No. 4 never got off at all. Four horses were shot before the gun could even be limbered. It was left in place, seized by either Read's men or troops from the 51st Virginia. No. 5 also had three animals struck, all badly wounded, but they managed to haul the gun back "600 yards" before collapsing. Ultimately that gun was also abandoned. No. 6 lost a caisson after several men and horses were hit but did manage to get off the field.[11]

---

10 Bruce, "Battle of New Market, Va," 554. In this account, written in 1907, Bruce was clearly mistaken about seeing Derrick's 23rd Virginia Battalion. The 23rd was not on the Confederate left, but instead all the way over on the right, nearly a mile distant.

11 Sigel, "Sigel in the Shenandoah Valley in 1864," 489; "Carlin's Battery," *Wheeling Intelligencer,* May 23, 1864.

Carlin's retreat left von Kleiser's New Yorkers as the only Federal guns still in action, holding position about halfway between the crest of the bluff on the Union right and the Valley Turnpike.

Colonel Shipp might have confined his report to a few terse words, but others would have much more to say about VMI's advance. Eventually to loom large in the lore of the war, VMI's participation here would draw praise from friend and foe alike. Captain Henry A. Wise, who inherited command of the cadets upon Shipp's wounding, ran down the cadet line from the flank (He had been leading A Company) to the battalion center. "Get up from here," Wise shouted, "and give the Yankees hell!" Up they went, but, ensconced behind a fence at the north end of the orchard, first the cadets had to scale that obstacle to close with their foe. To Cadet Pvt. John C. Howard of Richmond, aged 18, the task seemed daunting. "It was an ordinary rail fence, probably about four feet high, but as I surmounted the top-most rail I felt at least ten feet up in the air and the special object of hostile aim."[12]

The VMI contingent then surged towards von Kleiser's guns. Federal witnesses, their memories perhaps misted by time and reconciliation, praised the advance fulsomely. Lieutenant Colonel Lincoln of the 34th Massachusetts recalled that the cadets "marked time, dressed their ranks, and when again aligned on the left came forward in most admirable form. The whole thing was done with as much precision and steadiness as if on parade, and this while all the time subjected to a destructive fire. No one who saw it will ever forget it." Lincoln would have additional reason to remember the moment.[13]

Similar praise came from the pen of Howard Morton, a lieutenant in Captain Ewing's Battery G, the 1st West Virginia Light Artillery. It will be recalled that Ewing's guns had fallen back earlier, once their cavalry support was gone, and came to rest at some distance from the fight. "We look to the further end of the Rebel line," wrote Morton. "Out from an orchard steps a small body of gray-clad troops. Something about them attracts our attention. Their marching and alignment are perfect. . . .

12 William Couper, ed., *The Corps Forward: The Biographical sketches of the VMI Cadets who Fought in the Battle of New Market* (Buena Vista, VA: 2005), 234; John C. Howard, "Recollections of New Market," 59.

13 William S. Lincoln, "Battle of New Market," *Confederate Veteran*, vol. 26, no. 2 (February 1918), 85.

Their movements those of a crack battalion on dress parade. They look like boys; the [field] glasses show they are boys."[14]

Other Federals added their praise. Among them, Major Theodore Lang thought the charge "gallant." Captain Franklin Town, mounted and positioned behind von Kleiser's guns, described the charge as "wild" rather than precise, but was nonetheless mesmerized. "I . . . was so absorbed in the spectacle that it did not occur to me that I might be included in the capture. . . ."[15]

The cadets themselves recalled the affair as being considerably less than parade-worthy. Their descriptions of this final movement tallied more closely with Captain Town's "wild charge" than with Lincoln's or Morton's versions. Cadet Frank Preston of Company B noted that once over or through the fence, "the company organizations were gone, yet [we] rallied round the colors and formed some sort of a line as we advanced." Fourteen-year-old J. B. Baylor recalled that the fence was "demolished" where he lay, and that several Confederates from other units had climbed into a big tree nearby, "evidently picking off the gunners from the enemy's guns in front of us." The cadets, thought Baylor, were becoming a little "demoralized" while lying stationary, but responded with a will when ordered to move. "It seems to me that we advanced practically with unbroken ranks, and that as we charged, the men of the first line of battle charged *en masse* with us."[16]

Those men included the 62nd Virginia. As noted previously, the 54th Pennsylvania, out on the Union left, found itself taking fire from the front and both flanks after the collapse of the 1st West Virginia. Colonel George H. Smith, commander of the 62nd, ordered his regiment forward again once the fire of the 22nd and 23rd Virginia began to shred the Pennsylvanians' left. Smith always insisted that no other Confederates ever advanced ahead of his own men, or ahead of Col. Patton's (Echol's) forces, but, as Smith confessed in 1906, "my observation was not directed to the field west of me, to which the operations of [Edgar's 26th Virginia]

14 Howard Morton, "Cadets at New Market," *Richmond Dispatch*, November 17, 1895.

15 Knight, *Valley Thunder*, 198.

16 Preston Cocke, "New Market," *The Bivouac Banner*, online Civil War Journal, vol. 3, issue 1 (Spring 2004), www.bivouacbooks.com. accessed June 8, 2011; J. B. Baylor to Henry Wise, June 6, 1909, New Market Collection, VMI.

battalion and the corps of cadets were confined. As to that portion of the field, therefore, my mind is a perfect blank."[17]

Instead, Smith's attention was focused on the 54th Pennsylvania. Threatened with encirclement, Colonel Campbell reported that "I was reluctantly compelled to order my command to retire." Lieutenant George W. Gageby of the 54th recorded that "[we] stood our ground till all other regts and batteries had left, then as we were being outflanked, [we] left in disorder." Much later, in a letter to former Cadet Benjamin Colonna, Gageby jested that when "we discovered some of your people passing around our right . . . we acted on the principle that he who fights and runs away may live to fight another day."[18]

Meanwhile, General Wharton's efforts to get his whole line moving simultaneously were paying off. Captain Read's half of the 26th Virginia was scaling the bluff, Col. Edgar's portion was advancing, and the 51st was also moving again, savaging Carlin's battery. Still with the 51st's left, Wharton recalled that "I . . . moved forward as rapidly as possible, the whole command on my right [also] moving forward—on emerging from a grove or collection of large trees we were met with columns of infantry and rapid fire of grape and canister from the battery in my immediate front which was, it was supposed the extreme right of the Federal line. . . . Fortunately for those of us who were charging the battery, their firing was too low, the ground, a wheat field having been tramped over, was very muddy and soft. The balls when striking the ground did not ricochet, but threw up much mud, at times almost blinding us. . . . "Wharton, still with the 51st, surged up the hill where he could lay claim to "two guns."[19]

That accomplished, Wharton turned his attention to the 34th Massachusetts, which along with von Kleiser's guns represented the last vestige of Sigel's center. "I could see that I had turned the right flank . . . but that the center and right of my line was hotly engaged. . . . In a few minutes the gallant

---

17 Smith to Edgar, March 16, 1906, Edgar Papers, UNC.

18 *OR* 37, pt. 1, 86; George W. Gageby to Colonna, December 19, 1910, and May 27, 1911, New Market Collection, VMI.

19 Wharton, "Forty Years Ago," *Staunton Spectator*.

and daring Edgar had turned his battalion and coming up opportunely . . . broke the enemy's line."[20]

Colonel William Wells of the 34th Massachusetts was absorbed in the fight to his front. "The alignment [was] perfected and the men well at work [when] I was able to look about the field and saw, to my surprise, that the artillery had limbered up and was moving off . . . and that the infantry had gone, save one regiment [the 54th, itself about to retreat] gallantly holding its ground far to the left." Next Wells spotted "two [enemy] battle-flags on the hill" threatening his own right flank. "I ordered a retreat, but they either could not hear or would not heed the order. I was finally obliged to take hold of the color bearer, face him about, and order him to follow me."[21]

It is unclear when exactly von Kleiser's battery began their own retreat. Wells's reference to "the artillery" in his report refers to Carlin and Snow, not the New Yorkers, but he also specifies that the only force still in place to his left was "one regiment of infantry"—clearly the 54th. In any case, with the Rebels now atop Bushong Hill and enfilading the 34th's right flank, holding firm was tantamount to suicide. True to form, initially Wells attempted a slow, controlled withdrawal, halting periodically to deliver fire into the ranks of his pursuit, "but the rebels were coming on at the double-quick and concentrating their whole fire upon us. I told the men to run and get out of fire as quickly as possible, and rally behind the first cavalry line found to the rear."[22]

Now virtually all of Sigel's battle line was in shambles, falling back rapidly to the north. Here and there scattered bands of Federals attempted to reform—these included Wells's efforts, while Lieutenant Gageby recorded that the 54th Pennsylvania made similar interim stands three times—but the overall Union line had collapsed. Confederate Surgeon Isaac White of the 62nd Virginia marveled that "I never have seen such havoc."[23]

Havoc it was. All over the field, figures in blue were running, and gray figures gave chase, seizing prisoners and trophies. Von Kleiser's

20 Ibid.

21 *OR* 37, pt. 1, 84.

22 Ibid.

23 Knight, *Valley Thunder,* 203.

battery limbered hurriedly, getting off four of their five effective pieces. The last gun had to be abandoned, the stricken horse team unable to get it away. Cadet Sergeant Oliver Evans, the battalion color bearer, leapt astride the scorching gun, wild with excitement. Nearby, other cadets captured Lieutenant Colonel Lincoln of the 34th, wounded, but not so bad as to be incapacitated. Initially Lincoln thought to resist, a notion soon put to rest by the menace of cadet bayonets. He was not happy. Captain J. W. Parsons of the 18th Virginia Cavalry chanced upon him some time later, recalling that Lincoln, now under guard, "was very indignant at being a prisoner in the hands of the vile Rebels. He walked back and forth like a chained bear."[24]

This left the 12th West Virginia all alone, still in column of division, massed on the slope of Bushong Hill, behind the former position of Snow's and Carlin's batteries. Sigel was here as well; members of the 12th mentioned his presence. "Gen. Sigel is a brave man," marveled one of them, Lt. Milton Campbell. "[He] sat on his horse during the whole engagement, part of the time in front and part of the time in rear of our regiment. He was as cool as if he had been on review." Sigel himself noted that "my own position during the battle was in the line between the batteries on the right and the 34th Massachusetts (Colonel Wells), as on the right the principal attack of the enemy was directed."[25]

Sigel later described a curious situation with the 12th, which reflected badly on the West Virginians. In his description of the fight for *Battles and Leaders*, Sigel insisted that when the artillery was first threatened, "I immediately ordered two companies . . . to advance and protect the pieces, but to my surprise there was no disposition to advance; in fact, despite entreaties and reproaches, the men could not be moved an inch!" According to the German's narrative, this incident happened before Sigel observed the initial Confederate repulse and ordered Thoburn's brigade to charge, not as the guns were departing. This failure to engage, coupled with the incident where the 12th mistakenly followed him, were reasons

---

24 Knight, *Valley Thunder*, 199; J. W. Parsons, "Capture of Battery at New Market," 119.

25 Linda Cunningham Fluharty, ed., *Civil War Letters of Lt. Milton Campbell, 12th West Virginia Infantry* (Baton Rouge: 2004), 105; Hewitt, *History of the Twelfth Regiment*, 112.

Sigel felt he was "chained" to the right, and offered up as excuses why he could not manage the whole field.[26]

Now, with the blue line shattered and running, the 12th felt overwhelmed. Surging Confederates "were by this time nearly upon us," wrote Lieutenant Campbell, and "had flanked us on both right and left. Their line 3 columns (of 2 men) deep, ours only two, and their line extending halfmile beyond ours on both flanks. Their sharpshooters killed a number of horse attached to our artillery, and we were compelled to retire before them leaving 5 pieces of artillery in their hands."[27]

The collapse was now complete. Of the Federal senior officers, Colonel Moor had already gone in search of the elusive 28th and 116th Ohio, whom Sigel mistakenly believed (thanks to Captain Prendergast) would appear at any minute. In fact these Ohioans had not yet even reached Rude's Hill. General Sullivan was trying to restore order without much success. Finally, Colonel Wells of the 34th (who by this time was also wounded, hit in the shoulder and leg) met up with General Sullivan somewhere north of Bushong Hill, who told him that the new "line would be formed on the ridge [Rude's Hill] and no stand made before it was reached." Colonel Thoburn, embarked on a similar endeavor, told much the same thing to Campbell of the 54th Pennsylvania, who reported that he attempted "two stands . . . by a portion of the command, before passing beyond musket-range, and the whole of [the 54th] finally rallying and forming at a point indicated by the colonel [Thoburn] commanding the brigade."[28]

Sigel was doing his utmost to save cannons. At one point he came upon von Kleiser. The artillerist was trying to get one of his cannon across a small creek, unable to make any headway due to the mud. This gun was the piece disabled by Rebel shellfire earlier in the fight, now dismounted from its shattered carriage and slung under a limber. Sigel lent a hand. "I tried my best to save it," he recalled, "and was nearly made a prisoner by the enemy's skirmishers who followed us." Sigel escaped, but the damaged gun did not.[29]

---

26 Sigel, "Sigel in the Shenandoah Valley," 489.

27 Fluharty, *Civil War Letters of Lt. Milton Campbell*, 105.

28 *OR* 37, pt. 1, 85-86.

29 Sigel, "Sigel in the Shenandoah Valley." 490.

While admitting to "some confusion and scattering of our forces," Sigel insisted that "very soon order was restored." A new line formed "opposite the Dunker Church . . . west of the turnpike, . . . about three quarters of a mile from the battlefield." From "here we could see a dark line on Rude's Hill, and discovered the line of the 28th and 116th Ohio."[30]

These two regiments, plus Capt. Henry A. Dupont's Battery B of the 5th US Artillery were halted at Mount Jackson when Colonel Moor's messengers found them and ordered them to the front. Colonel James Washburn of the 116th took charge of this movement, leading the way with his own men and five companies of the 28th Ohio. The movement proved arduous. Lieutenant Colonel Thomas Wildes of the 116th recalled that "we had moved to the front in a violent rainstorm on the double quick, or run, for a distance of about four miles . . . arriving on the field in an exhausted condition, and too late to do anything, except cover the retreat of the broken up and defeated regiments." Upon reaching Moor atop Rude's Hill, Washburn "stated that he had ordered bayonets to be fixed to clear his way on the pike . . . through disgraceful fleeing masses of cavalry and straggling infantry."[31]

Captain Dupont, angry at being left behind when Sullivan was called forward earlier, made his own way to action. The sounds of the fight were clearly audible, and the 26-year old regular army captain wanted nothing more than to be in the thick of things. "Finally," he recalled, "after a delay which seemed endless, the order came, [and] the battery moved to the front at a sharp gallop, arriving . . . between 2:30 and 3:00 p.m." Dupont apparently moved up and over Rude's Hill without meeting either Moor, Sullivan, Sigel or Stahel. Instead, he recalled, "I was at once pounced upon by a number of young and inexperienced staff officers who proceeded to give me . . . the most absurd and contradictory orders. . . ." Ignoring them, Dupont instead deployed his battery by sections alongside the Valley Pike from south to north, each pair of guns about 500 yards apart. Dupont now employed the tactic, of "retiring by echelon of platoons," intending to provide cover for the withdrawing infantry. Returning to his lead section, commanded by Lt. Charles Holman, Dupont then engaged the Rebels "until we found ourselves

30   Ibid.

31   Wildes, *Record of the One Hundred and Sixteenth Regiment*, 38; *OR* 37, pt. 1, 80.

Brigadier General Jeremiah C. Sullivan.
Library of Congress

entirely alone. . . . Telling Holman that 'we had to get out of this,'" Dupont ordered a retreat. Holman was to "take the best position he could find" about 500 yards behind the last section, while Dupont retired to and fought with each of the other sections, successively, until all had disengaged. It was as cool and as capable a performance as any seen on the field that day, a testimony to the professionalism of the regulars involved.[32]

Realizing that his reinforcements were at last on hand, Sigel ordered his scratched-together line to fall back and form on the 28th and 116th. That was accomplished without further disruption. Once there, Sigel conferred with General Sullivan. Except for the two newly arrived regiments, all the men were short of ammunition and the southern slopes of Rude's Hill would be exposed to Rebel artillery fire. Neither officer wanted to renew the engagement with the swollen Shenandoah at their back, and with their sole line of retreat being the bridge. They decided to continue to retire all the way to Mount Jackson.[33]

Theywould do so unhindered. With the Federals in flight, John C. Breckinridge struggled to regain control of his infantry. At 3:15 p.m., he ordered a halt. "The men are a little scattered," Breckinridge informed Col. Edgar, "I want you to detail an officer and have him take some men

32 Du Pont, *The Battle of Newmarket*, 16-17. Du Pont was a brave and capable officer. He would be awarded the Congressional Medal of Honor for his actions at Cedar Creek the following October, but his version of the battle of New Market appears overblown. Du Pont claims, for example, that he was not part of the line on Rude's Hill, received no orders from any senior commander to retreat, and was acting entirely on his own authority until the army retreated to Woodstock, which seems highly unlikely. Du Pont's narrative was first published 59 years after the battle, when Du Pont was 84 years old.

33 Sigel, "Sigel in the Shenandoah Valley," 490.

with him to the rear and gather up the stragglers. . . ." The Kentuckian was not, however, ready to quit the fight: "I think the enemy is reforming on [Rude's] Hill, and we will have to charge them." Edgar complied, detailing Lt. William W. George of Company H for the task.[34]

That task proved daunting, for Rebels were finding good pickings all over the field. Discarded Union knapsacks, haversacks, and equipment lay everywhere. It was a fine opportunity for men with worn-out gear to re-equip themselves. Among the spoils was one item now rare and much prized in Confederate ranks. Virginia Sharpshooter John Schowen noted with satisfaction that "we made . . . coffee which we captured on the field, which I thought was very good." Fellow Virginian Thomas W. Fisher gloated over his gains in a letter home: "Most all our boys got oil cloths, overcoats and blankets, boots and so on. I got a splendid gum cloth."[35]

Additionally, there was the matter of ammunition. Like the Federals, many Rebels had emptied their cartridge boxes during the Bushong Hill fight. "After following the defeated and fleeing enemy nearly a mile," recalled General Wharton, "Gen'l Breckinridge ordered a halt to reform his line and supply the men with ammunition . . . [we] had to wait for the ordnance wagons to be brought up." Attending to these details took a long time—too long, in fact. By the time Breckinridge's line was ready to resume the advance, Sigel's army was departing.[36]

"As soon as the ammunition was distributed," Wharton continued, "we pressed forward again. [T]he enemy seem[ed] to be preparing to make a stand on Rude's Hill, and did fire a few shots, but before my skirmish line got within 1/2 mile they disappeared, and when we reached the top of the hill their rear was near the bridge and beyond our pursuit."[37]

Here again, Breckinridge missed his cavalry. General Imboden, it will be recalled, had taken Breckinridge's entire mounted force northward along the east bank of Smith Creek, looking for a crossing place, seeking to turn Sigel's left. That effort proved wholly unsuccessful. This decision left Imboden and his troopers as nothing more than spectators:

34 Knight, *Valley Thunder*, 210.

35 Schowen, "Civil War Diary," 7: Knight, *Valley Thunder*, 211.

36 Wharton, "Forty Years Ago," *Staunton Spectator*.

37 Ibid.

Witnessing as first Sigel's cavalry broke rearward, and subsequently, the blue-clad infantry followed suit. Frustrated at being unable to ford the swollen creek, Imboden finally turned back south tore-cross the water course on the Luray Road, where he encountered Breckinridge while the latter was reforming his line. There was no time for finesse; now Breckinridge ordered Imboden to lead the Confederate cavalry "straight down the pike towards the enemy" atop Rude's Hill. Before ought could come of this, however, Wharton's men occupied the crest and saw off the last the Yankees.[38]

By that time, most of the Federals were already across the turnpike bridge. Dupont's guns were covering the last of the retreat. Chapman's Virginia Battery, McClanahan's horse artillery, and the two outdated VMI guns unlimbered atop Rude's Hill to engage what was left of Sigel's bedraggled army. A short artillery duel ensued, though by now, gathering darkness limited visibility. One of McClanahan's gunners was sure their fire wreaked havoc among "panic-stricken" Federals, but in fact, little damage was done. Captain Dupont and one Union cavalry company were the last to cross; and once across, they fired the bridge. The battle of New Market was over.[39]

38 Woodward, *Defender of the Valley*, 112.

39 Knight, *Valley Thunder*, 212-213.

CHAPTER 10

Aftermath

The battle of New Market cost the Union army 97 men killed, 440 wounded, and 225 missing, most of which became prisoners; for a total of 762 losses. The Confederate toll was about 600. Though Sigel's army numbered more than 8,000 men, only about 60% of that force was engaged on May 15; no more than 5,400 infantry, cavalry and artillery. Of those, only about 2,750 infantrymen bore the greatest share of the fight and suffered the bulk of the casualties. Another 1,340 men—in the form of the 28th and 116th Ohio—were present for the final moments on Rude's Hill but fired few shots (if any) and suffered no losses. Even the 5,400 figure might be high, for Sigel's need to secure his rear made for numerous oft unaccounted-for detachments. In Moor's brigade, the 18th Connecticut had only seven companies present, the 123rd Ohio, six; similar shortages plagued other units, especially the cavalry.

Sigel's artillery fought well. Though the cavalry performed poorly throughout the campaign, their failure at New Market was largely due to Stahel's disastrous decision to launch a grand charge, which fizzled miserably. The infantry proved to be a mixed bag, as might be expected of largely untested units; it is worth noting that Sigel's poor management meant that when the battle was joined, two of his three best infantry units, the 28th and 116th, played no role in the fighting. The infantry did well in defense, though they were often poorly deployed, and proved steady enough to repulse the Rebel attack on Bushong Hill, but things

The 54th Pennsylvania Infantry Regiment's Monument at New Market. *Author Photograph*

fell apart when they tried to advance. That mishap quickly turned to a rout, characteristic of green troops.

Breckinridge brought about 5,300 men onto the field, of which about 4,700 were engaged. He had the advantage in infantry, with about 3,300 men in action. His force contained only 350 artillerymen and roughly 1,000 troopers. As it turned out, his cavalry played no more of a role in the battle than did the Federal horse. Stahel's blunder was partially offset by Imboden's own poor decision to move east of Smith Creek, where he was isolated from the fight by the swollen stream, unable to cross. Though outmatched, the Rebel artillery performed credibly, and had much to do with driving off those same Federal cavalrymen. Breckinridge's infantry provided the key to victory. Even when checked, they rallied and counter-attacked. Fortitude in the face of a reverse was often the critical difference between veterans and inexperienced troops, a reality that paid off for John C. Breckinridge on May 15.

Sigel informed Washington of the repulse as soon as he was able, portraying the disaster as beyond his control. At 8:00 p.m., he wired that "a severe battle was fought to-day between our forces and those . . . under Breckinridge. Our troops were overpowered by superior numbers. . . . Under the circumstances prevailing I find it necessary to retire to Cedar Creek." That retreat began immediately. "We marched all night," noted Cpl. Jonas Kaufman of the 54th Pennsylvania. It continued the next day, amid pouring rains. While it was a miserable, demoralizing march, Sigel's little army fell back "unmolested," reaching Strasburg on the 16th.[1]

Sigel halted at Edinburg on the 16th, where he received Crook's dispatch announcing Union success at Cloyd's Mountain, and the subsequent temporary destruction of the New River Bridge. That news prompted a wisecrack by Col. David Strother: "We are doing a good business in this department," he sniggered. "Averell is tearing up the Virginia and Tennessee Railroad, while Sigel is tearing down the Valley Turnpike." Strother's jibe elicited a good laugh at Sigel's expense and spread quickly through the department, but no one knew at the time that Crook's bedraggled army was at that very moment in very like circumstances; in full retreat, struggling to cross the swollen Greenbriar River, and desperately short on rations.[2]

1   *OR* 37, pt. 1, 76; Henry Wilson Storey, *History of Cambria County Pennsylvania,* 2 vols. (New York: 1907), vol. 2, 107; Entry for May 16, Campaign Journal, Sigel Papers.

2   Eby, *Virginia Yankee,* 229.

On the 17th there occurred one of the more curious exchanges of the campaign. By the middle of May, Grant's opening strategy had become largely undone. His own powerful Army of the Potomac had just finished one bloody battle in the Wilderness and was currently grappling with Lee at Spotsylvania Courthouse. Benjamin F. Butler's thrust towards Petersburg had been blunted, then stopped; now Butler was dug in at Burmuda Hundred, well short of his objective. Worse yet (though Grant had yet to learn of it) Crook and Sigel were both falling back. Grant, hoping to leverage Lee out of his Spotsylvania earthworks, wired Halleck on the afternoon of May 17: "Cannot General Sigel go up the Shenandoah Valley to Staunton? The enemy is evidently drawing supplies largely from that source, and if Sigel can destroy the road there, it will be of vast importance to us."[3]

Of course, Staunton was Crook's objective. Sigel's role was to merely provide the escort for Crook's re-supply train. Now Crook was forgotten. Even more oddly, based on the wording, Grant was apparently still unaware that a battle had been fought at New Market, or its outcome; why had Halleck not informed Grant of those pertinent facts? He did so now. Dutifully, at 10 p.m. that same day, Halleck passed on Grant's instructions: "Lieutenant General Grant expects that you will go up the Shenandoah Valley to Staunton and destroy the railroad there, so as to prevent General Lee's drawing supplies from there." However, Halleck warned Grant not to get his hopes up. "Instead of advancing on Staunton," Halleck sneered, Sigel was "already in full retreat [to] Strasburg. He will do nothing but run. He never did anything else. The Secretary of War proposes to put General Hunter in his place." With that dispatch, Sigel's fate was sealed.[4]

In his memoirs Grant spun Crook's role in the campaign as completely successful. The "western column," noted Grant, "advanced . . . at the appointed time, and with more happy results. They reached the Virginia and Tennessee Railroad at Dublin and destroyed a depot of supplies, besides tearing up several miles of [rail] road and burning the bridge over

3   *OR* 37, pt. 1, 475.

4   *OR* 37, pt. 1, 475; *OR* 36, pt. 2, 840.

New River. Having accomplished this they re-crossed the Alleghenies to Meadow Bluffs and there awaited further orders."[5]

Certainly, Crook had achieved the first of his objectives—Dublin and New River—but what of the rest? What about Crook's role in taking Staunton, once considered the main objective of the Valley campaign, and still squarely in Grant's thoughts as of May 17? What of uniting Sigel and Crook to operate against Lee's rear? Crook's initial success, solid as it was, was rendered moot by the retreat to Meadow Bluffs. Instead of a decisive stroke, Crook's expedition was a nuisance to the Confederacy, nothing more.

Edwin Stanton's suggestion of a new commander was heartily endorsed by both Grant and Halleck. Major General David "Black Dave" Hunter departed Washington for Harper's Ferry on May 20. The next day, he rode south to Cedar Creek, a 38-mile journey, and assumed command of the Department of West Virginia.[6]

This meeting, while it could not have been pleasant for Sigel, was at least cordial. Sigel described it as a "friendly conversation," with Hunter "express[ing] his desire that I should remain in the department and accept command either of the Infantry Division, or of the Reserve Division, comprising all the troops at Harper's Ferry and the lines of the Baltimore and Ohio." Hunter found Sigel "actuated by an earnest patriotism" and "anxious to take a division of this army or [willing] to attend to any other duties." The two agreed that Sigel would return to Harper's Ferry and assume command of the reserve component. He departed the next day.[7]

Hunter's command tenure would be brief. His rise and fall complete by July 15. He began well enough, re-organizing Sigel's battered army and reinforcing it heavily, bringing in both Crook's column and some of the troops now freed up by the newly-arriving 100 days men brought up to guard the Baltimore and Ohio. The Federals headed south again on May 26, now more than 20,000 strong, against negligible opposition.

5   Ibid.

6   Edward A. Miller, Jr., *Lincoln's Abolitionist General: The Biography of David Hunter* (Columbia, SC: 1997), 166.

7   Sigel, "Sigel in the Shenandoah Valley," 491; Miller, *Lincoln's Abolitionist General*, 167.

Almost immediately after his victory at New Market, Breckinridge was ordered east to join Lee, leaving only Imboden to defend the Valley. With a scant 2,000 men, Imboden was powerless to stop Hunter. Once again Confederates scrambled to meet a Federal invader. "Grumble" Jones brought up another 4,000 men, virtually all the force in southwest Virginia, to unite with Imboden north of Staunton. On June 4, Imboden and Jones, now 5,500 strong, met Hunter's van of 8,500 at Piedmont. This time there would be no New Market. Instead, it was a replay of Cloyd's Mountain, a Union victory that resulted in the death of Jones and 1,500 Confederate casualties, to the tune of 875 Federals lost. Staunton fell, the warehouses pillaged and destroyed. Hunter now turned east, moving against the Confederate depot at Lynchburg. Though he could ill spare it, of necessity Lee dispatched Maj. Gen. Jubal Early and most of a Confederate infantry corps to defend that point.

Then Hunter, feeling isolated and awash in rumors of a massive defeat inflicted on Grant by Lee (why else would troops from the Army of Northern Virginia be free to rush to Lynchburg?) again opted to retreat. Instead of moving to Staunton and then turning northward down the Valley, however, Hunter chose to continue westward towards Gauley, in a reprise of Crook's decision the month before. As a result, Hunter's army would be incommunicado for ten critical days. This decision opened the door for Early to seize the initiative, turn northward, and launch a daring campaign that took him into Maryland and to the fortified outskirts of Washington DC. Grant had no choice now but to detach troops from the Army of the Potomac and rush them northward in turn. Hunter paid for his poor decision to move into West Virginia, being relieved in mid-July. He was replaced by the man who would ultimately finish the war in the Shenandoah Valley once and for all: Philip Henry Sheridan; reinforced to 40,000 men, including the Union VI Corps and most of the Army of the Potomac's cavalry.

*   *   *

Franz Sigel certainly committed his share of mistakes, even outright blunders, in the New Market campaign, for which he has received a full measure of historical blame. Indeed, Sigel has largely become a mockery, the convenient scapegoat upon which to heap all blame. However, very little effort has gone into exploring the larger strategic questions of the campaign or look beyond Sigel's supposed buffoonery to fairly analyze either his performance of that of the other players involved.

Despite his prickly personality and touchy sense of honor, Sigel tried hard to fulfill Grant's various (and changing) directives, even when those directives were counter-productive. Sigel gave Edward O. C. Ord his full co-operation, despite his dismay at Ord's arrival and their mutual antagonism. Ignoring his own misgivings, Sigel struggled to assemble Ord's troops at Bevery, until Ord displayed his moral cowardice by ejecting himself from the campaign on the eve of active operations. Unfortunately, Ord's unexpected presence and equally unforeseen departure wasted at least two critical weeks of Union preparations while the men marched back and forth uselessly between Beverly and Martinsburg.

Then there was the question of Sigel's efforts to train his troops, who desperately needed such instruction. Sigel's drills and mock battles were viewed as foolish by many of his men, but it was the men who were being foolish. Colonel Wells's arrogance provides a case in point. He found Sigel's maneuvers so ludicrous that after the first day's effort he faked illness rather than take the drill field again with his 34th Massachusetts Regiment. Had he put aside that arrogance he might have learned something. The 34th was able to drill with precision, but in combat, Wells's lack of actual battle experience contributed to the unnecessary deaths of some of his men. In that fateful counter-attack on Bushong Hill, when the time came to advance, Wells immediately lost control of his men, who rushed forward without regard to formation. Wells only regained tactical control by physically grabbing the color-bearer. When he realized that the Union advance was uncoordinated, Wells ordered his men to about-face and retreat at the common-time. Wells should have ordered his men back at the double-quick, preserving their lives, to reform again at the gun line. Instead the 34th suffered severely as they painstakingly made their way back to their original position. The 34th lost a staggering 30 killed, 151 wounded, and 54 missing at New Market. Perhaps a little more realistic drilling might have saved some of those men.

Nor was Sigel's slow progress towards New Market in the days leading up to the battle a blunder. Far from it; that advance pulled Breckinridge northward and left Staunton exposed to Crook's force, exactly as intended. The plan would have been successful had Crook not taken council of his fears and retreated to West Virginia—a retreat Sigel could not know about.

The decision to fight at New Market cannot really be laid at Sigel's feet, either. Instead, Stahel and Moor must shoulder the blame. Sigel's orders to Moor were clear, and if they weren't sufficient, when Stahel arrived the instructions he came with were even more explicit: fall back on Rude's Hill or Mount Jackson. For reasons never really explained, neither man complied with those orders. Had they done so, Breckinridge's efforts to rush to New Market and win a quick, decisive victory would have come to naught. Many years later, Charles Lynch of the 18th Connecticut recalled that "Colonel Moore . . . commander of our brigade, came in for much censure by our boys, for bringing on a general engagement before the arrival of the main forces." Indeed, by the time Sigel reached the field a wholesale retreat in the face of Breckinridge's army had become a more dangerous proposition; Sigel ran an equal risk in staying to fight as he did in retreating to Mount Jackson.[8]

Of course, Sigel is not without blame. Perhaps his biggest blunder can be found in the constant meddling with the chain of command, attaching and detaching brigades, regiments, and even companies willy-nilly, without regard to unit cohesion. Repeatedly this practice wrought havoc. Boyd's expedition to New Market, via Luray, on May 14 was once such disaster. Another was the confusion inherent during the Federal retreat on the morning of the 15th, when Moor ordered his advanced line back, with two regiments halting at the Rice house while two more fell back to Bushong Hill. Even worse, Sigel personally did nothing to sort out that confusion, leaving the two forward regiments (the 18th Connecticut and 123rd Ohio) to face Breckinridge's main line alone. Sigel should have ordered both regiments to fall back to Bushong Hill and join the Union main line at once, but he failed to act, or apparently even notice the blunder.

Sigel's misplaced confidence in, and misuse of, Julius Stahel must also be acknowledged. Sigel's high opinion of Stahel seems to have been based more on the Hungarian's shared revolutionary roots than in any demonstrated military skills. Though Stahel was brave enough,

---

8   "My dear sir," August 27, 1912, Charles Lynch to B. A. Colonna, New Market Collection, VMI.

he was not the man to meld Sigel's disparate cavalry oddments into a real division. Sigel further complicated matters when he also made Stahel his chief of staff. Each position was a full-time job, requiring the office-holder's full attention; no one short of Napoleon could likely have simultaneously filled both sets of boots effectively – and Stahel was no Napoleon. Sigel never grasped that his subordinate was overwhelmed and ineffective in the dual role.

Similarly, Sigel failed to make better use of Brig. Gen. Jeremiah Sullivan. Sigel routinely bypassed Sullivan, issuing orders directly to Sullivan's subordinates. Notably, Sigel's only mention of Sullivan during the battle of New Market comes at the very end of the fight, when Sigel and Sullivan meet at the last line and agree to retreat.

Sigel's worst decision was in ordering the counter-attack on Bushong Hill, which revealed the underlying fragility in Union morale. Here Sigel was adhering blindly to doctrine, failing to consider his command's actual capabilities, which were not up to an assault. Thanks to Sigel's impulsive meddling Colonel Thoburn, the nominal brigade commander, failed to co-ordinate that advance or control his line. Each regiment lurched forward individually, came to grief, and broke, with some men routing completely. By that stage in the battle, Sigel's position was admittedly difficult, with both flanks vulnerable to being turned, but the failed attack only exacerbated matters. Had Sigel opted to stand pat, would Breckinridge's line have charged again into the teeth of a steady infantry and artillery line, blazing with fire? Breckinridge's own men were not elite troops, driven forward by *elan* and the confidence of past victories. They were veterans, true enough, but that would have only meant that they understood the cost of such an assault better than green men. And, as Sigel should have understood it, anything short of a Union rout was a Rebel defeat, assuming Crook was wreaking havoc in the Rebel rear. In short, Sigel didn't have to win decisively, he just had to keep from losing decisively. He failed to grasp that reality.

One other general must come in for a large measure of criticism for the failures of the campaign: Ulysses S. Grant. Grant's concept of a subsidiary operation in the Valley was certainly sound, and potentially decisive if handled properly. The Valley was Robert E. Lee's vulnerable flank during the opening stages of the Overland campaign. Lee understood this, as borne out by his various communications with Breckinridge during the period.

However, Grant's handling of the details in the valley showed carelessness. Grant erred in two ways: first, he repeatedly undermined Sigel and disrupted the latter's plans; and second, he set forth ambitious objectives without allocating sufficient resources, especially manpower.

It is understandable that Grant would prefer an officer of his choosing in place of Sigel, in whom the regular army establishment (especially Halleck) had no confidence. However, once that selection was made, undermining Sigel with the introduction of Ord was poor leadership; and an example of Grant's often misplaced sense of loyalty over judgment. Ord's subsequent behavior was unbecoming of a military officer; childishly shirking responsibility because he feared blame. That Grant accepted and even rewarded that conduct does not speak well of Grant. It would have been far better to have let Sigel conduct his own campaign right from the start.

As for manpower, Grant seriously under-estimated the effect of Confederate guerrilla operations, both against the B&O and Sigel's own ever-lengthening supply lines. Grant assumed that Sigel could strip the rail line and advance virtually unopposed up the Valley to Staunton. The commanding general then greatly compounded the manpower problem by creating a third column for his pet, Ord; when there really weren't sufficient troops for Crook's and Sigel's expeditions, let alone another force advancing from Beverly.

What would have been the outcome had Grant been willing to spare an infantry division and perhaps a veteran cavalry brigade, each solidly led, from the Army of the Potomac? If Sigel's expedition had numbered 15,000 instead of 8,000? An advance beyond Woodstock would then become much more feasible. It is worth noting that in the battle of the Wilderness Grant led 120,000 men against Lee's 65,000 troops, and in the close woods of that battlefield many of those Federals could not be brought to bear effectively. With such a surplus of manpower, applying some of that strength to Lee's vulnerable flank only makes sense. Of course this is speculation; it is possible that Sigel might still have blundered even with twice the numbers, but the idea of turning Sigel's and Crook's individual pinprick operations into a real flanking force had merit. Grant should have devoted more thought to the concept.

And what of the Confederate side of the ledger? The Confederate performance has received considerably more scrutiny and has usually been judged much more positively. Certainly John C. Breckinridge took enormous risks, but on the whole he performed very well. For the most part he was decisive, even in the face of conflicting information, and maintained his resolve. He did not shirk to commit his whole force at the critical moment. He was also very lucky. Crook turned away at precisely the right time to save Staunton, despite Breckinridge stripping that place of any defenders, and Sigel's May 15 blunders in Breckinridge's front made the New Market victory possible.

Even Breckinridge's curious hesitation on the morning of May 15, when he was trying to induce Sigel to attack him on Shirley's Hill, did not redound to his detriment. Had Sigel's orders been executed properly, of course, Moor and Stahel would have marched away at that moment, frustrating Breckinridge's ambitious plans for a quick knockout blow , and potentially (as far as Breckinridge knew) leaving the Rebels trapped between the upper and lower millstones of Sigel and Crook. Instead, Moor and Stahel stayed put, waiting until Breckinridge launched his own attack. Even this delay did not hurt the Confederate commander; for instead of using the time to concentrate the Union army and establish a coordinated defense atop Bushong Hill, the Federals' fumbling re-deployments meant that Breckinridge could use his whole force to strike Federal dribs and drabs, ensuring tactical superiority during each part of the engagement. It is to Breckinridge's credit that he seized those opportunities when offered.

*   *   *

Though many Union soldiers viewed Sigel's replacement as a positive, there was considerable dissenting opinion, as well. Even Colonel Strother, by no means a Sigel supporter, felt a flash of sympathy when he saw the little German for the last time. On May 22· wrote Strother, I "called on General Sigel and gave him my journal completed to date of yesterday with a full description of the battle. The tears were standing in his eyes and his lips were quivering. He said it was better to have died on that battlefield than to have suffered this disgrace. I felt touched by his appearance. He is a stranger who has come over here to fight for a sentiment and he seems utterly cast down by his failure. . . ."[9]

---

9   Eby, *Virginia Yankee*, 232.

Colonel Joseph Thoburn expressed similar thoughts, confiding them to his diary on May 22: "Maj. Gen'l. Sigel was relieved yesterday by Maj. Gen'l David Hunter. I rejoice at the change; Hunter will be a very poor Gen'l indeed if he is not better than Sigel. The latter is a well-informed military man, honest and devoted to our cause, but he lacks the practical common sense that enables a man to adapt himself to circumstances. He has courage; still he becomes flurried when in action and his orders are not clear and prompt. I feel kindly toward the Gen'l—yet I would rather he would never have another command."[10]

Within the army, some regarded the battle as little more than a temporary check. Private Aungier Dobbs of the 22nd Pennsylvania Cavalry was not in the battle, being one of those detached to guard the railroad, but he was relieved that he could deny some of the initial rumors. Writing home on May 19, Dobbs was upbeat. "I hear the War news is favorable. Segle was not whipped as first reported it was only his advance guard that suffered."[11]

Sigel's relief engendered considerable comment. On May 22, as Hunter's arrival and Sigel's replacement became generally known, Fabricus A. Cather of the 1st West Virginia Cavalry felt that there was "much dissatisfaction among the troops, who have the greatest confidence in Maj. Gen. Sigel." Maryland gunner John Gray of Snow's battery, naturally enough, blamed the Union infantry for the defeat: "Had [they] stood their ground and charged the rebels after their lines had been broken, the battle of New Market would have been a victory for Sigel instead of Breckinridge." Additionally, however, Gray went out of his way to praise the German, insisting that "it was [only] by Sigel's cool generalship that he was able to save all his artillery."[12]

In his diary, Charles Lynch also thought the trade of Sigel for Hunter a bad one. On May 20 Lynch wrote: "General Sigel relieved of command. A good officer. Kind to his men. From the soldier's view we need more

---

10   Thoburn, Joseph, and Martin Beer, ed., *Hunter's Raid 1864. From the Diary of Colonel Joseph Thoburn* (Wheeling, WV: Thomas Beer, 1914), 6.

11   Ralph Haas and Philip Ensley, eds., *Dear Esther, the Civil War Letters of Private Aungier Dobbs, Centerville, Pennsylvania, Company "A," the Ringgold Cavalry Company, 22nd Pennsylvania Cavalry, June 29, 1861 to October 31, 1865.* (Apollo, PA: 1991), 211.

12   "Entry for May 22, 1864," Cather diary, West Virginia University; Gray, "New Market," *National Tribune*, March 14, 1895.

men in this, the Shenandoah Valley. Major General David Hunter now in command. Dark complexion, black moustache, stern looking." Gloomily, Lynch concluded, "we don't like his looks." Corporal Andrew Powell agreed. On May 23, 1864, Powell reported that "Gen. Sigel was relieved of his command yesterday by Maj. Gen. Hunter, so we no longer 'fights mit Sigel.' This change of commanders throws a deep gloom on the troops here as we were all strongly attached to and had the utmost confidence in our little Dutchman, and the past career of Gen. Hunter is famous for defeats and blunders. . . ." Hunter's very first orders, continued Powell, "displays the genius of a lunatic more than that of a man . . . able to . . . keep the same discipline of a Sigel."[13]

Even a soldier-correspondent in the 1st West Virginia echoed the support for their previous commander. In a *Wheeling Intelligencer* letter published on May 23, 1864, the correspondent provided a detailed description of the fight, finishing with these lines: "The soldiers in this command are highly pleased with the Gen'l commanding, and all see[m] glad of an opportunity to 'fight with Sigel.'" As for the battle, noted the writer, "the soldiers in this army are not demoralized over their late defeat, as they were not whipped, but overpowered by numbers; the enemy's force being ten . . . [or] twelve thousand while the entire force on our side did not exceed four thousand men."[14]

That supposed disparity of numbers became a common Union theme for explaining the outcome of the battle, exaggerated until, much as portrayed by the anonymous 1st West Virginian, Sigel faced imaginary odds of three-to-one. While the image of overwhelming Rebel numbers certainly helped salve Federal consciences, of course the reality was much different. Breckinridge brought no more men to the fight than did Sigel; he just employed them more effectively. In 1884, Lt. Col. Thomas Wildes of the 116th Ohio grasped the essential problem, though he did still accept the Federal conventional wisdom of being outnumbered. After New Market, remembered Wildes, "very few of us wanted to fight any more 'mit Sigel.' His army was beaten in detail. A small force was first sent into the fight, which was allowed to be first beaten, when another small force would be sent in, to be in turn beaten. Had he gotten his

---

13 Lynch, *Civil War Diary*, 62; "Brother Israel and dear friends," May 23, 1864, Powell Letters.

14 "Letter from the 1st West Virginia Regt," *Wheeling Intelligencer*, May 23, 1864.

army well in hand at first, and given battle with it, he might have been victorious, though the enemy under Breckinridge outnumbered us."[15]

Perhaps the *New York Times* said it best regarding this matter of overwhelming numbers:

> "We have one more victim of 'superior forces' to add to the long list which already adorns our military annals. Gen. SIGEL on Sunday last, 'fought the forces of ECHOLS and IMBODEN under BRECKINRIDGE, at New-Market,' and in consequence of the enemy's forces being superior in number, 'he gradually withdrew from the battle-field, having lost five pieces of artillery and six hundred killed and wounded.' Translated into simpler English, this means that he was well beaten, though not routed.
>
> One does not need to be a professional soldier to arrive at the conclusion, from what has happened in the course of this war, that fighting 'superior forces' of the enemy is a losing business. Some of our Generals are constantly doing it, and whenever they do it they are defeated.
>
> When a General, therefore, coolly informs us—and how many Generals have done so!—that he voluntarily, and with the choice of staying quiet or retreating open to him, assails a much heavier force than his own, and gets badly thrashed, it is simply a euphemistic mode of informing us that he is either a very stupid or a very inhuman person.
>
> Our advice to them is—and we offer it with becoming deference, and with the full knowledge that it is not to be found in JOMINI—that whenever they find the enemy in greatly superior force (and they find him in this condition apparently very often) they had better let him alone. He is apt under these circumstances to be dangerous."[16]

Dangerous indeed.

---

15 Wildes, *Record of the One Hundred and Sixteenth Regiment*, 87-88. Of course, much of that piecemeal generalship Wildes lamented should really be laid at the feet of Moor and Stahel.

16 "Gen'l Sigel's Repulse – Its lesson," *New York Times*, May 19, 1864.

Appendix: Order of Battle

CONFEDERATE
Maj. Gen. John C. Breckinridge

Echol's Brigade: Brig. Gen. John Echols
22nd Virginia Infantry: Col. George S. Patton
23rd Virginia Infantry Battalion: Lt. Col. Clarence Derrick
26th Virginia Infantry Battalion: Lt. Col. George M. Edgar

Wharton's Brigade: Brig. Gen. Gabriel C. Wharton
30th Virginia Infantry Battalion: Lt. Col. J. Lyle Clark
51st Virginia Infantry: Lt. Col. John P. Wolfe

Northwestern Brigade: Brig. Gen. John D. Imboden
18th Virginia Cavalry: Col. George W. Imboden
23rd Virginia Cavalry: Col. Robert White
62nd Virginia Mounted Infantry: Col George H. Smith
Co. A, 1st Missouri Cavalry: Capt. Charles Woodson
Davis's Maryland Cavalry Company: Capt. T. Sturgis Davis
2nd Maryland Cavalry Battalion: Maj. Harry Gilmor

Chapman's Battery: Capt. George B. Chapman (6 guns)
Jackson's Battery: First Lt. Randolph H. Blain (4 guns)
McClanahan's Battery: Capt. John McClanahan (6 guns)
VMI Cadet Battery (1 Section): Cadet Capt. Collier H. Minge (2 guns)

UNATTACHED
VMI Cadet Battalion: Lt. Col. Scott Ship
Co. E, 3rd Confederate Engineers: First Lt. M. W. Long
Rockingham and Augusta County Reserves: Col. William Harman

UNION
Maj. Gen. Franz Sigel
First Infantry Division: Brig. Gen. Jeremiah C. Sullivan

First Brigade: Col. Augustus Moor
18th Connecticut Infantry (7 companies present): Maj. Henry Peale
28th Ohio Infantry: Lt. Col. Gottfried Becker
116th Ohio Infantry: Col. James Washburn
123rd Ohio Infantry (6 companies present): Maj. Horace Kellogg

Second Brigade: Col. Joseph Thoburn
1st West Virginia Infantry: Lt. Col. Jacob Weddle
12th West Virginia Infantry: Col. William B. Curtis
34th Massachusetts Infantry: Col. George D. Wells
54th Pennsylvania: Col. Jacob M. Campbell

First Cavalry Division: Maj. Gen. Julius Stahel
First Brigade: Col. William B. Tibbits
1st New York (Lincoln) Cavalry: Lt. Col. Alonzo W. Adams
1st New York (Veteran) Cavalry: Col. Robert F. Taylor
21st New York Cavalry: Maj. Charles G. Otis
1st Maryland Cavalry Potomac Home Brigade: Maj. J. T. Daniel
14th Pennsylvania Cavalry: Capt. Ashbel F. Duncan

Second Brigade: Col. John E. Wynkoop
15th New York Cavalry: Maj. H. Roessler
20th Pennsylvania Cavalry: Maj. R. B. Douglas
22nd Pennsylvania Cavalry: Lt. Caleb McNulty

Artillery: Capt. Alonzo Snow
Battery B, 1st Maryland: Lt. G.A.C. Gerry (6 guns)
Battery B, 5th U.S.: Capt. Henry A. Dupont (6 guns)
30th New York Battery: Capt. Alfred von Kleiser (6 guns)
Battery D, 1st West Virginia: Capt. John Carlin (6 guns)
Battery G, 1st West Virginia: Capt. Chatham T. Ewing (4 guns)

Bibliography

Manuscripts

Army Heritage and Education Center (AHEC) Carlisle Pennsylvania
    Albert Artman Diary (14th Pennsylvania Cavalry)
    William M. Ellis Letters (123rd Ohio Infantry)
    Peter Gamache Memoir (34th Massachusetts Infantry)
    George W. Imboden Letter (18th Virginia Cavalry)
    David Powell Memoir (12th West Virginia Infantry)
    George W. Thompson Diary (34th Massachusetts Infantry)

Bowling Green State University, Bowling Green Ohio
    Leander M. Coe Diary, Dorothy Ringle Papers (123rd Ohio Infantry)

East Carolina University, Greenville North Carolina
    George Duncan Wells Letterbook (34th Massachusetts Infantry)

Jasper County Public Library, Rensselaer Indiana
    Robert H. Milroy Papers

Lake Forest College, Lake Forest, Illinois
    William Mays Recollections (22nd Virginia Infantry)

Library of Congress, Washington DC
    Julius Stahel Papers

Ohio Historical Society, Columbus Ohio
    Josiah Staley Papers (123rd Ohio Infantry)
    Henry W. Ocker Letters (28th Ohio)

Rutherford B. Hayes Presidential Library, Fremont Ohio
    Andrew Powell Letters (123rd Ohio)

Stanford University, Stanford California
    EOC Ord Papers

University of California, Bancroft Library, Berkeley California
    EOC Ord Papers

University of Illinois, Illinois Historical Survey, Urbana Illinois
    Augustus Moor Papers, Henrich Rattermann Collection

University of Iowa: Digital Collections
    Henry Brockway Diary (34th Massachusetts Infantry)

University of North Carolina, Chapel Hill North Carolina
    George M. Edgar Papers. (26th Virginia Infantry Battalion)
        George H. Smith Letter (62nd Virginia Mounted Infantry)
        Henderson Reid Letter (26th Virginia Battalion)
        Thomas C. Morton Letter (26th Virginia Battalion)

Virginia Military Institute, Preston Library, Lexington Virginia
    Michael Auer Letter (15th New York Cavalry)
    J. B. Baylor Letter (Cadet Battalion)
    John C. Breckinridge, Report of Operations
    B. A. Colonna Letter (Cadet Battalion)
    G. W. Dunford Letter (51st Virginia Infantry)
        "As a private saw the New Market fight."
    George M. Edgar Letter (26th Virginia Battalion)
    George W. Gageby Letters (54th Pennsylvania Infantry)
    James Haggerty Letter (18th Connecticut Infantry)
    James Hardin Papers (22nd Pennsylvania Cavalry)

    George W. Imboden Papers (18th Virginia Cavalry)

    J. Stoddard Johnson, "Sketch of Operations" (Breckinridge Staff)

    Theodore F. Lang, "Personal Recollections of the Battle of New Market."

    Charles Lynch Letter (18th Connecticut Infantry)

    Peter J. Otey file, address, "The War Cadets." (Cadet Battalion)

    John A. Porter Letters (51st Virginia Infantry)

Julian Pratt Letter (18th Virginia Cavalry)

C. H. Richmond Letter (18th Connecticut Infantry)

George H. Smith Letter

Virginia Polytechnic Institute, Blacksburg Virginia
    Henry C. Carpenter Letters (45th Virginia Infantry)
    Jacob Cohn Diary (54th Pennsylvania Infantry)
    Isaac White Letters

West Virginia State Archves, Charleston West Virginia
    Civil War Collection
        Theodore Cook Diary (2nd West Virginia Infantry)
        John N. Waddell papers and correspondence (12th West Virginia Infantry)
    John Prager Papers (1st West Virginia Infantry)

West Virginia University, Morgantown West Virginia
    Fabricus A. Cather Diaries (1st West Virginia Cavalry)

Western Reserve Historical Society, Cleveland Ohio
    Franz Sigel Papers

Newspapers

Abingdon Virginian (VA)
Johnstown Tribune (PA)
New York Times
Northampton Free Press (MA)
Oswego Times (NY)
Tiffin Weekly Tribune (OH)
Troy Daily Times (NY)
Wheeling Intelligencer (WV)

Published Primary Sources and Regimental Histories

Baldwin, Helene L, Michael Allen Mudge, and Keith W. Schlegel, eds. *The McKaig Journal: A Confederate Family of Cumberland.* Cumberland, MD: Allegany County Historical Society, 1984.

Beach, William H. *The First New York (Lincoln) Cavalry: From April 19, 1861 to July 7, 1865.* New York: The Lincoln Cavalry Association, 1902.

Bonnell, Jr., John C. *Sabres in the Shenandoah, the 21st New York Cavalry, 1863-1866.* Shippensburg, PA: Burd Street Press, 1996.

Brown, Joseph Alleine. *The Memoirs of a Confederate Soldier.* Abingdon, VA: Forum Press, 1940 (22nd Virginia Infantry).

Bruce, David H. "Battle of New Market, Va." *Confederate Veteran* 15, no. 12 (December 1907): 553 (51st Virginia Infantry).

Clapp, Henry S. *Sketches of Army Life in the Sixties and "The Mansion by the Spring," a Civil War Story of the Shenandoah.* Newark, OH: Mary Belle Clapp Cline and Kathrine B. Clapp Horton, 1910.

Clark, William H. *The Soldier's Offering.* Boston: J.C. Clark Printing, 1875 (34th Massachusetts Infantry).

Colonna, Benjamin A. "The Battle of New Market, VA." *Journal of the Service-Institution of the United States* no. 51, (November - December, 1912): 343-49 (Cadet Battalion).

Crook, George, and Martin F. Schmitt, eds. *General George Crook: His Autobiography.* Norman, OK: University of Oklahoma Press, 1946.

Delauter, Roger U. *18th Virginia Cavalry.* Lynchburg, VA: H. E. Howard, Inc., 1985.

——. *McNeill's Rangers.* Lynchburg, VA: H. E. Howard, Inc., 1986

——. *62nd Virginia Infantry.* Lynchburg, VA: H. E. Howard, Inc., 1988.

Dickenson, Jack L. *Diary of a Confederate Sharpshooter: The Life of James Conrad Peters.* Charleston, WV: Pictorial Histories Publishing Co., Inc., 1997 (30th Virginia Battalion Sharpshooters).

Donald, Robert Bruce. *Manhood and Patriotic Awakening in the Civil War. The John E. Mattoon Letters, 1859-1866.* Lanham, MD: Hamilton Books, 2008 (21st New York Cavalry).

Drickamer, Lee C., and Karen D. Drickamer, eds. *Fort Lyon to Harper's Ferry: On the Border of North and South with "Rambling Jour": The Civil War Letters and Newspaper Dispatches of Charles H. Moulton (34th Mass. Vol. Inf.).* Shippensburg, PA: White Mane Publishing, 1987.

Driver, Robert J. *The Staunton Artillery - McClanahan's Battery.* Lynchburg, VA: H. E. Howard, 1988.

Du Pont, Henry A. *The Battle of Newmarket, Virginia, May 15, 1864.* Washington, DC: H. A. Du Pont, 1923 (Battery B, 5th U.S. Artillery).

Duncan, Richard R., ed. *Alexander Neil and the Last Shenandoah Campaign.* Shippensburg, PA: White Mane Publishing, 1996 (12th West Virginia Infantry).

Early, Jubal Anderson. *Autobiographical Sketch and Narrative of the War Between the States.* Philadelphia: J. B. Lippincott Company, 1912.

Eby, Jr., Cecil D. ed. "With Sigel At New Market: The Diary of Colonel D. H. Strother," *Civil War History* 6, no. 1 (March, 1960.): 73-83.

Eby, Jr., Cecil D., ed. *A Virginia Yankee in the Civil War: The Diaries of David Hunter Strother.* Chapel Hill: University of North Carolina Press, 1961.

Farrar, Samuel Clarke. *The Twenty-Second Pennsylvania Cavalry and the Ringgold Battalion 1861-1865.* Pittsburgh, PA: The Twenty-Second Pennsylvania Ringgold Cavalry Association, 1911.

Fitz-Simmons, Charles. "Sigel's Fight at New Market, VA." *Military Order of the Loyal Legion of the United States,* (70 vols), Vol. 12. Wilmington, NC: Broadfoot, 1992..

Fluharty, Linda Cunningham, ed. *Civil War Letters of Lieutenant Milton B. Campbell, 12th West Virginia Infantry.* Baton Rouge, LA: Linda Cunningham Fluharty, 2004.

Gatch, Thomas B. "Recollections of New Market." *Confederate Veteran* 34, no. 6 (June, 1926): 210-12.

Gilmor, Harry. *Four Years in the Saddle.* London: Longmans, Green and Co., 1866.

Grant, Ulysses S., with John F. Marsalek, ed. *ThePersonal Memoirs of U. S. Grant. The Complete Annotated Edition.* Cambridge, MA: Harvard University Press, 2017.

Gray, John J. "New Market," *National Tribune*, March 14, 1895 (Battery B, 1st Maryland Light Artillery).

Grant, Ulysses S. "Preparing for the Campaigns of '64," *Battles and Leaders of the Civil War* 4, New York: Thomas Yoseloff, 1956.

Haas, Ralph, and Philip Ensley, eds. *Dear Esther, the Civil War Letters of Private Aungier Dobbs, Centerville, Pennsylvania, Company "A," the Ringgold Cavalry Company, 22nd Pennsylvania Cavalry, June 29, 1861 to October 31, 1865.* Apollo, PA: Closson Press, 1991.

Heatwole, John L. *"Remember Me is all I Ask," Chrisman's Boy Company, A History of the Civil War Service of Company A, 3rd Battalion, Virginia Mounted Reserves.* Bridgewater, VA: Mountain and Valley Publishing, 2000.

Hewitt, William. *History of the Twelfth West Virginia Volunteer Infantry, the Part It Took in the War of the Rebellion 1861-1865.* Charleston, WV: The Twelfth West Virginia Infantry Association, 1892.

Howard, John C., "Recollections of New Market." *Confederate Veteran* 34, no. 2 (February, 1926): 57-59 (Cadet Battalion).

Imboden, John D. "The Battle of New Market, VA, May 15th, 1864." *Battles and Leaders of the Civil War,* 4 vols. New York: Thomas Yoseloff, 1956.

Keyes, Charles M. *The Military History of the 123rd Regiment Ohio Volunteer Infantry.* Sandusky, OH: Register Steam Press, 1874.

Laine, J. Gary, and Morris M. Penny. *Law's Alabama Brigade in the War between the Union and the Confederacy.* Shippensburg, PA: White Mane Publishing Company, 1996.

Lang, Theodore F. *Loyal West Virginia from 1861 to 1865, With an Introductory Chapter on the Status of Virginia for Thirty Years Prior to the War.* Baltimore: The Deutsch Publishing Co., 1895.

Lincoln, William S. *Life with the Thirty-Fourth Mass. Infantry in the War of the Rebellion.* Worcester, MA: Noyes, Snow and Co., 1879.

William S. Lincoln. "Battle of New Market." *Confederate Veteran* 26, no. 2 (February, 1918): 84-85.

Lowry, Terry D. *22nd Virginia Infantry.* Lynchburg, VA: H. E. Howard, 1988.

———, *26th Battalion Virginia Infantry.* Lynchburg: H. E. Howard, 1991.

Lynch, Charles H. *The Civil War Diary, 1862-1865, of Charles H. Lynch, 18th Connecticut Volunteers.* Hartford: The Case, Lockwood & Brainard Co., 1915.

Mays, William. *Four Years for Old Virginia.* Los Angeles: Swordsman Publishing Co., 1970 (22nd Virginia Infantry).

Morton, Howard. "Cadets at New Market." *Richmond Dispatch*, November 17, 1895 (Cadet Battalion).

O'Ferrall, Charles T. *Forty Years of Active Service.* New York: The Neale Publishing Company, 1904 (23rd Virginia Cavalry).

Parsons, J. W. "Capture of a Battery at New Market." *Confederate Veteran* 17, no. 3 (March, 1909): 119 (18th Virginia Cavalry).

Phillips, Edward L. *Wheeling's Finest: A History Of Battery "D" First West Virginia Light Artillery, From The Wheeling Daily Intelligencer.* Wheeling, WV: Edward L. Phillips, 2002.

Potts, J. N. "Who Fired the First Gun at New Market?" *Confederate Veteran* 17, no. 9 (September, 1909): 453.

Rawling, Charles J. *History of the First Regiment Virginia Infantry. Being a Narrative of the Military Movements in the Mountains of Virginia, in the Shenandoah Valley and East of the Blue Ridge during the War of the Rebellion, of the First Regiment Virginia Infantry Volunteers - Three Months' and Three Years' Service.* Philadelphia: J. B. Lippincott Co., 1887.

Schowen, John. "Civil War Diary of John Schowen," *The Vandalia Journal,* (October 1984, and January, 1985), 1-9 (30th Virginia Battalion Sharpshooters).

Scott, Johnny Lee. *23rd Battalion Virginia Infantry.* Lynchburg, VA: H. E. Howard, Inc. 1991.

Sigel, Franz. "Sigel in the Shenandoah Valley in 1864." In *Battles and Leaders of the Civil War,* 4 vols, edited by Robert Underwood Johnson, and Clarence Clough Buel. New York: Thomas Yoseloff, 1956.

Simon, John Y., ed. *The Papers of Ulysses S. Grant*, 31 vols. Carbondale, IL: Southern Illinois University Press, 1982.

Smith, George W. "More on the Battle of New Market," *Confederate Veteran* 14, no. 11 (November, 1908): 570 (62nd Virginia Infantry).

Snyder, Edmund P. *Autobiography of a Soldier of the Civil War*. Privately Printed, 1915 (123rd Ohio Infantry)

Stanard, Beverly, John G. Barrett, and Robert K. Turner, Jr., eds. *Letters of a New Market Cadet*. Chapel Hill: University of North Carolina Press, 1961.

Stephenson, Darl L. *Headquarters in the Brush: Blazer's Independent Union Scouts*. Athens: Ohio University Press, 2001.

Stevenson, James H. *"Boots and Saddles": A History of the First Volunteer Cavalry of the War Known as the First New York (Lincoln) Cavalry, And Also as the Sabre Regiment, Its Organization, Campaigns, and Battles*. Harrisburg, PA: Patriot Publishing Company, 1879.

Storey, Henry Wilson. *History of Cambria County Pennsylvania,* 2 vols. New York: Lewis Publishing Co., 1907 (Includes diary of Jonas B. Kauffman, 54th Pennsylvania).

Swiger, Elizabeth Davis, ed. *Civil War Letters and Diary of Joshua Winters*. Parsons, WV: McClain Printing Company, 1991 (1st West Virginia Infantry).

Thoburn, Joseph, and Martin Beer, ed. *Hunter's Raid 1864. From the Diary of Colonel Joseph Thoburn*. Wheeling, WV: Published by Thomas Beer, 1914.

Thompson, Edwin Porter. *History of the Orphan Brigade*. Louisville, KY: Lewis N. Thompson, 1898.

Walker, William Carey. *History of the Eighteenth Regiment Conn. Volunteers in the War for the Union*. Norwich, CT: Published by the Committee, 1885.

Warner, Charles. "Who Fired the First Gun at New Market?." *Confederate Veteran* 17, no. 5 (May, 1909): 237.

Wert, Jeffry D. *Mosby's Rangers*. New York: Simon and Schuster, 1990.

Wharton, Gabriel C. "Forty Years Ago," *Staunton Spectator and Vindicator*, May 20, 1904.

Wildes, Thomas Francis. *Record of the One Hundred and Sixteenth Regiment, Ohio Infantry Volunteers in the War of the Rebellion*. Sandusky, OH: I.F. Mack & Bro. Printers, 1884.

Williams, Edward B., ed. *Rebel Brothers: The Civil War Letters of the Truehearts*. College Station, TX: Texas A & M University Press, 1995.

Wilson, Robert B. "The Dublin Raid," in *G.A.R. War Papers*. Cincinnati, OH: 1891.

Wise, John S. *Battle of New Market, Va. May 15th, 1864.* Lexington, VA: Hall of the Dialectic Society, n.p., 1882.

Secondary Sources

Ackinclose, Timothy R. *Sabres and Pistols: The Civil War Career of Colonel Harry Gilmor, C. S.A.* Gettysburg: Stan Clark Military Books, 1997.

Bennett, Jr., Charles W. *"Four Years with the Fifty-Fourth" The Military History of Franklin Bennett, 54th Pennsylvania Volunteer Regiment, 1861-1865.* Richmond, VA: Charles W. Bennett, Jr., 1985.

Bright, Simeon Miller. "The McNeill Rangers: A Study in Confederate Guerrilla Warfare." *West Virginia History* 12, no. 4 (July, 1951): 338-87.

Collins, Darrell L. *The Jones-Imboden Raid.* Jefferson, NC: McFarlands, 2007.

Connelly, Thomas Lawrence. *Autumn of Glory: The Army of Tennessee, 1862-1865.* Baton Rouge: Louisiana State University Press, 1971.

Couper, William, ed. *The Corps Forward: The Biographical sketches of the VMI Cadets Who Fought in the Battle of New Market.* Buena Vista, VA: Mariner Publishing, 2005

Davis, William C. *The Battle of New Market.* New York: Doubleday, 1975.

Davis, William C. *Breckinridge: Statesman, Soldier, Symbol.* Baton Rouge: Louisiana State University Press, 1992.

Duncan, Richard R. "The Raid on Piedmont and the Crippling of Franz Sigel in the Shenandoah Valley." *West Virginia History* 55, (1956): 25-40.

Engle, Stephen Douglas. *Yankee Dutchman: The Life of Franz Sigel.* Fayetteville: University of Arkansas Press, 1993.

Feis, William B. "Grant's Relief Man: Edward O.C. Ord." In edited by Steven E. Woodworth, *Grant's Lieutenants from Chattanooga to Appomattox.* Lawrence: University of Kansas Press, 2008. 173-194.

Gordon, Larry. *The Last Confederate General: John C. Vaughn and his East Tennessee Cavalry.* Minneapolis: Zenith Press, 2009.

Gottfried, Bradley M. *The Maps of Gettysburg.* New York: Savas-Beatie, 2007.

Hallock, Judith Lee. *Braxton Bragg and Confederate Defeat,* Vol. II. Tuscaloosa: University of Alabama Press, 1991.

Knight, Charles R. *Valley Thunder: The Battle of New Market and the Opening of the Shenandoah Campaign, May 1864.* El Dorado Hills, CA: Savas Beatie LLC, 2010.

McManus, Howard Rollins. *The Battle of Cloyd's Mountain: The Virginia and Tennessee Railroad Raid, April 29 - May 19, 1864.* Lynchburg, VA: H. E. Howard, 1989.

Magid, Paul. *George Crook: From the Redwoods to Appomattox*. Norman: University of Oklahoma Press, 2011.

Miller, Jr., Edward A. *Lincoln's Abolitionist General: The Biography of David Hunter*. Columbia, SC: University of South Carolina Press, 1997.

Newton, Steven H. *Lost for the Cause: The Confederate Army in 1864*. Mason City, IA: Savas Publishing Company, 2000.

Piston, William Garrett, and Richard W. Hatcher III. *Wilson's Creek: The Second Battle of the Civil War and the Men Who Fought It*. Chapel Hill: University of North Carolina, 2000.

Quarles, Garland R *Occupied Winchester 1861-1865*. Winchester, VA: Winchester-Frederick County Historical Society, 1991.

Ramage, James A. *Rebel Raider: The Life of General John Hunt Morgan*. Lexington: University Press of Kentucky, 1986.

Robertson, James I. *Stonewall Jackson: The Man, The Soldier, The Legend*. New York: McMillen Publishers, 1997.

Sears, Stephen W. *Gettysburg*. Boston: Houghton Mifflin, 2003.

Shea, William L., and Earl J. Hess, *Pea Ridge: Civil War Campaign in the West*. Chapel Hill: University of North Carolina, 1992.

Smith, Theodore Clarke. *The Life and Writings of James Abram Garfield*, 2 vols. New Haven, CT: Yale University Press, 1925.

Snell, Mark A. *From First to Last: The Life of Major General William B. Franklin*. New York: Fordham University Press, 2002.

Toomey, Daniel Carol, and Charles Albert Earp. *Marylanders in Blue: The Artillery and the Cavalry*. Baltimore: Toomey Press, 1999.

Turner, Edward Raymond. *The New Market Campaign, May, 1864*. Richmond, VA: Whittet & Shepperson, 1912.

Warner, Ezra J. *Generals in Blue: Lives of the Union Commanders*. Baton Rouge: Louisiana State University Press, 1964.

Woodward, Harold R. *Defender of the Valley: Brigadier General John Daniel Imboden C.S.A. Shenandoah Valley*. Berryville VA: Rockbridge Publishing Co, 1996.

Online Resources

Charles J. Rawling, *History of the First Regiment Virginia Infantry*, accessed 1 July 2013, http://www.lindapages.com/wvcw/1wvi/1wvi-20.htm.

Accessed 5 June 2013, http://newmarketbattle.blogspot.com/2010/07/alfred-von-kleisers-other-gun-lost-at.html.

Accessed 26 January 2016, http://www.shenandoah.stonesentinels.com/Mount_Jackson/ A26-Cavalry_Engagement.php.

Preston Cocke, "New Market," *The Bivouac Banner*, online Civil War Journal, 3, no. 1 (Spring 2004), accessed 8 June 2011, www.bivouacbooks.com.

R. F. Taylor to Wife, Camp near Strasburg Va., May 17, 1864, online auction catalogue, accessed 18 April 2010, http://www.mqamericana.com/Col_Taylor_1st_NY_Vet_Cv.html.

Thomas Winton Fisher Papers, accessed 18 November 2012, http://ted.gardner.org/ twfhome.htm.

Index

Altman, Albert, 111, 128
Artillery, Confederate, 41
Artillery, Union, 61, 199
Auer, Michael, 127-128
Averell, William W., 50, 57, 65, 69, 73-74, *photo, 85;* fails to take objectives, 85-86

Babcock, Orville E., 50-51
Baltimore and Ohio Railroad, 2, 11, 29-30, 47, 54, 90, 91, 208
Banks, Nathaniel P., 7-8
Baylor, J. B., 190
Beach, William L., 109, 118-119
Belle Grove, 100
Berryville Virginia, 101
Beverly West Virginia, 45, 47, 62
Blain, Randolph, 174
Blazer, Richard R., 69
Blazer's Scouts, 69, 71, 73
Boyd, William H., 109-110, 111, 114, 117, 118-120, recklessness of, 122
Bragg, Braxton, 34, 35, 79, 123
Breckinridge, Fort, 76
Breckinridge, John C., assigned to command, 33, *photo, 33;* background of, 33-35, 36, 37, 38, 41, 70, 74, 75, 78, 79, 99, 102, 103, 105, 123, meets with Imboden, 124; 133, 135, 138-139, hides deployments, 140-141; decides to attack, 150; addresses cadets, 151; 174, 178, 196, 198, 201, 204; evaluation of, 209
Bristol Tennessee, 29
Brockway, Henry, 142
Brough, John, 93
Brown, Joseph A., 161
Bruce, Daniel H., 171-172, 188
Buckner, Simon B., 36-37
Buell, Don Carlos, 2
Bunker Hill West Virginia, 64, 89
Butler, Benjamin F., 7-8
Bushong Hill, 134, 136, 141, 158, 166, 168, 183, 188, 194
Bushong House, 169, *photo, 179*

Campbell, Jacob, 96, 181, 182, 191
Campbell, Milton, 193-194
Carlin, John, 158, 183, 188
Carter, John J., 175
Cather, Fabricus A., 102, 210
Cedar Creek, 100
Chapman, William, 112
Charlestown West Virginia, raid on, 30
Chase, Katherine, 21
Chickamauga, Battle of, xii
Christianburg Virginia, 84
Clapp, Henry S., 160, 161

Clark, William, 148, 180
Clausewitz, Karl, 7
Cloyd's Mountain, 79, 80-81, casualties
  at, 82; news of, 201
Coe, Leander, 142
Colonna, Benjamin A., xi, 138, 191
Confederate units: *Engineers, 1st,* 38
Connecticut units: *Infantry, 18th,* 51,
  53, 54, 111, 125, 145, 147, 148,
  152, 154, 157, 162, casualties, 163;
  168, 199
Coverstone, Andrew, 121
Cowan, Robert, 121
Crabill, "Davey," 117-118
Crawford, James S. A., 76
Crook, George, 43-44, *photo, 43;* 45,
  49, 51, 65-66, 68, 69, 71, 77, at
  Cloyd's Mountain, 80-82; decides
  to retreat, 84-85; 86, 101, 106,
  108, 144, 201, 203
Culver, Benjamin, 54
Cumberland Maryland, 11, 45, 98-99

Davis, Jefferson, 74,
Davis, Sturgis, 102-103, 113,
Davis, William C., historian, x, 107,
  140,
Derrick, Clarence, 175,
Desertion, 40,
Dickenson, Crispin, 79,
Dogs, 55,
Dobbs, Aungier, 209,
Douglas, Robert W., 129,
Droop Mountain, battle of, 39-40,
Du Pont, Henry A., 61, 195-196,
Dunford, George W., 133, 172,
Dublin Virginia, 70, 78, 80, occupied
  by Federals, 83; 105,

Early, Jubal A., 32, 204
East Tennessee, Confederate
  Department of, 36
Echols, John, 40, 70, health of, 124;
  138, *photo, 139;* 181

Edgar, George M., 137, 139-140, 150,
  169, 178, 187, 197
Edinburg Virginia, 88, 115, 117,
  125, 144, filled with stragglers,
  145-146; 201
Emancipation Proclamation, 3
Evans, Oliver, 193
Ewell, Richard S., 13

Fayettesville West Virginia, 71
Fisher, Thomas W., 33, 197
Fitzsimmons, Charles, 96, 164
Fort Donelson, battle of, 40
Fort Valley, 115, 121
Franklin, William B., 8
Front Royal Virginia, 88, 106, 110

Gageby, George W., 191, 192
Garfield, James A., 21
Gauley Bridge West Virginia, 69, 204
George, William W., 197
German-Americans, 16-17, 22
Gerry, Lucius A. C., 186
Gettysburg campaign, 28
Gilmour, Harry, 30-31, 103-104,
  113-114
Grafton West Virginia, 62
Grant, Ulysses S., xii, 1, 3-4, 6-7,
  photo, 5; 43, plans Valley
  Campaign, 44-45; 48, 50,
  reportedly defeated at battle of
  the Wilderness, 84, 101, 106; 202;
  criticism of, 207-208
Gray, John J., 186, 210
Griswold, John A., 60

Haggerty, James, 158, 162
Halleck, Henry W., 1, 4-5, 13, pre-war
  reputation of, 20; 93, 202
Hardin, James, 40
Harper's Ferry West Virginia, 27
Harrisonburg Virginia, 88
Hawkinstown Virginia, skirmish
  at, 113

Hayes, Rutherford B., 66, *photo, 67;* 73, 83
Heintz, Carl, 149
Hewitt, William, 54, 171
Higgins, Jacob, 93, 97, 98, *photo, 98;* errors of, 122
Hill, A. G., 155
Hoffman, R. C., 142
Holman, Charles, 195-196
Hooker, Joseph, 21, 57
Howard, John C., 155, 189
Hunter, David, 203

Imboden, Francis, 28
Imboden, George W., 28, 124
Imboden, John D., 9, background of, 26-27; *photo, 27, 135;* assigned to command, 29, criticized by Lee, 31-32, 88, 98, 107, 114, 119, 122, meets with Breckinridge, 124; 129, 131, 135, 139, executes feint, 140; 151, 164, 165, 197-198

Jackson, Thomas J., "Stonewall," 2
Jackson, William L., 31, 70
Jenkins, Albert G., 70, *photo, 75;* 75-76, 79, 81, mortally wounded, 83
Johnston, Joseph E., 6
Jones, John H., execution of, 40
Jones, Samuel, 29, 31, *photo, 32;* replaced, 32-33
Jones, William E. "Grumble," 9, 28, 37, 78, 80, 204

Kaufman, Jonas, 201
Kelley, Benjamin F., 9, *photo, 10;* 12, 144
Kellogg, Dwight, 161
Kellogg, Horace, 53, 125, 160
Kentucky units, Confederate: *Cavalry, 5th,* 80, 83
Kirkpatrick, J. D., 39
Kerr, Robert, 147

Knight, Charles R., historian, x, 107, 178
Knoxville Tennessee, 29

Lacey Spring Virginia, 124, 133
Lang, Theodore F., 52, 136-137, 146-147, 148, 154, 190
Lee, Robert E., 2, 29, 30, 38, 74-75, 105, 123, 204
Lester, Jacob, 174
Lewisburg West Virginia, 66, 70, 71, 74, 144
Lexington Virginia, 71
Lincoln, Abraham, 1, 13
Lincoln, William S., 55, 89, 170, 189, 193
Longstreet, James, 29, 36, 101
Luray Valley, 106, 110, 117
Lynch, Charles H., 111, 132, 147, 162, 206, 210-211
Lynchburg Virginia, 204

Manor's Hill, 134
Martinsburg, 2, 61, 91, 122
Maryland units: *Artillery, B, 1st,* 61, 126, 158, 186, 188; *Cavalry, 1st Potomac Home Brigade,* 58
Massachusetts units: *Infantry, 34th,* 51; and dogs, 55; 62, 89, 94, 95, 125, 130, 134-135, 142, 148, 158, 166, 169, 170, 179-180, casualties, 181; 184, 205
Massanutten Mountain, 88, 115, 117
Mattoon, John E., 176
Mays, William, 104, 175
McCausland, John C., 70, 74, 79, 83-84, 105, 141
McClanahan, John, 102, 164
McClellan, George B., 2
McCracken, William V., 53
McLaughlin, William, 141
McNeill, John Hanson "Hanse," 11, 30, 31, 56, raids Piedmont, 92; *photo, 92*

McReynolds, Andrew T., 60
Meade, George G., 4, 68
Meadow Bluff West Virginia, 84, 86
Meldrum, Norman H., 115
Mick, John, execution of, 41
Middleton, Gabriel, 60
Milroy, Robert H., 9, 13, 15-16,
    photo, 14
Minge, Collier, 174
Missouri units: *Cavalry, 1st,* 138, 173
Moor, Augustus, 51, 52, 115-116,
    117, 125, 126, 130-131, 134, 136,
    photo, 137; inaction, 143-144;
    148, 159, 163, 168, 194, 206
Moorfield West Virginia, 97
Morton, Howard, 189
Morton, Thomas C., 178
Mosby, John S., 11, 89, *photo, 91*
Moulton, Charles H., 62
Mount Crawford Virginia, 88, 123
Mount Jackson Virginia, 104, 106, 114,
    128, 145, 146, 168

Neil, Alexander, 61-62, 63, 167
New, Edwin, 111, 118-119
New Market, battle of, and losses, 199
New Market Virginia, 88, 106, 108,
    114, 123, 125, 128, described,
    133-134; 143, 144
New River Bridge, 44-45, 49, 78, 83
New York units: *Artillery, 30th,* 61,
    156, 157, 163, 166, 189, 193;
    Cavalry, 1st (Lincoln), 58-59, 101,
    109, 110, *1st (Veteran),* 58-59, 110,
    121, 174, *15th,* 58-59, 93, 97, 126,
    129, *21st,* 58-59, 60, 93, 96, 97,
    101, 110, 112, 115, 126, 165, 176
Noble, Asa, 165

O'Farrell, Charles, 118, 119
Ohio units: *Infantry, 12th,* 66, 73, *23rd,*
    66, 76, 82 *28th,* 51, 52, 56, 115,
    117, 125, 145, 168, 195, 199, *34th,*
    68, *36th,* 49, 66, *91st,* 68, 69, *116th,*

51, 53, 54, 95, 112, 125, 168, 195,
    199, *123rd,* 51, 53, 54, 64, 100,
    125, 134, 142, 145, 156, 157, 160,
    161-162, casualties, 163; 199
Ord, Edward O. C., 9, background of,
    22-23; 24, 44, 45-46, 47, *photo,
    48;* requests transfer, 48, 50, 205
Otey, J. H., 68
Otis, Charles G., 112-113, 114, 127-128

Parsons, J. W., 150, 193
Partisan Rangers, 28, and harboring
    deserters, 31; potential
    disbandment, 32
Patton, George S., 138, 175, 181
Peale, Henry, 54, 147, 157, 162
Pennsylvania units: *Cavalry, 7th,* 60,
    12th, 90, 93, *13th,* 112, *14th,* 58-
    59, 111, 128, *20th,* 49, 58-59, 60,
    129, *21st,* 109, *22nd,* 58-59, 93,
    97, 131; *Infantry: 3rd Reserves,*
    66, *4th Reserves,* 66, 77, *54th,* 51,
    56, 96, 131, 158, 166-167, 181,
    casualties, 182; 191, 192, 194,
    Monument photo, 200; 201
Peters, James C., 40
Peterson, Charles, 120-121
Philippi West Virginia, 62
Piedmont West Virginia, 92
Piedmont Virginia, battle of, 204
Pleasonton, Alfred, 57
Potts, James, 120, 129
Powell, Andrew, 64, 100, 156, 160,
    161, 163, 211
Pratt, Julian, 102
Prendergast, R. G., 168
Preston, Frank, 155, 190
Preston, Robert L., 123
Princeton West Virginia, 69, 74, 76

Quinn, Timothy, 115-117, 126, 129

Read, Edmund S., 172, 184, accused
    Wharton of cowardice, 185; 186

Reynolds, John F., 68
Rice House, fight at, 157-158, 160
Richmond, Calvin, 154
Roanoke Virginia, 3
Roessle, Henry, 129
Rogers, Robert S., 91
Romney West Virginia, 11
Rosecrans, William B., 2
Rude's Hill, 106, 109, 117, 128, 134,
    141, 153, 163, 168, 195, 198

St. Matthews Church and Cemetery,
    143
Salt works, 37
Saltville Virginia, 40, 69, 77, 80, 85
Scammon, Eliakim P., 12
Schenk, Robert, 9, 13
Schowen, John, 104, 133, 142, 152,
    197
Semple, Charles, 178
Shenandoah Valley, 2, 6, description of,
    25-26
Sheridan, Philip H., 204
Sherman, William T., 3
Shipp, Scott, 103, 151, 155, *photo, 187*
Shirley's Hill, 128, 134, 135, 137, 139,
    151
Sickel, Horatio G., 66
Sigel, Franz, xi, xii, 9, background
    of, 15-20; *photo, 18;* at Bull Run,
    20-21; resigns, 22; 42-43, 45-46,
    47, 48, 49, 50, 63, 66, 88, seeks
    new orders, 89; 93, and training,
    94-95; 99, 105, dividing his forces,
    106-107; 108, 110, 112, 114, lack
    of cavalry, 122; 125, 131, 144-
    145, orders Moor to retreat, 146;
    149, decides to fight, 150; 152,
    chastises Lang, 154; overwrought,
    159; generalship of, 165-166; 168,
    and 12th West Virginia, 171, 177;
    193, 194-195, 196, 201; relieved
    of command, 203; evaluation of,
    204-207

Smith, D. Howard, 80
Smith, Francis H., 88, 103
Smith, George H., 102, 128, 139, 169-
    170, 172-173, 190
Smith, William F. "Baldy," 8
Snow, Alonzo, 61, 183, 186, 187
Snyder, Edmund P., 160, 161
Snyder, Edwin, 161
Spaulding, William, 152
Spencer, James G., 158
Sperry, Kate, 87
Stahel, Julius, 57-58, 88, 125, 126,
    145, sent to take command at New
    Market, 146; *photo, 148;* takes
    command, 149; 154, orders a
    cavalry charge, 173; 176, 206-207
Stairwalt, Andrew, 76
Stanard, Beverly, 123
Stanton, Edwin M., 1, 203
Staunton Virginia, 3, 37, 71, 78, 84,
    104, 107-108, 123, 202; captured,
    204
Stephens, Edward W., 56
Stevenson, James H., 110, 118-120
Strasburg Virginia, 88, 99, 111
Stringfellow, Charles E., 81
Strother, David M., 12, 57, 94, 97, 107,
    photo, 127; 145, 152, 159, 201, 209
Sullivan, Jeremiah C., 51, 125, 194,
    photo, 196; 207

Taylor, Robert F., 126, 175
Tazewell Virginia, 69, 76
Thoburn, Joseph, 51, 52-53, 102, 158,
    photo, 159; 177, 194, 207, 209
Thompson, George, 134, 180
Tibbets, William B., 58, 60, 149, *photo,
    176*
Tomlinson, Abia A., 71, 73
Town, Franklin, 190
Truehart, Henry, 92
Turchin, John B., 3
Turner, Edmund Raymond, historian,
    x, 107

United States units: *Artillery, B, 5th US,* 61, 195

Valley District, 29, 39
Vaughn, John C., 78-79
Vermylia, Isaac D., 110
Vicksburg Mississippi, 79
Virginia and Tennessee Railroad, 37
Virginia Central Railroad, 37
Virginia Military Institute, x, 39, 71, 88, 103
Virginia units: *Artillery: Chapman's,* 142, 174, *Jackson's,* 142, *McClanahan's,* 128, 142, 165, 174, *Ringgold Light,* 79, *VMI,* 142, 174; *Cavalry: 5th,* 68, *7th,* 68, *8th,* 74, *14th,* 70, 73, *17th,* 76, 79, *18th,* 28, 98, 102, 117, 119, 120, 135, 137, 143, 150, *23rd,* 98, 102, 118, 137; *Infantry: 22nd,* 39, 104, 123, 137, 161, 170, 175, 181, *23rd Battalion,* 39, 40, 123, 137, 161, 170, 175, 181, *26th Battalion,* 39, 40, 137, 150, 160, 169, 172, 178, 184, 186, 191, *36th,* 39, 40, *45th,* 39, 40, 78, 80, 81, *45th Battalion,* 39, 40, *51st,* 33, 39, 40, 133, 137, 151, 155, 160, 169, 171-172, 178, 191, *59th,* 40, *60th,* 39, 40, *VMI Cadet Battalion,* 103, 151, 155, 178-179, 186, 187; *Mounted infantry: 62nd,* 28, 41, 102, 117, 129, 137-138, 155, 161-162, 169, 172-173, 181, 190; *Sharpshooters: 30th,* 39, 40, 104, 133, 137, 142, 152, 161, 171
von Kleiser, Alfred, 61, 148, 163-164, 165, 194

Wampler, John, 188
Warner, Charles, 143
Washburn, James, 195
Weber, Maximilion E., 90
Weddle, Joseph, 177
Wells, George D., 55, feigns illness, 95-96, 126, 155-156, 166, 170, 176, 179, *photo, 180;* 192, 194
West Virginia, Department of, 9, strength in, 10-11, 42; 43
West Virginia units: *Artillery; Battery D, 1st,* 61, 115, 158, 188, Battery *G, 1st,* 61, 126, 164, 166, 189; *Cavalry: 1st,* 102; *Infantry: 1st,* 51, 56, 100, 125, 134, 136, 156, 158, 179, 211, *5th,* 71, *9th,* 68, *11th,* 68, *12th,* 51, 53, 54, 61, 101, 115, 117, 125, 145, 158, 166, 168, 169, fires on own men, 170; 176, 184, 187, 193-194, *14th,* 68, *15th,* 68
Wharton, Gabriel C., 70, 151-152, 160, 173, 184; accused of cowardice, 185; *photo, 185;* 191, 197
White, Carr B., 66
White, Isaac, 192
White, Robert, 109
Wildes, Thomas F., 54, 95, 195, 211
Wilson, Robert B., 73, 77
Winchester, 2; battle of, 13-14; 45
Winchester Virginia, 87-88
Winters, Joshua, 100
Wise, John A., xi, 104-5, 124, 155, 189
Woodson, Charles A., 138
Woodstock Virginia, 88, 101, 108, 114, 126, 144
Woolworth, R. H., 77
Wyncoop, John E., 58, 59-60, 126, 129, 149
Wytheville Virginia, 77

Acknowledgments

Writing a manuscript is often a solitary endeavor. Turning that manuscript into a publishable book is very definitely a team sport. This work is my seventh volume published by Savas Beatie, and each such effort only reinforces that understanding more completely. Accordingly, I wish to thank several people who helped guide this humble volume on that path.

My wife Anne continues to be the soul of support and patience. In many ways small and large she has helped me to pursue my dream of writing and has witnessed it from inception to fruition. Each time I finish a project, I vow I will take some time to just relax; she laughs, for she knows full well that within a week I am already itching to start the next effort. I love you, Annie.

I also want to thank, collectively, the Virginia Military Institute. I matriculated there in August 1979, a skinny high-school kid from the suburbs of Chicago, uncertain of what to expect. In May 1983, I walked across the stage to receive my diploma, A Bachelor of Arts in History. I experienced tremendous growth at VMI: mentally, physically, and emotionally. Who knew that upperclassmen yelling at you all the time could be so rewarding? Seriously, the Institute played a huge role in making me who I am today. I learned respect for history, for VMI had a long and revered history. I learned leadership. I learned how to deal with adversity. I experienced highs and lows at the Institute, as any college-age person will, but my college environment was quite different than that of most of my peers. VMI is not for everyone, but I thrived there. And it introduced me to New Market, as well as to the field of living history. I would like to thank classmates Joe Leonard and Carl Gibeault, two of my Brother Rats who shared those interests and have remained good friends throughout our subsequent lives. I would also like to thank Richard Keister and Ron McGovern, class of 1982, both of whom spurred my interest in Civil War living history. Weekends away from the Institute to stay at the Bushong House, immersed instead in the 1860s and surrounded by the battle of New Market, certainly fired my interest in the topic.

As I write this my father turns 90 years old, and a very fine nine decade run it has been. His curiosity about the American Civil War sparked my own interest, and for that I am grateful. The first books on the war I ever read were his, from American Heritage and Bruce Catton. I have never regretted that interest. Thank you, Dad.

A legion of fellow Civil War scholars, both academic and amateur, helped me along the way. In this project, three of them stand out. My good friend Eric Wittenberg, award-winning author and Civil War Cavalry expert nonpareil, provided encouragement and key detail concerning some of the individuals described within. Charles R. Knight and Scott Patchan both read the manuscript, offering up their opinions and corrections where needed. Charles's book on New Market, *Valley Thunder* (Savas Beatie, 2010) is a superb tactical study of this small but fascinating battle. Scott's numerous works on the Shenandoah in 1864, including *The Last Battle of Winchester: Phil Sheridan, Jubal Early, and the Shenandoah Valley Campaign, August 7 - September 19, 1864* (Savas Beatie, 2013) informed many of my own opinions concerning those operations. Scott's discourses concerning George Crook have been especially fascinating. I extend my thanks to these fine authors for informing this Western Theater writer, when appropriate, where he went wrong.

All the people at Savas Beatie do an incredible job of publishing and marketing fine books, an even more impressive effort given today's difficult retail literary climate. First and foremost, I must thank its owner and managing director, Theodore P. Savas, who has repeatedly shown great faith in my writing. Given that Savas Beatie had already published what is arguably the definitive account of the battle of New Market in *Valley Thunder* just eight years before, chancing a second book on that campaign would, at first blush, seem counter-productive. I certainly felt that there was room for another work on the campaign focusing on the Federal side of the hill, but did anyone else agree with me? To my great delight, Ted did. The result is now in your hands.

I wish also to thank my publisher's marketing director, Sarah Keeney, and sales account director, Donna Endacott, for working so hard to keep my books on the shelves across the country, and to everyone else there who has a hand in running the shop. Designer Ian Hughes, to whom Savas Beatie usually turns for its outstanding jacket designs, is due a special thanks. *Union Command Failure in the Shenandoah Valley* is my favorite cover of all the books I have written. Thanks also and especially to the artist, Andy Thomas, whose image of Franz Sigel graces the cover of this work.

In each of my books, I try and dig into as much primary source material as possible; New Market is no exception, as the bibliography will attest. Three repositories proved especially invaluable. VMI's archives contain an enormous amount of material from participants on both sides, first collected and catalogued by cadet veterans of the battle themselves. The records are now housed at the Preston Library on the VMI Campus, where Archivist Mary Kludy made accessing these documents easy and productive. Second only to the VMI collections is the Franz Sigel Papers at the Western Reserve Historical Society in Cleveland, Ohio, which yielded a trove of important documents, including the record I have labeled (for ease of use) the Franz Sigel Campaign Journal. This document was extremely helpful, given that it was compiled at Sigel's headquarters while events were happening, rather than written years later with the benefit of hindsight. Finally, the Edgar Papers at University of North Carolina, Chapel Hill, produced another mini-trove of battle accounts gathered by Colonel Edgar of the 26th Virginia Battalion. Edgar's interest was driven by the need to claim what he viewed as proper credit for his own battalion in that fight; and in doing so he gathered several very useful accounts of the battle.

As ever, any mistakes and errors remain mine alone.

David A. Powell graduated from the Virginia Military Institute (Class of 1983) with a BA in history. He leads tours to Civil War battlefields, loves tramping the battlefield of Chickamauga, and runs a popular blog on the Chickamauga battle and campaign (chickamaugablog.wordpress.com). He is married and lives and works in Chicago, Illinois.

In addition to magazine articles and more than fifteen historical simulations of various battles, Dave is the author of many books, including the magisterial trilogy *The Chickamauga Campaign: A Mad Irregular Battle: From the Crossing of Tennessee River Through the Second Day, August 22-September 19, 1863* (Savas Beatie, 2014), *Glory or the Grave: The Breakthrough, the Union Collapse, and the Defense of Horseshoe Ridge, September 20, 1863* (Savas Beatie, 2015), and *Barren Victory: The Retreat into Chattanooga, the Confederate Pursuit, and the Aftermath of the Battle, September 21-October 20, 1863* (Savas Beatie, 2016). His groundbreaking cavalry command study *Failure in the Saddle: Nathan Bedford Forrest, Joseph Wheeler, and the Confederate Cavalry in the Chickamauga Campaign* (Savas Beatie, 2010) was awarded the Atlanta Civil War Round Table's 2010 Richard Barksdale Harwell Award, as was *Glory or the Grave* in 2016, making him the first two-time recipient of this prestigious award.

Dave also wrote (with David A. Friedrichs, cartographer) *The Maps of Chickamauga: An Atlas of the Chickamauga Campaign, Including the Tullahoma Operations, June 22-September 23, 1863* (Savas Beatie, 2009), part of the Savas Beatie Military Atlas Series™ and is working on two other volumes in that series (the Chattanooga and Atlanta campaigns). Dave has also authored a pair of books for the award-winning Emerging Civil War Series: *Battle Above the Clouds: Lifting the Siege of Chattanooga and the Battle of Lookout Mountain, October 16-November 24, 1863* (Savas Beatie, 2017), and *All Hell Can't Stop Them: The Battles for Chattanooga, Missionary Ridge, and Ringgold, November 24-27, 1863* (Savas Beatie, 2019).